A Class
by Themselves

A Class by Themselves

THE UNTOLD STORY OF THE GREAT SOUTHERN FAMILIES

William Stadiem

CROWN PUBLISHERS, INC.   NEW YORK

Inquiries should be addressed to Crown Publishers, Inc.

One Park Avenue, New York, New York 10016

Printed in the United States of America

Published simultaneously in Canada

by General Publishing Company Limited

Library of Congress Cataloging in Publication Data

Stadiem, William.

A class by themselves.

Bibliography: p.

Includes index.

1. Upper classes—Southern States—History.

2. Southern States—Social conditions. I. Title.

HN79.A13S8   301.44'2   79-24878

ISBN: 0-517-537354

Design by Camilla Filancia

10 9 8 7 6 5 4 3 2 1

First edition

Contents

[v]

Contents

Contents

photographs follow pages 84 and 180

Acknowledgments

The great pleasure of writing a book about the South is the charm and hospitality of the people one meets in the process. Among the hundreds of people who have contributed advice, assistance, and anecdotes to this book, I would like to express special thanks to the following:

Virginia: Langhorne Gibson, Dr. and Mrs. Howard Hamilton, Mrs. Parthy Stevens, and Miss Olivia Taylor

North Carolina: Caesar Cone, The Duke University Library, the East Carolina University Library, and the Z. Smith Reynolds Foundation

South Carolina: Mrs. Chester Carré, Harry Rutledge Hampton, Mrs. C. Pinckney Roberts, Miss Elise Pinckney, and the South Carolina Historical Society

Georgia: Malcolm Bell, the Georgia Historical Society, Mills Lane IV, Abraham Minis, Charles Rippin, and Albert Scardino

Tennessee: Mrs. Richard Leatherman

Mississippi: Mrs. Frank Boggess, Miss Eleanora Gralow, Mrs. Robert Haltom, James Lambert, and Ron Tomlin

Louisiana: Bethany Bultman, Mrs. Joseph Rault, Mrs. Hugh St. Paul

Acknowledgments

England: Rodolphe d'Erlanger, Mrs. Nancy Lancaster, and Mrs. Alice Winn

France: Mrs. Gillette Lecocq

New York: Timothy Beard, Frank Bradley, Douglas Caverly, William Astor Chanler, Wilson Randolph Gathings, Brendan Gill, Ralph McAllister Ingersoll, Mrs. Alfred Winslow Jones, William M. V. Kingsland, Elizabeth McGehee, the New York Historical Society, Daniel Okrent, and Orme Wilson

Finally, I would like to thank my editors, Mimi Koren and Nancy Fields, the staff of Crown Publishers, and my agent, Joan Raines.

W. S.

A Class
by Themselves

Introduction

The South possesses an aura all its own. No other region of America has such a powerful mystique, such a special ambience. The Southern image is one of white-columned plantations, courtly drawls, mint juleps, magnolias and camelias, liveried blacks, and crinolined belles. This aristocratic image typifies the South. In fact, the South's proudest feature is its aristocracy, an extraordinarily colorful ruling class that has given the area its unique character. The story of this aristocracy and of the vivid personalities that shaped it is the real story of the South.

The Southern aristocracy has been, in every sense, a family affair, a pantheon of entrenched, intermarried dynasties dating back to the founding of their particular regions, boasting enormous landed wealth, political power, and social prestige. Each dynasty proudly claims to have endowed American history with at least one mythic figure, and mythic is the only word for a life-style whose glamor, elegance, and unabashed sybaritism have never been equaled in this country. This plantation society, the pinnacle of the American dream of success, was the triumph of these great families. It was also their tragedy, and that of the entire South as well.

The Southern dream, founded on slavery, was impossibly elitist and provided the greatest good for the smallest number. The Civil War (referred to in the South as the War Between the States) was less a matter of North versus South than of North versus the great families of the South. Yet the more prosaic Southern masses never seemed to resent their subjugation. They felt an obligatory loyalty to their lords and ladies. They fought and died for them. They suffered stoically through decades of postbellum blight because of them. And they still worship them.

But why in a nation whose hallmark is democracy did the South become an aristocracy? Who were these great families? How did they forge their elite? What was great about them? And how have they mesmerized the South through the years, even to the present day?

The answers began in colonial Virginia. Unlike the Pilgrims and Puritans of the North, the first families of the Old Dominion were anything but persecuted outsiders. The early Virginians were the quintessence of upward mobility: lower gentry or upper bourgeoisie chafing at the impossible specter of stately homes and hereditary titles they could never acquire in the mother country. Virginia, with its lavish land-grant incentives, offered the perfect outlet for the pretensions of these aspiring establishmentarians.

The prospect of becoming the landed lords of a new domain, but still an *English* domain, impelled the more intrepid of these status seekers to brave the hardships of the wilderness. Their pioneer tribulations were eased considerably by white indentured servants, whose passage was paid by the more solvent colonists, and by slaves, who were purchased outright. Thus, beginning with the boat ride across, the class lines were being sharply drawn. Even after the poor whites had become unindentured, they and their descendants remained in social thrall.

While elite classes were forming in the North as well, these were classes founded upon trade. But in the South it was land, not trade, that "made" a gentleman. Of course, the first Virginians were not immune to trade, but whereas in New York or Pennsylvania trade was an end in itself, in Virginia trade was only a means to an end—land. Virginians looked upon commerce as a necessary unpleasantry in the process of acquiring capital with which to buy slaves and acreage.

In building their estates, the Virginia Cavaliers were ever mindful of the English model, hence the importance of the dynastic line. Because there was only a relative handful of socially acceptable immigrants, most marriages took place within this self-consciously circumscribed group. Some matches were even made within the same family—better to hazard the genetic risks of consanguinity than the social ones of a union beneath one's station.

Family became the all-consuming passion, the separator of "them" from "us," the keystone of the aristocratic ruling order. Within these aristocratic families everything was Anglicized, from afternoon tea to Oxford educations. If it seems somewhat incongruous that so many of the greatest Revolutionary leaders had such Anglophilic roots, it should be remembered that by 1776 Virginia had grown so haughty that she saw herself not as a colony but as a kingdom.

A similar coalescence of transplanted social climbers was occurring in the rice fields around Charleston and in the sugarcane fields around New Orleans. In both places there developed an aristocracy (founded on land) forgetful of its own, predominantly mercantile, origins, and utterly disdainful of the businessmen in its urban midst and of the plutocracy of trade that characterized the North. Both cities had megalomanic identity problems; they thought they were, respectively, London and Paris. Their families likewise had grand delusions of being royal houses akin to the Hanoverians and the Bourbons.

Charleston rapidly became a completely closed shop. A few select plantation dynasties formed the tightest-knit society in America and, incidentally, produced some of the country's greatest statesmen. With their countless slaves doing all the work, these gentlemen had ample time for higher pursuits. No city anywhere was more mannered, more proper.

New Orleans was, by comparison, rather raffish and fluid. The lusty port's Rabelaisian emphasis on food and sex was reminiscent of Marseilles in its heyday. Perhaps the repressions of Catholicism produced a backlash of sensuality. The languorous Delta days of the great Creole families featured mass in the morning, Antoine's in the evening, and mulatto mistresses in between.

Despite their superficial impermeability, the Creoles had an unusual open-door policy whereby untitled but talented outlanders were maritally inducted into their inner sanctum. A suitor's future was all that mattered; his past was not important. Consequently, New Orleans became a second-chance El Dorado for ambitious men with scandal-tinged backgrounds. Because the *haute* Creoles regarded America as alien, English, and altogether quite mad, sordid details were generally greeted with an amused, knowing wink.

The United States from the beginning accepted the diversity of Southern pretensions at face value. Democracy notwithstanding, a native aristocratic myth seemed to meet some psychic need. Furthermore, behind the pose lay the power, enormous landed power, wielded by monumental, arrogant leaders. Still, how did the pockets of privilege of Tidewater Virginia, Charleston, and New Orleans come to set "the" standard for the entire South? After all, Georgia began as a debtors' colony. North Carolina, without a lavish land-grant system, was a decidedly plebeian colony peopled by small farmers, not great planters. Tennessee, Alabama, and inland South Carolina comprised a rugged, forbidding wilderness filled with mountain men, coarse flatboaters, wild bears, and wilder Indians. Mississippi was an uncharted malarial swamp.

Once again, Virginia, along with Eli Whitney, provided the answer. By the time of the Revolution, the once-cozy Cavalier nobility had proliferated beyond the colony's capacity. Ever-English Virginia had adopted the common law's system of primogeniture, under which the firstborn took all. The tobacco land that was there for the taking had been exhausted by destructive farming methods. Consequently, there was a large group of disgruntled, empty-handed blue bloods and an even larger group of superfluous slaves. An exodus to the more fertile frontier of the area that was then the Southwest provided the solution.

The ominous wilderness became the greenest of pastures with the advent of Whitney's cotton gin. These cotton fields, sprawling from the Carolinas to the Rio Grande, would produce the biggest cash crop the nation would ever know. Here then was a new New World, whose class structure was waiting to be determined by the outcome of the initial land grab, a cotton olympics joined with equal zeal by both Northerners and Southerners.

Despite the diversity of the participants, the Virginians predominated, and the Virginia social model prevailed. The preeminent families of each region all sprang from Old Dominion stock. Both the non-firstborn of the Virginia aristocracy and the lower born émigrés, who had aspired for generations to the Cavalier ideal, agreed that they would translate the gracious life along the James into the idioms of the new territories. Those who succeeded in the cotton fields knew exactly what they wanted. Those who failed knew their place.

Thus the inland South became the Cotton Kingdom, with its own royal city, Natchez, and its own royal families, who were the spiritual and often temporal cousins of the first wave of Southern aristocrats. The wealth and the pleasures the kingdom afforded America's first millionaire leisure class were staggering. The cotton families enjoyed grand tours of Europe, interspersing their quest for culture with shopping sprees for art and antiques. They brought home entire cellars of champagne to wash down twelve-course dinners highlighting canvasback duck and terrapin. Inspired by *Ivanhoe,* the most popular book in the South, they held costume balls and even jousting tournaments. They sojourned to New Orleans for grand opera and grand bordellos.

While their husbands were off politicking, gambling, shooting, or whoring, the wives took control of the entire social order. Superficially belles but essentially matriarchs, these omnipotent women devoted themselves to developing the plantation society to a fine art and to arranging noble nuptials that would perpetuate the elite. And everywhere, making this whole world possible, were the slaves.

Eventually all this consumption became too conspicuous. The Civil War was very much a clash of life-styles: Dixie self-indulgence collided with Yankee self-denial. Because slavery was the prop, the mere prospect of its abolition engendered a rampant paranoia among the patrician masters. Far better to secede than to have their agrarian Camelot disrupted by the jealous Shylocks of the North, they reasoned. Given that the aristocracy controlled public office and public opinion, the adulation of the aristocrats by the unprivileged masses was a conditioned response. The call to arms to preserve the rich man's civilization was answered unquestioningly, except in isolated pockets where the aristocratic charisma had never been felt. Most upper-class Southerners were blithely oblivious to the guilt of slavery. Their life was simply unimaginable without it.

The leaders of the new Confederacy actually believed that the showdown with the North could be won by bloodlines rather than by bloodshed. If imitation was the sincerest form of flattery, the South had every reason to assume that class-conscious England and France would empathize with the Confederate cause. The Europeans would intervene, it was believed, on behalf of their social soul brothers and bring the parvenu Yankees to their knees. Besides, England and France desperately needed Southern cotton. Giddy with visions of a glorious triple entente, the South's planter-statesmen sailed to Europe to seal the alliance. Regrettably, the club they planned to join ultimately refused to admit them. The Europeans were more than willing to lend their sympathy, but not their support. The social implications of the rebuff were devastating to the Southern patrician ego. Failure at St. James's and at Versailles proved to be as fatal a blow as the one at Gettysburg.

The end of the war was the end of the world. With slaves freed, mansions ravaged, money valueless, the Southern aristocrats had nothing to fall back upon except their own gentility. It was difficult, to say the least, to stay genteel during the horrors of Reconstruction, that most inapposite appellation for the most devastating episode of American history. Three courses of action were available.

The first was to leave. The graceful exit was chosen by the best and the brightest, as well as by the most charming. Southern courtliness was an exotic commodity, especially in a North dominated by semibarbaric robber barons. These plutocrats needed a social establishment to use as a mechanism for embellishing their wealth. Transplanted Southern men were delighted to play this court-jester–court-snob role. For the women of the Dixie diaspora, the "right" marriage was perhaps the surest means of personal reconstruction. No woman was more coveted, by Yankee millionaires and by European noblemen, than the Southern belle. She served as an invaluable primer on strategic conjugality for later generations of women in search of a title or, at least, a bank account.

The second alternative for the old aristocracy in the postbellum South was to stay and to try to establish a career. Moldy law degrees, previously acquired solely for prestige rather than gainful employment, provided the most popular new source of income. Some tried small-scale farming, enlisting former slaves as sharecroppers. Others essayed various sorts of business, particularly brokerage operations where their contacts provided leverage. But because the South was virtually bankrupt until the early twentieth century, these feeble efforts of the Old Guard to succeed in a new guise were usually in vain.

The third avenue, and the road most often taken, was to do nothing at all. Before the war, such occupational indolence had been eminently respectable and financially feasible—the badge of the proud aristocrat. Now it was a function of malaise and depression. These people were equipped for nothing except lavish wealth. Without it they were lost. They sat on their rotting verandas, staring at the desolation, waiting for a change of fortune. Selling off their immense acreage to feed themselves, the dispossessed elite were eventually left with little more than their family heirlooms, their names, and their kin.

In the old South these links with the great tradition might alone have been enough to facilitate a comeback. The doldrums of Reconstruction left the South with nothing but the embellished reveries of its golden age. Here were survivors, links to the fabled past, who could have won public office by the mere incantation of their names. But they were too dispirited even to try. The planter class was destitute without its slaves. It would never recover from the traumatic reality of its vanished utopia.

Because the aristocrats were unable to retain their mantle of leadership, a power vacuum came to exist. Any aspirant to fill this void had to make a vivid impression: hence, the screaming evangelists and screaming demagogues who captured the mind of the South with their fantastic promises of a much-needed salvation. Behavior that was normally considered indecorous, tasteless, or outrageous, now became acceptable, a sad sign of the hard times. The South became a sideshow of decaying eccentrics, hooded Klansmen, frenzied blacks, and a thousand and one bizarre varieties of "poor white trash."

The romantic, aristocratic ideal was never forgotten; in fact, the return to the status quo antebellum was the South's "great white hope." The dream was suppressed only for want of a means of expression and a lack of money. When Dixie finally began to revive, there arose a New South, whose prosperity was couched in Northern industrial terms.

Now the South's social awareness and intense nostalgia were focused upon its new capitalists, who produced items the nation wanted. The Candlers gave America Coke, the Cones corduroy, the Cannons towels, the Dukes and Reynoldses cigarettes. To these families was handed the dynastic gauntlet: give us the aristocracy we used to know. The New South wanted desperately to be respected. But these people were merely hard workers, up from the yeomanry or the piney woods. They didn't want to become aristocrats; they wanted to become rich.

The dynastic challenge basically overwhelmed these families. They were labeled the great families of the New South, but they bore no relation and little similarity to the great families of the Old. Their proletarian roots not having prepared them for their gargantuan success, they were awkward, insecure. They spent and spent, but spending was not enough. They looked back to the plantation for inspiration, yet their interpretation of the Southern dream was embarrassingly clumsy. Long on cash, short on style, this arriviste plutocracy was simply unable to resurrect the glory of the Old South. That era was lost forever.

I

Slow Dirge for the Old South

It was a singular murder, even for Natchez. By 1932 formal duels had become rather antiquated; but plain, old-fashioned shootings remained in vogue. So many townspeople sported pistols, and used them with abandon, that a visitor might think he was in the Wild West. This was, however, anything but the Wild West. In one hand was a pistol, in the other, a mint julep. This was the Deep South, the Old South, and Natchez was its quintessence and crowning glory, the queen city of the Cotton Kingdom.

Although the Civil War had destroyed this empire that slavery had built, above the mighty Mississippi, the lords and ladies of the realm, sitting in their white-columned castles—bearing such names as Dunleith and D'Evereux—could never quite come to grips with this reality. The Cotton Kingdom was dead. The great families, whose fabled life was predicated upon the kingdom, were struggling to avoid fading away. Thus when Miss Jane Surget Merrill was found shot through the head in a poetically appropriate location, a clump of camelia bushes on her plantation, it was more than a murder. It was a dramatic coda for the old order that had come to an end.

The ordinary folks of Natchez could shoot each other to their hearts' content, but the great old families were different, exalted and exempt from the rules of this bloody game. Yet no families in Natchez were greater or older than those involved in this murder. And no scions, anywhere, were stranger.

First, the victim. The blood that drenched the camelias on the sweltering evening of August 4, 1932, was the bluest in Natchez. Jane Surget Merrill had all the prerequisites to be considered the grandest of Natchez's grandes dames. At sixty-eight, Jennie, as she was called, still possessed the petite, fragile beauty that had made her a legendary belle in her youth. Her appearance was in keeping with her lineage. Her mother was one of the Surgets, Natchez's first family and, at their peak, the richest cotton planters in the United States. Her father, Ayres Merrill, was the American Minister to Belgium.

After growing up among the ruling elite of two continents, Jennie had returned to the South to claim her birthright as head of Natchez society. However, she was forced to abdicate her social throne because of an incestuous love affair with the man who discovered her body that fateful August night. Duncan Minor, at sixty-nine, was an aging Ashley Wilkes, a refined, handsome, prototypical Southern gentleman. Beginning with his great-grandfather, who had been the Spanish royal governor of Natchez, the name Minor was synonymous with the grandeur of the Cotton Kingdom. In fact, Duncan Minor would have been the perfect choice to be the consort of Princess Jennie, had he not been her cousin. Undaunted that their relatives had beaten them to the altar, the couple turned away from society and took their romance underground. They kept it there for over forty years.

Jennie became a recluse, locked in a fin de siècle time warp. While she frolicked about her antique-filled mansion, Glenburney, dressed in Gay Nineties' costume, Duncan sat with his ageless, forbidding, but unsuspecting mother at his Oakland plantation, anxiously waiting for nightfall. Then he would steal away to Jennie's on his silent horse, for a clandestine rendezvous that became a nightly ritual. These nocturnal trysts continued unchanged from gilded youth through frayed senescence, until the secret idyll was ended by the slaying.

If Jennie grew increasingly eccentric in her self-imposed, arrogant solitude, Duncan, too, rebelled against the passage of time. His reaction was economic. Despite his being perhaps the wealthiest man in Natchez, he was also the cheapest. Known as the Mississippi miser, Duncan refused to acknowledge post-1890 inflation. Accordingly, he spent almost nothing and lived in inexorably crumbling elegance. As the sole beneficiary of Jennie's huge estate, and as a man who possibly preferred money over love, Duncan Minor was, at first glance, the only person with a motive for his mistress's demise.

Yet the normally laconic Duncan was quick to direct the authorities to another motive and two other suspects. The motive was revenge. The suspects were Jennie's and Duncan's former friends from Glenwood, the plantation adjacent to Glenburney, Octavia Dockery, sixty-eight, and Richard H. (Dick) Dana, sixty-two, also charter members of the Southern aristocracy but relative newcomers to Natchez itself. Octavia Dockery was from old Arkansas plantation stock and a true daughter of the Confederacy. Her father was a dashing Confederate brigadier; through her mother she was a relative of Varina Howell, wife of President Jefferson Davis. Dick Dana was the son of Natchez's high priest, the Episcopal minister, and was descended from one of the most revered New England clans. Despite these distinguished antecedents, Octavia and Dick, along with Jennie and Duncan, ranked high among the odd couples of Southern society.

Octavia and Dick were victims of, among other things, the fiscal doldrums that had plagued the South in the postbellum period. Haughty, horsy, altogether imposing, Octavia was a destitute ex-debutante as well as a poetess manquée who was forced to support herself by raising chickens and goats. Her intense devotion to her flock won her the nickname, "goat woman of Natchez." Dick was unique. His appearance was that of an Eastern establishmentarian gone astray, a slightly deranged Ivy League philosophy professor. Once a dashing playboy, Dick was a gifted pianist who was destroyed when an accident mangled his hand and extinguished a concert career. He became the "wild man of Natchez," spending much of the three decades preceding the murder gamboling in the woods, sporting only a gunnysack and a three-foot beard.

Glenwood, the Dana barony, had been inherited by Dick. He lived there with Octavia in such incredible squalor that it gave a new dimension to the concept of decadence. Their life-style, if one can call it that, provided the basis for the alleged act of vengeance. In the grand dining salon of Dick Dana's once stately mansion resided Octavia's large and cherished herd of goats. The animals were detested by Jennie Merrill, who claimed that the goats left their posh abode to trespass on the hallowed Merrill grounds. Worse yet, they ate her shrubs. For all her femininity, Jennie was also a crack shot. Over that last year she had used her rifle to redress this beastly impertinence, felling several of the goats. Her marksmanship precipitated a state of siege with Octavia and Dick, who had reveled with Jennie and Duncan in the better days of the last century.

Thus, at Duncan Minor's accusing finger, Octavia Dockery and Dick Dana were arrested for the murder of Jane Surget Merrill, the products of noble families at war not over cotton, nor slaves, nor honor, but goats. Was it possible that the Cotton Kingdom could have come to this? The motive was surreal, as were the people involved and the remarkable scenario that followed the arrest. There is nothing the South outwardly so despises, yet thrives on so ghoulishly, as a scandal involving its standard-bearing great families. As such, the Merrill affair is the nonpareil.

ORIGINS

The symbiosis between Surgets and Minors antedated Jennie and Duncan and can be traced back to the founding of Natchez in the late 1700s. The patriarchs of the two dynasties, Pierre Surget and Stephen Minor, were close friends and allies in carving up a wilderness that would prove to be an El Dorado. Their respective origins as a stowaway and a mercenary soldier are testimony to the opportunities for upward mobility in the new American nation. They also provide insight into the roots of our aristocracy.

Jennie Merrill's great-grandfather, Pierre Surget, like so many of the progenitors of our first families, had come to America to escape religious persecution. Pierre's oppression was atypical; he wanted freedom *not* to worship. His French parents had issued an edict that he become a Catholic priest. Having a member of the first estate in the family was a status symbol highly coveted by Pierre's bourgeois merchant father in La Rochelle. However, the atmosphere of that port, then booming with the foreign trade of the 1760s, was hardly conducive to the taking of any vows, except those to see the world. Pierre escaped the cloister and his wrathful parents by stowing away on a ship bound for New York.

Pierre achieved moderate prosperity in Manhattan. Working his way up from stowaway to captain, he eventually saved enough money to buy a small, old ship. He also took a wife, ironically enough a minister's daughter from New Jersey. Still, Pierre's primary devotion was to his financial self-aggrandizement. Following the lead of other Easterners in the 1780s, he headed his prow toward the Gulf of Mexico and the economic Promised Land of New Orleans. Unfortunately, even this Mecca was becoming saturated with hungry seafarers, forcing Pierre to sail up the Mississippi in search of more unfettered opportunity. He found it in Natchez, where the white sea of cotton looked far more alluring than the blue ones.

Possibly inspired by Peter Minuit, the Dutch administrator who bought Manhattan from the Indians with trinkets in 1624, Pierre Surget obtained a huge tract of land from the local Indians in exchange for a load of pig iron. These were massacre days, and the iron was most likely destined for weapons production. Pierre was undismayed. Land in hand, he now set off to create a dynasty.

When Pierre arrived, the Natchez territory was something of a political football, in a game that was being expertly plotted at all points of the field by Stephen Minor. The French, who first held the territory but never settled, had ceded it to the British in 1763 as spoils of the French and Indian War. The British had sent the first colonists, mostly expatriate Virginians who had exhausted their tobacco lands in the Old Dominion by very unscientific farming methods. The Virginians brought their slaves with them, to clear the wilderness and to establish the rudiments of the gracious planter civilization that was soon to begin to blossom.

While Britain was otherwise preoccupied during the American Revolution, Spain seized control of the area in a rearguard action to which Stephen Minor had sold his participation. An itinerant Pennsylvania mercenary, the affable young Minor was the perfect liaison with the growing American community. Consequently, the Spanish awarded him high posts in their Natchez administration, culminating in the royal governorship. They also gave him a new name, Don Estevan Minor. It was a title belying his plebeian background, and one that has confused latter generations of Natchezians into exalting him as Spanish royalty.

Natchez may have been light-years distant from El Escorial but, as in the rechristening of Stephen Minor, the Spanish administrators were intent on transforming their new territory in the image of the mother country. They began a major effort to convert Natchez to Catholicism, using imported Irish priests as proselytizers. At the same time, they arranged an elaborate array of balls and gala dinners evocative of the grandee life in Iberia, and precursory to the sybaritic society that would distinguish the Cotton Kingdom.

Pierre Surget was fairly entranced by all the Spanish glamor, and by the prospect of further self-advancement. Furthermore, in Don Estevan Minor, decades his junior, he found a very simpatico fellow opportunist. Pierre rediscovered his long-lost Catholicism and, with Minor's assistance, insinuated himself into the good graces of the ruling class, winning grants of several thousand more acres in the process. While Pierre was building his network and his plantation, Cherry Grove, he lived on his boat, where two of his eleven heirs and heiresses were sired. One of the keys to founding a great family is quantity, a criterion Pierre more than fulfilled.

In addition to issue, Pierre was also amassing slaves. Virginians, finding that humans were more valuable than depleted land, were sending their superfluous servants down the outlaw-infested Natchez Trace for auction to the prospering planters of the black belt. This band of dark clay soil in Mississippi and Alabama was the most fertile in the entire country. Pierre, overflowing with offspring, chattels, and acres, had become, within a decade of his arrival, the toast of Natchez.

By 1798 the Americans had displaced the Spanish, with Don Estevan presiding over the transition and maintaining his position, even if unofficially, as the leader of the community. The recently invented cotton gin now precipitated a "white gold" rush. Hordes of Eli Whitney's fellow Yankees joined the Virginians and other ambitious Southerners en route to this fabled frontier. Cotton planting became the dream occupation of the nineteenth century. Pierre died at the then ripe age of sixty in 1796, but his family took his place, along with Don Estevan Minor, at the head of the welcoming committee.

In the early 1800s, the Natchez-style reception was so expansive that it frequently involved marriage to the most socially prominent of the newcomers. Many were prominent indeed. Regardless of their colonial social status, citizens of the new nation were very vulnerable to the siren of wealth symbolized by the immense mansions that were being built as the townhouses or, more accurately, palaces of the owners of the cotton fields up, down, and across the Mississippi.

If strategic conjugality was the name of the game in burgeoning Natchez, the master gamesman was Don Estevan Minor. Basking in his Spanish mystique among the readily impressed arriving pioneers, the debonair Minor was so engaging that, within a relatively brief period, he had wed three daughters of the most prominent settlers. The first two died soon after their respective nuptials, yet some locals whispered that Juan, rather than Estevan, might be the more fitting forename.

Not content to rest on his own highly profitable altar-hopping, Minor insisted on leading his numerous offspring down the same calculating path. One of his greatest triumphs occurred with the marriage of his fourteen-year-old daughter Mary to William Kenner, a Louisiana sugar planter. The wedding forged a formidable alliance between cotton and cane. Mary's seventh baby, Duncan Kenner, killed the exhausted child bride and he was raised by the Minors. Duncan grew up to become the sugar king of Louisiana. The Minors were also maritally entwined with the Croesus-rich Duncans (hence the Christian name for Messrs. Kenner and Minor). The Duncan fortune stemmed from a young Pennsylvania physician who came south and quickly involved himself in two brilliant cotton marriages in succession and a booming medical practice in sickly Natchez. (The city was one of America's yellow fever capitals.)

Although the Surgets were so wealthy that they didn't *have* to marry well, they rarely passed up an opportunity to burnish the family's social status through judicious matchmaking. One of Pierre's daughters, for example, married the highborn Adam Bingaman, whose sister was Don Estevan Minor's second late wife. Adam squandered at least his wife's share of the Surget fortune on horses. So passionate a sportsman was Bingaman that he was buried beneath the turf of the New Orleans track where his mounts had distinguished themselves. The Surgets joined the Minors in carrying Bingaman's equine tradition to new heights. One of their most famous steeds was Henry Clay, named after their Whig idol and frequent houseguest.

Another of the patrician arrivals embraced by the Surgets was Ayres Merrill II, who married Pierre Surget's granddaughter, Jane Surget, and fathered Jennie. Ayres was the son of a leading Massachusetts surgeon. Like his father, Ayres had gone to Harvard, where he studied law. The bitter Cambridge winters must have fueled his fantasies about the magnolia paradise where a Harvard man could just as easily marry a fortune as make one himself. Natchez had developed a reputation as Nirvana for male adventurers, with lonely, lovely cotton heiresses beckoning from behind every Greek Revival column. Smitten by the idea, Ayres packed up his degree, his lineage, and his best manners, and followed the well-beaten path down the Natchez Trace. The time was the early 1840s.

Ayres immediately did the "right" thing professionally, by apprenticing himself to Sargent Prentiss, Mississippi's leading advocate and most dazzling orator. Prentiss himself was a Maine transplant who had won his place in Natchez society by a combination of Galahad graciousness and Herculean drinking capacity. Eventually Ayres developed his own very respectable practice. Nevertheless, law, and medicine as well, were here only temporary callings, providing stopgap social acceptability until the great leap forward into the cotton fields could be made.

Within a short while, the Harvard dreams came true. Ayres wooed and won the biggest cotton heiress of all, enabling him to abandon Blackstone for Eli Whitney. The new bride's father, Frank Surget, had ridden the crest of father Pierre's initial wave to become the greatest planter in Mississippi history. Together with his brother James, he controlled nearly 100,000 acres in Mississippi, Arkansas, and Louisiana, as well as thousands of slaves. As a wedding present, Frank gave the young couple their own mansion, Elms Court. The house was furnished with the Surget surplus of elegant European furniture, tapestries, statues, paintings, and rare books, not to mention a complement of cooks and servants. Another notable, and inevitable, wedding took place when, in 1857, James Surget's daughter Catherine married John Minor, grandson of Don Estevan. Natchez's two greatest clans were finally entwined. From this union came Duncan Minor.

The extended plantation honeymoon was totally shattered by the Civil War. Natchez itself had never been terribly sympathetic to the secessionist cause. True, the grand manner there was predicated upon slavery, but there were many relocated Northerners like Ayres, whose allegiances extended above the Mason-Dixon line. Also, a large number of native Southerners, including the Surgets and Minors, were conservative Whigs who firmly believed in the Union. Such federalism was not at all unusual for gentlemen who relied on Philadelphia for furniture, Cincinnati for farm implements, Boston for servants' uniforms, New Haven for tutors, and New York for other luxuries that were not imported from abroad. James Surget represented Natchez at the 1861 Mississippi Secession Convention. Preferring the lush status quo to the vagaries of war, James voted a ponderous nay.

Alas, the fire-eaters had their way, bombasting the state into the Confederacy. Meanwhile, the Surgets, Minors, Merrills, and others of the Natchez elite were responding in a less than patriotic manner. None mounted white stallions to lead troops; instead, they hired mercenaries to fulfill their military obligations. Even more reprehensible was the behavior of this nonbelligerent aristocracy when the Union forces took the city, without a fight, in 1862. The preservation of their mansions and blockaded cotton took precedence over the Confederacy. Accordingly, the spoils of Southern hospitality were lavished upon the federal invaders. Led by Frank Surget and Ayres Merrill, the storied Natchez party life went into high gear. Every night saw a different ball or banquet. And because few true Natchezians could refuse a good party, even rabid secessionists scurried for invitations. The Elms Court circle became, in the eyes of the rest of the South, the Cliveden Set of its day.

There was one fatal breach of etiquette. Frank Surget's wife, Charlotte, somehow overlooked the chief Union engineer in preparing the guest list for a dinner honoring all federal officers. So splendid was the food and wine, so beguilingly belleish was the female company, and so miffed was the engineer, that the morning after Frank received a counterinvitation that he couldn't refuse. It was an order to vacate his cherished Clifton. The engineer had decreed that the house be demolished to make way for a federal fort on the prime location atop the Natchez bluff. Adding insult to injury, the jilted guest initialed one of the harsher eviction notices: the Surgets had a scant three days to dismantle a treasure house that had taken decades to assemble.

Never had eminent domain been so remorseless. A desperate Frank threw himself upon the mercy of his guest list. He even took Lincoln's oath of allegiance, a guarantee of ignominy among other Southerners. The engineer, still rankling over unrequited gustatory fantasies of canvasback, terrapin, and oceans of Madeira, was unyielding. Surrounded by Hepplewhites and Chippendales, the Surgets and their twenty-two house servants watched and wept as the Union soldiers dynamited the mansion into legend.

Frank had prepared a fallback position at war's outbreak by transferring all his money to banks in France, his annual holiday destination. Frank and Charlotte soon sailed for the ancestral homeland, where his cache would certainly have placed the Surgets in the French fiscal nobility, to the posthumous delight of the upwardly mobile forebears at La Rochelle. Sadly, Frank became despondent and died on the voyage. Charlotte stayed abroad. She never saw the Deep South again.

Frank's tribulations notwithstanding, Ayres and Jane Surget Merrill kept up the good show. With Clifton demolished, Elms Court reigned supreme as the social center of Natchez. The festivities were crowned in 1864 by the birth of Jane Surget Merrill, Natchez's most celebrated war baby. But the Emancipation Proclamation meant that the party was over. The Natchezians, first stripped of their cotton, now lost an even more valuable commodity, the one that made the leisure life possible: their slaves. Furthermore, the freedmen, incited by their abolitionist liberators, did not comprehend the distinction between freedom and license. As an inducement to leave their masters, posters showing batter cakes drenched in molasses exhorted the blacks to lay down their plows and pick up the weapons of the Union Army. Such a precipitous change of status turned out to be a temporary catastrophe for all concerned.

Thousands of ex-slaves, worth millions of dollars, descended upon federal headquarters in Natchez. And thousands died from drinking the disease-bearing waters of the Mississippi, on whose banks they camped out. James Surget saw three hundred of his former slaves die of malaria and yellow fever within six months in 1864. Those who survived joined white soldiers in periodic pillaging of the great mansions they, as slaves, had worked so hard to build. This degeneration came after the transfer of the refined General Walter Gresham, who had been a powerful restraining influence. True enough, the party life of peaceful coexistence under this commander may have tainted Natchez as Vichy-on-the-Mississippi. Still, it was one thing to invite a Union officer to drink your Madeira, and it was quite another for your slaves to loot your home and for common soldiers to quarter their mules in your drawing room. The rest of the South could now gloat that Natchez was getting her just desserts. Among Natchezians themselves, fond memories of the hospitality of the Gresham era gave way to an unvarnished loathing of all Yankees.

Natchez during Reconstruction was a wretched place, a queen who had been raped. With lands confiscated, homes wrecked, and earning power crippled, Natchezians had to resort to radical belt-tightening. For people who had never needed to comprehend the concept of economy, this retrenchment was painful. One of the rare occasions for cheer was the arrival, in 1866, of the Reverend Charles Bacchus Dana, whose middle name inadvertently gives some hint of the secularity of religion in Natchez. During Reconstruction, the Episcopal Church, rather than the decaying plantations, was the social center and rallying point of the old nobility. (Catholicism seemed to have vanished with the Spaniards.)

Reverend Dana was well qualified to lead the social revival. In the tradition of Ayres Merrill and so many other Natchezians, Dana was a New Englander. His old-line family included such luminaries as the famous editor Charles A. Dana, of Brook Farm and later the *New York*

Sun, and Richard Henry Dana, great maritime lawyer, author of *Two Years Before the Mast,* and the namesake of the reverend's son Dick. Reverend Dana was educated at Dartmouth and the Andover Theological Seminary. Before coming to Natchez, he had grounded himself in Southern gentility as the rector of Christ Church in Alexandria, Virginia, ministering to the Lees and other FFVs (First Families of Virginia, as they refer to themselves). The Danas' Glenwood, with its vast library and numerous cultural events, was a fine setting for the childhood of a Renaissance man-to-be like little Dick.

While the rest of the reverend's congregation was bitterly trying to accommodate themselves to their reduced circumstances, the Merrills and their home went miraculously unscathed. A possible explanation for this exemption was Ayres's close friendship with Ulysses S. Grant, both before the war and during the federal occupation, when the general was hosted at Elms Court. The Merrills' good fortune hardly endeared them to anyone in Natchez, including the remaining Surgets and Minors, who fared far less well. Within a short time after Appomattox, the mounting hatred, even threats, rendered Natchez an impossible place to raise young Jennie and her brothers and sisters.

Giving the townspeople new material for their animosities, the Merrills moved to New York, where Ayres prospered as a commission merchant for the huge mass of cotton that was now being freed up (though often in the hated hands of Northern confiscators) for sale to the starved New England and European mills. Money that Ayres's assiduously cultivated Yankee connections had allowed him to funnel out of Dixie enabled the Merrills to simulate their glorious Natchez existence. They acquired two magnificent homes, one a townhouse on Washington Square, the other a Newport "cottage." The Merrills surely provided a useful model for Ward McAllister, transplanted Savannahian and social arbiter *extraordinaire,* who was orchestrating the development of the upstart society of New York's gilded age along Southern lines. In fact, the Merrills' Newport retreat was later sold to one of the Vanderbilts, a family that was able to shed its coarse image through several marriages to some very enterprising Southern belles.

In forging his Southern-accented high society, McAllister had, in addition to the Merrills, a superabundance of aristocratic inspiration.

Nearly as devastating to the South as the Civil War itself was the postwar talent drain, which saw an exodus of many of the brightest sons of Dixie, in search of financial salvation up north. One of these was Brigadier General Thomas Paine Dockery, father of Octavia. To the plantation born, Dockery had been one of Arkansas' largest cotton producers, as well as the moving force behind the development of that state's railway system for speeding the product to market. After the war, the general's fields were confiscated and he, like so many of the dispossessed leaders, fell back on his charisma.

Capitalizing upon Dockery's stature and reassuring presence, the city of Houston, Texas, hired him to market its municipal bonds in the financial centers of the North and Europe. The family moved from their devastated Lamartine, Arkansas, estate to Manhattan, in the spirit of Southern service, rather than the self-service of Ayres Merrill. Nonetheless, like Merrill, General Dockery quickly developed a propitious friendship with Ulysses S. Grant. The relationship was so close that Grant escorted young Octavia at a grand Gotham ball. General Dockery was an honorary pallbearer for the President in 1885, a curious distinction that went to only one other of Grant's Confederate adversaries.

While General Dockery was wheeling and dealing in the bond market, Ayres Merrill got still another plum from President Grant—the appointment as Minister to Belgium. The 1876 assignment was one of the final gestures of Grant's scandal-torn, grab-bag second administration. It must have appeared especially treacherous to the people of Natchez. The diplomatic mission made for the most glamorous of whirls for the teenaged Jennie Merrill. Her grand tour of Europe was climaxed by her presentation at the Court of St. James's.

Back in New York, Octavia Dockery was having a fling of her own. She attended the exclusive Comstock School for Girls on then-haughty Forty-second Street, grew up into a classic beauty, dressed in gowns by Worth of Paris, and danced away one night after another. Dick Dana, too, found his way to the splendors of Manhattan. His cultured parents had encouraged him to study music, which he pursued at prep school in Mississippi, at Vanderbilt, and finally in New York, where he sang in the noted choir of Christ Church. Dick had entree to the best of New

York society, not only through his cousin Charles Dana at the *Sun,* but also through artist cousin Charles Dana Gibson, whose new wife, Irene Langhorne, of the Charlottesville Langhorne beauties, was the inspiration for the Gibson Girl symbol of American chic.

Only young Duncan Minor remained patiently behind in Natchez, saving, watching, and waiting for better days. Yet by the late 1880s, Duncan was joined by the three other youths. For each of them, the return to the South proved to be ill-fated.

JENNIE AND DUNCAN

Jennie's regal adolescence was cut short by the death of her mother abroad and by the serious illness of her father in 1882. Why Ayres came back to Natchez to die is something of a mystery. Perhaps he felt that the passing years and end of Reconstruction had diluted the resentment that had driven him away. Certainly Elms Court, with its jasmine-scented gardens, was the most serene of his several residences. In any event, the house was filled with new European *objets d'art.* Wrought-iron trellises from Belgium further set the mansion apart from the neighbors' decaying plantations. Nonetheless, hospitality triumphed. Ayres's death soon after his return seemed to have exorcised the demon of his Unionism. The parties began anew, with Jennie presiding as Natchez's favorite hostess.

That Jennie would be anointed the town's princess is readily understandable. She was an amalgam of Southern charm and European sophistication. She was beautiful. Barely five feet tall, under one hundred pounds, with curly reddish hair cascading down her shoulders, and the olive skin and dark features that were the hallmark of the Surgets, Jennie was a Gallic Dresden doll. And she was rich. Ayres had left each of his seven children $200,000 in cash, as well as a great deal of cotton land. None of this was lost on the men of Natchez or, for that matter, the entire South. From the city of Louisville alone Jennie received proposals from three self-declared "millionaires." Kentucky colonels notwithstanding, Jennie's heart was gradually captured by her second cousin, the calm and courtly Duncan Minor. An uproar soon ensued.

Incest may have been a way of life among the First Families of Virginia. In lean postwar Natchez, however, the official marriage policy was one of divide and conquer. After all, Southerners everywhere were reconstructing themselves by splendid marriages. Alva Smith of Mobile had married a Vanderbilt *and* a Belmont. Richard and Grace Wilson of lowly Loudon, Tennessee, had wedded their children to a Vanderbilt, a Goelet, an Astor, and a British ambassador. Why shouldn't the noble Surgets and Minors do as well? Catherine Surget Minor, Duncan's mother and Jennie's cousin, saw the rapidly budding romance as a matter of duplication, not expansion. Icily, she cast an irrevocable veto.

Further interference came from Catherine's brother, James Surget II. James's daughter Carlotta had affianced herself to a wealthy outsider named David McKittrick, exactly the path the elders were pleading with Jennie and Duncan to take. Consanguinity be damned, the young lovers replied. They were inseparable. Something drastic had to be done, and it was. Through some sleight of hand of Mississippi real property law, James Surget discovered that he held a mortgage on Elms Court. He now decided to follow planter tradition and bestow the house upon his daughter as a wedding present, just as his Uncle Frank had done for Jennie's mother. Piqued as much by the Merrills' un-chivalric Yankee getaway as by Jennie's intransigent hold on Duncan, James foreclosed as ruthlessly upon his cousin as the Union engineer had blown up his uncle's Clifton. Dispossession had killed Frank Surget; it now killed Jennie Merrill's cotillion life and drastically altered her future.

This family warfare lasted through the end of the 1890s, whose gaiety was rapidly fading everywhere in Natchez. Railroads had delivered a fatal blow to the steamboat age on the Mississippi. Because the planter-esthetes refused to deface their Camelot with tracks and round-houses, Natchez at the turn of the century sat in splendid isolation. The economic situation was exacerbated by plummeting cotton prices and soil exhaustion, to say nothing of the reduced scale of operations resulting from Emancipation. The scions of the gentry continued to seek better fortune in the despised North, including Jennie's brothers and sisters. Through it all, Jennie and Duncan stayed on to continue their now clandestine romance. The furor succeeded only in driving them into secrecy. Duncan lived at home with his mother. Jennie rented, for a pittance, a succession of the vacant great houses, finally settling at the forty-five-acre Glenburney.

The trauma of eviction had its effect. Jennie became increasingly reclusive except, of course, to Duncan. He and his mother would eat dinner every evening around six, after which Mrs. Minor would retire. Then at the dot of eight, Duncan would sneak out the back door, mount his horse, and ride the two and a half miles to Glenburney. The trip always took precisely forty-five minutes; Duncan didn't want to arouse suspicion by an overeager gallop. The morning after Duncan would make the return trip at the crack of dawn to meet his unsuspecting mother at the breakfast table of their Oakland plantation. It was strange behavior for a man of thirty, far stranger for a man of sixty. The ritual never ceased. In 1932, the couple's routinized lives were almost identical to the way they had been in the 1890s.

During the day, while Duncan and his mother lolled about Oakland (in the Southern-aristocratic nonworking tradition), Jennie presided over her beautifully furnished Glenburney and its extensive gardens. She usually dressed in the diaphanous robes of Diana of the Hunt, or some other classical goddess, on her way to one of her costume balls of the nineties. Jennie cherished that period and her life then. She simply couldn't stand the thought of what had happened afterward. The time lock had its virtues: Jennie was said to look a good fifteen years younger than her age. Even at her death, her hair had no trace of gray.

When Jennie did venture out of her controlled environment, which boasted neither telephone nor electricity, she was almost totally oblivious to the world around her. (Luckily, Natchez was itself old-fashioned; a more progressive metropolis would have been too much for her.) In 1919 Jennie did purchase a car, but blithely ignored stoplights and pedestrians. She expected curb service from all the stores. All obliged her, including the banks, where tellers ran outside at the beep of her horn. She never cashed checks larger than three dollars at a time, a sum adequate for the nineties but not the soaring twenties. When she returned home, Jennie would always have one of her several black servants completely envelop her little auto with brown wrapping paper. Although it was parked under her porte cochere, the fastidious Jennie wanted to ensure its total protection from the elements.

Duncan, too, had his idiosyncrasies. Rain or shine, he always carried an umbrella over his head when riding his horse. Despite a reputed inheritance of $750,000 (confiscated lands had been recovered, and cotton prices had improved) from his mother in 1926, Duncan, who was never wanting, rarely spent a cent. (His nocturnal circuit continued out of sheer force of habit.) Oakland itself was in dreadful repair. In 1917 Duncan had splurged by buying a load of shingles to patch the badly leaking 1838 roof (perhaps the basis for the umbrella habit). Fifteen years later, at the time of Jennie's murder, the shingles lay rotting in his yard. Local rumor had it that the price of nails had gone up enough to discourage Duncan from completing the enterprise. Oakland, majestically situated at the end of an avenue of ancient oaks, was famous for its pink brocade drawing room, its black marble tables from Don Estevan's Spanish era, and its paintings of the great horses of the Bingaman-Surget-Minor stables. Still, two of the pillars supporting the front portico were about to fall, and the front steps had collapsed. Duncan had to enter Oakland by means of a ladder, which actually seemed more suited to his surreptitious modus operandi.

OCTAVIA AND DICK

In spite of its seediness, Oakland was Versailles compared with Dick Dana's Glenwood. And Jennie and Duncan seemed almost conventional compared with Octavia and Dick. The four had all been friends and fellow partygoers in the late 1880s. Octavia had come to Natchez at that time, after the death of her mother in New York and the marriage of her older sister Alice to a major planter in nearby Fayette, Mississippi. Because of General Dockery's all-consuming preoccupation with the bond business, the relationship between the two sisters was especially close. Had it been less so, Octavia, who had matured into a statuesque, perfect-featured WASP, might have been more reluctant to forsake the glitter of Manhattan and the chance of winning her own Astor or Vanderbilt.

Returning south to live with sister Alice was not, at first, without its social compensations. Given her family ties to the Confederate oligarchy, Octavia received from Natchez a magnolia-carpet greeting. She rode the Vicksburg-New Orleans cotillion circuit with much acclaim, rivaling that lavished upon Jennie Merrill herself. Yet in contrast to Jennie, Octavia was no delicate flower of the South. An avid equestrienne, she eschewed the demure sidesaddle and rode astride, like a man. She cut her hair iconoclastically short, like a man. Above all, she rapidly grew bored with the party life and desired a career, like a man and unlike most Natchez aristocrats of either sex. Her ambition was to become, not a plantation matriarch, but a writer. Octavia thus began composing articles and poetry, published in the *Natchez Evening News,* and also in the prestigious *New Orleans Picayune,* which presaged a widening, possibly national, audience.

For intellectual stimulation, Natchez was hardly a match for Paris. Nonetheless, Octavia found a sensitive kindred spirit in Dick Dana, several years her junior. Dick, whose cultivated appearance and keyboard skills had made him the man most wanted at holiday parties, had also just returned from New York, around 1890. The successive deaths of his father, mother, and brother, who worked for cousin Charles at the *Sun* and had died on assignment in Puerto Rico, had left Dick the sole heir to Glenwood, a splendid retreat from the bustle of the North.

Dick kept intending to return to New York, but economics, inertia, and the dispiriting sudden death of a summer love in New Hampshire's White Mountains conspired to keep him in Mississippi. Meanwhile, in 1893 Octavia's beloved sister, who had grown close to Dick, died shortly after her husband also passed away. (The lower Mississippi was one of the unhealthiest of areas; in addition to yellow fever, malaria and other swampy diseases abounded, thus accounting for the staggering mortality rates.) In both the good Christian and gallant Southern gentleman traditions, Dick gladly acceded to a death-bed request that he let Octavia live with him at Glenwood, whose forty-five acres adjoined those of Jennie's Glenburney. The then-good neighbors were separated only by Jennie's well-manicured hedges.

Noting that Glenwood's grounds were spacious enough for numerous agricultural endeavors, Octavia decided to supplement her precarious income as a writer by starting a chicken farm. Poetry and poultry proved incompatible; the writing was abandoned early in the new century. Dick's artistry also suffered a fatal setback. As he was repairing a window, the sash crashed upon his right hand, severing the forefinger at midjoint. This accident threw Dick into a serious depression. Another incident drove him mad. On their way home from a party, some of Dick's inebriated contemporaries grabbed his pistol (even artists carried them here), and accused him, in jest, of violating the honor of a local maiden. Dick, still brooding over his lost career, did not perceive the joke and grew terrified. Perhaps there was a ring of truth. Dick had a reputation as a rake, though his relationship with Octavia was ostensibly platonic. There was enough room at Glenwood so that their lives didn't have to intersect. In any case, the joke escalated out of control. A mock-angry mob chased Dick to the roof of Glenwood, where he retreated for two entire days without food or water, circling the parapet like a trapped animal.

He never recovered. For many years, he would dash into the woods at the mere sight of any human other than Octavia. He dressed only in a burlap potato sack, with holes cut out for head and arms. As a complement to this new habit, Dick let his hair grow to his shoulders, his beard nearly to the ground, perhaps for camouflage. Youths considered it the height of local sport to chase the "wild man" and watch him climb trees to escape. When, as time passed, Dick occasionally put on street clothes and met his once-admiring public, he denied who he was. Dick Dana was in New York, singing in the Christ Church choir, he'd say wistfully. Who was he? Just a friend.

Dick began collecting pets, including at one point nineteen cats, plus sundry dogs, ducks, and pigs. Octavia had supplemented her chickens with a herd of goats, for milk. Both Dick's inheritance and her own had been depleted. General Dockery had suffered sharp reverses in his latter years. He died in New York in 1898, at sixty-five. The couple's only living now would depend solely upon what little Glenwood could produce. Preoccupied with and exhausted by her outdoor chores, Octavia let the house—a veritable Noah's Ark of local fauna—fester in mounting squalor. A barometer of her distraction was her cessation of attendance at meetings of the Daughters of the Confederacy. The visits next door to Glenburney also ended. As with Jennie and Duncan, all friends faded away. Here then were four people, the flower of Southern youth and repository of generations of noble family tradition, devastated by the coming of the twentieth century.

THE MURDER

None of their lives had been at all momentous since 1900, until that sultry August 4, 1932. As Duncan was about halfway to his ritual rendezvous, one of Jennie's servants ran up to him screaming that he had heard shots earlier that evening and that Miss Jennie was nowhere in sight. For the first time ever Duncan threw down his umbrella and actually galloped through the forest to Glenburney. After several hours of searching the forty-five acres, the sheriff's search party and bloodhounds led Duncan to the body of the eccentric dame, in the camelias. One .32-caliber bullet was in her head, two in her chest. Her classical costume party had turned into a Greek tragedy.

Duncan remained as impassive as ever, intently following the authorities' every movement. Fingerprints were found in the dried blood splattered on the bedroom walls. A dragnet went out. Over a hundred years before, Jane Surget White, Pierre Surget's eldest daughter and Jennie Merrill's great aunt, died mysteriously in her bed, the largest fourposter in Natchez, after a magnificent champagne ball. The occasion was the opening of Jane's immense Arlington, an odd Doric-Georgian creation still a Natchez landmark. Speculation as to the cause of Jane's demise ranged from strangulation by a servant to acute indigestion. Whatever, Natchez was not going to let the death of another Surget go unanswered.

All the evidence, marshaled feverishly through the night with Duncan's meticulous assistance, pointed next door, across the dried-up bayou to murky Glenwood. The friendship that had once bound Jennie and Octavia had degenerated into vitriol over Octavia's goats. The herd, now more than a hundred strong, was accused of foraging over

Jennie's sacred gardens and destroying the hedges separating the two estates. So incensed was Jennie at these intrusions that several years before her death, she purchased a .22-caliber rifle, and killed several of the goats. She also owned a small revolver and prided herself as a sure shot, Natchez's answer to Annie Oakley. Her guns were so integral a part of Glenburney life that most of the servants who heard the shots on August 4 simply assumed that Miss Jennie was either shooting goats or taking target practice.

Octavia's goats meant even more to her than the gardens did to Jennie. Their loss had brought her out of the shadows and into the courts to seek redress in a suit that was never resolved. Was she now playing vigilante? Only a few months ago, Jennie had been attacked, from behind, in her gardens, by an unidentified assailant. Speculation led next door, but there was no evidence other than animosity. Now the bloody fingerprints indicated a missing digit. Sheriff "Book" (as in "throw the . . .") Roberts and his men descended upon Glenwood.

The visitors were the first in decades. The approach was hardly inviting—a weed-clogged, steep incline leading to the graceful, soot-gray citadel. Climbing over fallen columns and skirting rotted floor-boards, the sheriff's party encountered filth rivaled only by the Augean stables. Goats, pigs, cats, chickens, and ducks had replaced the belles and beaux who used to pass through the Doric pilasters into the main entrance hall. Eggs were everywhere. Suffocating dust covered massive accumulations of newspapers and catalogs thirty years old. The dining room had become a goat pen, overseen by highboys full of fine china and silver that had gone unused for ages. Myriad cobwebs and cock-roaches heightened the ambience. Downstairs there were only two signs of human existence. First were the shiny pedal tips of Dick's discordant upright piano. The second was a greasy frying pan atop a makeshift wood fire in Reverend Dana's study. The rosewood-paneled library, with its faded portrait of the austere rector, its bust of Dickens, its many rare volumes (an ancient Greek Bible, Cicero's *Orations,* the *Index Expurgatorius Vaticanus),* was now covered with lard buckets and rusted coffee cans.

Dick was in the back. In a household where soap and water were alien, he was engrossed in the incredible, and incredibly damning, task of washing a shirt. The lawmen immediately assumed that he was washing out Jennie Merrill's blood. They questioned him intensely. With a characteristically mad glint in his bright, wide eyes, Dick ingenuously replied that he hadn't seen Jennie since 1915. He had gone over then to retrieve his "red, white, and blue" pet hog named Sandy Great. Screams? Of course he heard screams that evening, but a black tenant in a nearby cabin regularly beat his wife at that hour. Screams were nothing unusual around Glenwood, nor were bizarre responses from Dick. At least he hadn't dashed off into a tree.

The police found Octavia upstairs smoking goat meat on old bedsprings. For her own bed, she inexplicably slept on a mildewed mattress supported by two splintered chairs and an upright dresser drawer, rather than the fine mahogany fourposter in the same room. Dick slept on a mattress on the floor next to a similar antique bed in another room. The entire floor was covered with feathers, from disintegrating bedding as well as hens. Trunks littered the halls, overflowing with Reverend Dana's sermons, petticoats, and men's dress suits, as wasps buzzed about menacingly.

Embarrassed by the unexpected callers, Octavia tried to explain her life-style. It was simply a matter of no money and much fatigue. Octavia told how she worked outside all day and how she had to walk three miles just to get drinking water for the house. She was too enervated by the requirements of the chickens, goats, and Dick to be concerned with the luxury of cleanliness. Octavia also had heard screams and had paid no attention to them. Nothing, she said, could budge her from her bedraggled mattress at the end of the day. She then spoke longingly about her proud past and her hopes for a better future, which never came.

The sheriff and his men were too eager to close the case to be sympathetic. A fingerprint expert from Jackson announced categorically that those in Jennie's room belonged to Dick and Octavia, who at once were removed from Glenwood and held incommunicado in the Natchez jail. There they joined six other suspects, five of whom were blacks routinely rounded up by the local constabulary whenever there was a breach of the peace. (These were days when due process was little more than a meaningless abstraction.) The sixth suspect was John

Geiger, an unemployed logger who was discovered to be the owner of a heavy Army overcoat found on the floor of Jennie's dining room.

Geiger had been living on the Glenwood grounds in a cottage picturesquely named Skunk's Nest. Until it was closed by state authorities a month before, Skunk's Nest had been a notorious roadhouse of the Prohibition era. Sin was nothing new to superficially pristine Natchez. During the reign of King Cotton, "Under the Hill," the port section along the Mississippi, was one of the lustiest prostitution and gambling centers in America. This was paradise indeed for the raw Kentucky flatboatmen, the motley crews of the big paddlewheelers, and assorted Mississippi gamblers. Under the Hill was also an essential component of the lives of the atop-the-hill gentility. The many brothels, with their exotic mulatto handmaidens, enabled the young cotton princes to have their fun and at the same time preserve the virtue of Southern womanhood. The demise of the river trade had driven Under the Hill aboveground to places like Skunk's Nest, on the consecrated grounds of the Episcopal rectory. It was yet another symbol of the changing times.

Geiger's coat was a pivotal piece of evidence. The only witnesses who had surfaced were a couple taking their evening constitutional. They reported seeing a man in a dark overcoat lurking near Jennie's house. Geiger, who, strangely enough, also had a deformed finger, testified that he had been evicted from Skunk's Nest for rent arrears the very day of the murder. Dick and Octavia, in an unusual display of efficiency, had immediately confiscated his household effects as well as his overcoat. Only one man in Natchez would be mad enough to wear a heavy topcoat, even for a disguise, on a steambath August night. Further, long gray hairs and feathers were found on the coat, again leaving but one inference. Geiger was released. On August 8, Dick and Octavia were indicted for the murder of Jane Surget Merrill.

Southerners normally subscribe to the Hebraic eye for an eye code of justice. But Dick and Octavia failed to engender any desire for revenge. Despite the evidence, the people of Natchez did not *want* to believe that the couple were guilty. To begin with, Dick and Octavia didn't seem like murderers. A photo of them taken at the jail is more that of a Boston Brahmin and a dowager clubwoman dressed like sharecroppers for a Walker Evans spoof. They may have acted like Jukes and Kallikaks; they surely didn't look like them. The heartstring tugs began with the circulation of one of Octavia's poems that had been published in 1893. Entitled "Ignis Fatuus," it began:

> Dancing on the stream of life
> Beauteous maiden in your boat.
> Hast thou thought of destination, whither bound?

A fairly eloquent ode to a futile search for happiness, the poem proved tragically prophetic.

Another melancholy touch was a revelation that just an hour before the murder occurred, Dick was playing sad classical airs on the piano of the empty Auburn Golf Club. (His hand may have prevented his becoming another Liszt, but he had refused to abandon his music.) This was a community center in Duncan Park, named for Duncan Minor's family, which Dick had begun to frequent in his seniority. Less afraid of the public, he had retired his potato sacking, except for special occasions, in favor of more conventional overalls. And while Dick was allegedly shooting poor Jennie in the head, he said that he was watching the sunset at Glenwood, lost in reveries of the lost love of his last happy summer, in the White Mountains.

As if these disclosures could not elicit sympathy, several family heirlooms appeared which made the couple virtually unassailable. These items were found by the hordes of reporters and curiosity seekers who had deluged Glenwood and rechristened it Goat Castle. The first was the tattered cavalry cape of Brigadier General Dockery, obviously cherished by a woman who was not just the daughter of a great soldier but one of the Confederacy and American Revolution as well. Octavia's patriotic lineage was further burnished by her possession of a number of antiques that had belonged to Varina Howell Davis, the First Lady of the Confederacy. Through her mother, Octavia was related to the Natchez Howells, who had bequeathed the treasures to the history-sensitive poetess.

The coup de grace was the affirmation that Dick, as a baby, had slept in the same cradle that had rocked Robert E. Lee. In Alexandria the Lees had been parishioners of Reverend Dana, who had christened many of the Lee children. So highly were the Danas regarded that when they moved to Natchez the Lees insisted on furnishing Glenwood with many of their family heirlooms. That the holy bassinet had been sold for fifteen dollars did not detract from Dick's enshrinement. There was absolutely no way that Natchez would convict as a common murderer a man who had slept in the cradle of Robert E. Lee!

By 1932 the beleaguered South had elevated the Civil War and its generals to Arthurian legend. Natchez's own Vichyesque relations with the North had been forgotten, and the city now prided itself as the ultimate monument to all that was good and great in Dixie. The amnesia, however, was selective; the collaboration and craven departure of the Merrills was recalled with controlled disgust. Nor did Jennie's well-known "secret" romance with Duncan endear her memory to the populace. One could have such affairs, of course. But one was supposed to be married to *someone else* while having them. Jennie had shirked her all-important propagational duties.

Moreover, Duncan was the sole beneficiary and executor of Jennie's will. He would receive an estate estimated from $100,000 to $250,00, plus Glenburney and two large Louisiana plantations. Jennie had totally neglected her sisters, still living in Europe, as well as her Surget relatives in Natchez. Regardless of internecine hostilities, great Southern families were supposedly true to themselves, especially in bequests. Finally, while Dick and Octavia could be excused for their eccentricities, Jennie Merrill had committed the one unpardonable Southern sin. She was antisocial.

Southern hospitality was now what Natchez was all about. The Natchez Pilgrimage had just been organized that very April, an institutionalization of living in the past. Natchez may have lacked commerce and industry, but it did have its great homes. The Depression, though, was taking its toll. By establishing a special week for visiting the houses and charging an admission fee, the owners could raise enough money for maintenance. After all, if Venice could survive on its past, why couldn't Natchez? Some traditionalists objected to what they considered a prostitution of cordiality, yet eventually the dollar had its say. Pilgrimage was a smashing success, putting Natchez boldly on the tourist map as a special destination all through the year.

The penny-wise grandes dames who organized the affair were appalled that two figures from fine old families and a fine old mansion were generating so much adverse publicity. That they might be guilty was irrelevant. Mr. Dana and Miss Dockery simply couldn't be murderers. That would be bad for the Natchez image.

Almost immediately upon their incarceration, assistance was mobilized. Reverend Joseph Kuehnle of the Episcopal Church voiced his support, creating a public symbol of Dick's old church ties. A steady stream of prominent Natchezians came to the jail to pay their respects. Typical was Mrs. J. Leslie Carpenter, one of the state's richest women, who sent her chauffeur with a huge box of red and white American Beauty roses for Octavia, along with a sympathy note. The best lawyer in the state came to the defense. Lawrence T. Kennedy was a tall, white-suited, classic Southern gentleman, known as "tiger man" for his tenacity. He was chairman of the Mississippi legislature's Appropriations Committee. The case that Sheriff Roberts had just closed was now reopened.

Kennedy and the Episcopalians had been involved with Glenwood once before, in 1917. The house had been put up for auction because of twenty-eight dollars in delinquent taxes which Dick and Octavia simply couldn't meet. The buyer was none other than Duncan Minor, who may have been tired of his horseback ride. Duncan might have won his proximity to Jennie had the church not discovered that it had a vested interest. Dick's mother's will provided that in the event of Dick's death, Glenwood would go to the Episcopal Church for use as an orphanage. Kennedy was retained. He had Dick declared mentally incompetent and hence unable to be held responsible for all those taxes. Octavia was appointed Dick's formal guardian, Duncan was thwarted, and the church began making plans for its new legacy.

THE SOLUTION

With the tiger man again in the corner of Dick and Octavia, the sheriff's office sought desperately for a new culprit. More blacks were corraled and held incommunicado, yet this procedure ran afoul of the Pilgrimage's exaltation of the Natchez style. Natchez blacks, went the party line, were just as obedient, well behaved, and blissfully happy as they had been in the good old days on the plantations. It was unthinkable that one of them could kill one of their masters. No, it couldn't be a Natchez black. Accordingly, a search went out for a sinister "Chicago-Detroit Negro" who had been in town the week of the murder. Duncan Minor, obviously discomfited at the attention and suspicion that his inheritance had created, hired Mayor Sol Laub as his attorney and offered new evidence.

Jennie, he said, had told him of a "Northern" black in his fifties who had come to her house claiming to have worked for her twenty-five years ago, when he lived in Natchez. He had asked for some money for tobacco, but since Jennie didn't believe that blacks should have such vices, she gave him food instead. On that same day, the black encountered Duncan on his way to Jennie's, introduced himself as a former Natchezian, and told how he had moved to Chicago, saved several thousand dollars, and lost it all in a bank failure. Now he had returned home to seek employment. He had once worked at Oakland as a yard boy and was wondering if Duncan could give him another job. Duncan certainly could have used a yard boy, but he was far too miserly. Instead, he turned him down because, Duncan complained to the authorities, the man was "insolent."

Duncan's story hardly described a calculating assassin, but that magic word was a red flag. This had to be the man. An all-points alert went out. Almost instantaneously came a report from Pine Bluff, Arkansas. An armed black man from Chicago had been shot and killed while resisting arrest. And his weapon was a .32-caliber revolver, the kind that was used on Jane Surget Merrill. Who could ask for anything more? The actual details of the incident, while never widely disseminated, were telling. In response to the Natchez sheriff's bulletin, an Arkansas patrolman noticed the man at the train station, waiting for the St. Louis express. The solitary traveler was carrying a small bundle of his belongings. The officer ordered him to unwrap it. He obliged. When the policeman saw a gun among the possessions, he shot the black man five times. The victim never fired a shot. Aside from his ticket, he had forty cents in his pocket. His body was taken to Chicago for burial.

The incident was very convenient. On August 15, the tiger man, assisted by Sophie G. Friedman, an activist Memphis attorney, whose mother, a Mrs. Goldberger, lived in Natchez, brought a habeas corpus proceeding on behalf of Dick and Octavia. When the judge ordered the pair released on their own recognizance, pandemonium broke out in the courtroom. A cheering crowd followed Dick, Octavia, and their attorneys back to Goat Castle. The extensive publicity had made them celebrities, cult figures. In a congratulatory gesture, the local wholesale grocer had stocked the house with provisions. Hundreds of fan letters awaited them, as did a new litter of kittens. They had a victory supper of bananas and sardines. Dick had been invited to give a postprandial speech to his new host of admirers, but he declined. The banquet had given him "the quakes," he explained. His new life would have to begin tomorrow.

There was a radical change indeed. Dick accepted a local barber's offer to cut his hair and beard. The same tonsorial artist had trimmed Dick's beard years before, gratis, when it was over a yard long. A Natchez beauty parlor proffered similar assistance to Octavia, who declined. The adulation had little effect on her. Delighted to be re-united with her goats, she was outraged that so many people had tramped through Glenwood and taken some of her dusty effects. "Ghouls and vandals," she denounced them. The police, very much at her service, mounted a successful retrieval. Some cajoling was necessary for Octavia to accept a new blue dress from one of her well-wishers. None was needed for Dick to don the obligatory white planter's suit, with white suede shoes to match.

The sartorial transformation was considered de rigueur for Natchez's new notables. A committee of local society had been formed to act as guardians-*cum*-promoters of their new stars. There was talk of a concert tour for Dick and a syndicated life story for Octavia. His shyness gone forever, Dick began giving daily concerts to packed houses at Duncan Park. Goat Castle supplanted Dunleith as *the* house to see in Natchez, and visitors flocked in from across the country.

Rakes, brooms, brushes, and ultrastrength industrial chemicals, along with two full-time janitors, were sent to Glenwood to beautify it for the tourist onslaught. There was little concern that any of its raffish charm might be lost in the cleansing. An admission charge of a quarter was established to enter the now-mowed grounds. (The castle itself was still by invitation only.) Dick, now playing grand seigneur to the hilt, objected to the fee as excessive in Depression times, even to view such a cultural landmark. He was overruled by his advisers.

Still, Dick and Octavia remained officially under indictment for the murder. This placed intense pressure upon the authorities to build their case against the late "Chicago-Detroit Negro." That unfortunate man was found to be one George Pearls, also known as Lawrence Williams. Pearls had been in Natchez during the crucial period. In fact, on the very day of the murder, Pearls was seen looking very Chicago-Detroit ominous, in navy shirt, black slacks, and a black Stetson hat. But lurid visions of a black Al Capone weren't quite enough evidence to warrant dismissing the charges against Natchez's fun couple. Hadn't their fingerprints been "unmistakably" identified? The aberrant shirt-washing episode? The overcoat with Dick's hair and feathers? The vengeance motive regarding the goats? The police had a difficult case to disprove.

A new round-up took place, with eight new blacks held incommunicado. When a reporter asked a prosecutor how long a man could be held in jail without preferring charges, the reply was "Until he bucks up." To encourage the men to "buck up," all the resources of Southern interrogation procedures were mobilized. Bloodcurdling screams from the jail pierced the city's normal hush. The police explained that some of the blacks were "having fits" or just "being crazy." The incisive questioning led the police to the boardinghouse where Pearls had stayed. There they found a trunk containing what they described as "burglary tools."

Now Emily Burns, the black woman proprietor, was on the firing line. Intensive interrogation elicited testimony that, mirabile dictu, Pearls also had a deformed hand. That could explain one set of prints. Then, after a number of escorted trips to Glenburney to refresh her memory, Emily made a "confession." Yes, Pearls was the culprit. He, Emily, and another of her lodgers, a black undertaker named Edgar

Newell, had hatched a boardinghouse plot to rob Miss Jennie. Pearls, of course, had pulled the trigger, while wearing the overcoat, which he had stolen from Glenwood's front porch. A neat explanation, but what about those definitive fingerprints? Sheriff Roberts brushed this aside, saying that they had never been officially verified. Robbery here was, at best, a dubious motivation. Everyone in Natchez, black and white, knew that Jennie never carried more than three dollars in cash. Nothing at all had been taken from the house. Nevertheless, a confession was a confession.

On November 15, 1932, a grand jury convened and indicted Emily Burns as an accessory to George Pearls in the murder of Jane Surget Merrill. The undertaker was not indicted, nor were Dick and Octavia. A speedy, pro forma trial was held on November 25. The court appointed counsel for Emily, who now recanted. Pleading that all she knew about the case was what she had read in the tabloids, Emily accused the police of dragging her to Glenburney and coercing her to reenact the crime according to their own scenario. Then, she said, she was locked in a tiny room in the jail with a whip on the table and told that she had thirty minutes to make her "confession." Nonsense, boomed the battery of local officials, who had escorted Emily. The confession was entirely voluntary. After a brief of deliberations, the jury convicted Emily Burns. She was sentenced to life in prison.

A free man and Natchez's center of attention, Dick was basking in a case of terminal megalomania. The community had bought him a new upright piano, and he posed for pictures in his natty plantation whites. Many folks now addressed him as "Colonel Dana," to his obvious pleasure. Preening that he was "no stick with the ladies," Dick insisted on letting his hair grow out a bit, on grounds of artistry as well as virility. He soon added a Buffalo Bill mustache and a goatee, and supplemented his new wardrobe with a frock coat, a string tie, and a slouch hat. Here was an artist, a planter, and a riverboat roué, all in one, the compleat Natchezian. The only casualty of this celebrity were the goats. Old Ball, the patriarch of the flock, was so annoyed by all the commotion that he led his tribe out of Glenwood to graze in silent contempt on a neighboring bayou.

AFTERMATH

What finally became of everyone? Jennie's will made a new man of Duncan Minor. Although he would have never spent Minor money, Merrill lucre was an altogether different matter. He traded in his old mare for a sleek roadster and tooled about the land. He was on his way to becoming a bon vivant in the Minor family tradition. Sadly, the metamorphosis must have been too much for him. He died after a few years of high living. The woman Duncan's testimony about black insolence had ultimately implicated, Emily Burns, was released from the penitentiary after about eight years. Cries of frame-up had proliferated until they were too loud to be ignored. Pardoned by the Governor of Mississippi, Emily returned to Natchez and a quiet life.

As for Dick and Octavia, the attention never ceased. While the syndicated life of Octavia never came to pass and the national concert series was canceled when only three dollars in subscriptions was netted, the tourists continued to pour into Goat Castle. Admission was raised to fifty cents, more than enough to keep the couple in bananas and sardines, and to hire a servant and handyman as well. An attempt to secure another windfall by suing Sheriff Roberts for over $25,000 for false arrest and other personal damages proved less than successful. He retaliated by indicting Dick and Octavia once again, even though they quickly dropped their suit. However, it was impossible to convene a jury to try them. They were Natchez's most popular citizens.

Before the murder, Isaac Zerkowski, a New Orleans real estate speculator, had acquired the mortgage on Glenwood. The Natchez establishment had shamed him from foreclosing, but his heirs felt no such compunction. Dick's payments were dilatory, then nonexistent. In 1942 the Mississippi Supreme Court upheld foreclosure proceedings. Yet decisions were one matter, evictions another. Dick and Octavia would not be moved, and there wasn't a sheriff in the Deep South who would dare try to move them.

A Milwaukee millionaire, desiring a warm, gracious winter retreat, thought that he could overcome their passive resistance. He would acquire and restore Glenwood, and build Dick and Octavia their own home on the estate. The fatal catch was the goats, with whom Dick'and Octavia had achieved a rapprochement under which the herd had returned to the house. The man from Wisconsin was mortified at the couple's insistence that the goats live under whatever roof he built for them. The deal fell through. Obviously the insensitive Milwaukeean did not belong in Natchez.

Dick died of pneumonia in October 1947 at the age of seventy-seven. The next February Octavia went to court to obtain full title to Glenwood. Despite five decades of mutual disclaimers of romance or any physical involvement between the decadent duo, Octavia's petition boldly asserted that her claim rested upon her being Dick's common-law wife. The strain of litigation overwhelmed her. Octavia was taken to a nursing home where she died at eighty-four that April, right after one of the busiest Pilgrimages on record.

Today Goat Castle is no more. Somehow the plans for an orphanage got lost in the profit motive. The hilly estate is now a posh subdivision, grandly named Glenwood. There modern homes sell for upward of $75,000, often much more. Across the way, Glenburney is boarded up, awaiting its demolition by some ambitious developer whose only concession to the original ambience may be to throw up an occasional Southern colonial mock-mansion among the sprawling split-levels. A new, nondescript nursing home already occupies part of the estate.

Subdivisions aside, Natchez still is much the same. The obligatory Holiday Inn, McDonald's, and shopping mall may mar the approach, but the center of town is a trip back to the Cotton Kingdom. Pilgrimage is going stronger than ever, while throughout the year the great manors are flooded with suitably impressed visitors who come by car, bus, and even special tourist steamboat from New Orleans, in quest of the antebellum.

Most of the old families are gone, or at least are absentee mansion owners. In their place are Houston oil barons, Chicago meat barons, and the like, who were not born into, but have bought a piece of, the grand manner. At two dollars a shot, fifteen minutes of Southern hospitality is dispensed to any and all comers, by the smiling, drawling, and undeniably charming matrons of the city's various garden clubs. These women, some natives, some adoptive Southerners, all committed to the ideal of the Old South, are the force that makes this perennial festival of homes possible.

When they have finished giving their necessarily mechanistic whirlwind tour of Duncan Phyfe, Wedgwood, and Aubusson, these hoopskirted hostesses are pleased, between tour groups, to tell you whatever they know of the histories and families of the home they are showing. The main problem is that their repertoires invariably terminate at 1860. Afterward? A sad look, a shrug of the shoulders, an oblique reference to "the war."

Nonetheless, if you press hard enough, in a genteel way, and show that you're *really* interested in postbellum Natchez, some of the ladies might suggest a visit to Elms Court. See the caretaker, they say. He knows a lot. Mrs. MacNeil, the elderly widowed daughter of Carlotta Surget McKittrick, for whose wedding present Jane Surget Merrill was evicted, is rarely around. But do go, they urge. You can learn some interesting family history. The good hostesses, off to greet the next tourists, never tell you what or why.

II

The First Gentlemen

THE BYRDS

[*APRIL 21, 1710*]

I rose at 5 o'clock and read two chapters in Hebrew and some Greek in Homer. I said my prayers and ate milk for breakfast. I had abundance of people come to see me. About 8 o'clock I went to see the President and then went to court. I settled some accounts first. Two of the Negroes were tried and convicted for treason. I wrote a letter to England and then went to court again. About 3 o'clock I returned to my chambers again and found above a girl who I persuaded to go with me into my chambers but she would not. I ate some cake and cheese and then went to Mr. Bland's where I ate some boiled beef. Then I went to the President's where we were merry till 11 o'clock. Then I stole away. I said a short prayer but notwithstanding committed uncleanness in bed. I had good health, bad thoughts, and good humor, thanks be to God Almighty.

[*JULY 30, 1710*]

I rose at 5 o'clock and wrote a letter to Major Burwell about his boat which Captain Broadwater's people had brought round and sent Tom with it. I read two chapters in Hebrew and some Greek in Thucydides. I said my prayers and ate boiled milk for breakfast. I danced my dance. I read a sermon in Dr. Tillotsen and then took a little nap. I ate fish for dinner. In the afternoon my wife and I had a little quarrel which I reconciled with a flourish. Then she read a sermon in Dr. Tillotsen to me. It is to be observed that the flourish was performed on the billiard table. I read a little Latin. In the evening we took a walk about the plantation. I neglected to say my prayers but had good health, good thoughts, and good humor, thanks be to God.

[*NOVEMBER 13, 1711*]

I rose about 7 o'clock and read nothing because of my company. However, I said a short prayer and drank chocolate for breakfast and ate some cake. Then Mr. Graeme and I went out with bows and arrows and shot at partridge and squirrel which gave us abundance of diversion but we lost some of our arrows. We returned about one o'clock but found that Frank Lightfoot had broken his word by not coming to us. About 2 o'clock we went to dinner and I ate some venison pastry and were very merry. In the afternoon we played at billiards and I by accident had almost lost some of my fore teeth by putting the stick in my mouth. Then we went and took a walk with the women and Mr. Graeme diverted himself with Mrs. Dunn. In the evening . . . we played at cards and drank some pressed wine and were merry till 10 o'clock. I neglected to say my prayers but rogered my wife, and had good health, good thoughts, and good humor, thank God Almighty.

[*FEBRUARY 5, 1712*]

I rose about 8 o'clock, my wife kept me so long in bed where I rogered her. I read nothing because I put my matters in order. I neglected to say my prayers but ate boiled milk for breakfast. My wife caused several of the people to be whipped for their laziness. I settled accounts and put several matters in order till dinner. I ate some boiled beef. In the afternoon I ordered my sloop to go to Colonel Eppes' for some poplar trees for the Governor and then I went to visit Mrs. Harrison. . . . She entertained me with apples and bad wine and I stayed with her till evening and then I took a walk about my plantation. When I returned I learned Peter Poythress had been here. At night I read some Latin. I said my prayers and had good health, good thoughts, and good humor, thank God Almighty. I rogered my wife again.   —MARION TINLING and LOUIS B. WRIGHT, eds., *The Secret Diary of William Byrd of Westover, 1709–1712*, pp. 168, 210, 437, 481.

Such were days in the life of William Byrd II, the First Gentleman of Virginia. Byrd was undoubtedly the best educated and most cosmopolitan man in all the original colonies—and, in his day, he was America's number one bon vivant. No man was better at balancing passion and reason. Byrd had an English education. He had English manners. He had English wives. Yet he was a Virginian. Land, tobacco, and slaves made him rich and supported his Anglophilia. And just as England served as the model for Virginia, Virginia, in turn, was the model for the South. As the quintessence of the landed Virginia Cavalier, William Byrd thus established a tone and style that the Southern aristocracy would emulate for centuries to come.

The rise and fall of the Byrd dynasty is a classic case study, the paradigm for other Southern rises and falls in the centuries that followed. It is the story of a quest for aristocracy and all that such aristocracy, Southern-style, entailed. It is the story of high living, often to the point of decadence, of calculated marriages, of political ascendancy, of scholarly accomplishments. But, above all, it is the story of money as the curse of the aristocrat.

THE EARLY BYRDS

In view of their symbiotic ties to the mother country, most Virginians had severe identity crises. Although they wanted desperately to be card-carrying English, they were still colonials, slightly second-class citizens. Yet only as colonials could they enjoy a country-squire existence, which was closed to them in England. They preferred an upper-class status in the New World to middle-class life in the Old. To be "aristocratic," whatever the locale, was the key ambition of most Virginians. The Byrds were no exception.

The first William Byrd had come to Virginia in 1670, at the age of seventeen. He didn't arrive as a brave pioneer, eager to carve out a home in the wilderness. In fact, had it been up to him, he probably wouldn't have come at all. He was merely obeying his parents' orders. His dying, childless uncle on his mother's side, one Captain Thomas Stegge, promised to leave Byrd his Virginia estate on the condition that the prospective heir come to America to oversee it. Since Byrd's father, John Bird (William later changed the "i" to the more patrician "y") was a humble London goldsmith, and since legacies, however distant, were hard to come by, the Birds felt this was an offer they could not afford to refuse. William was rushed to the first available ship across.

Stegge, who died shortly after William's arrival, left a fine estate indeed—many acres along the James River, where Richmond now stands. Stegge's father had been one of the earliest arrivals in the colony and, accordingly, had taken the best land he could. Stegge, Sr., had prospered mightily as a merchant, as well as landowner. He had later been Speaker of the House of Burgesses and a member of the Council of State, the highest governing body. Consequently, William Byrd inherited excellent social position along with the land. That his father remained mired in the English bourgeoisie could be easily forgotten. This was the New World and, in it, Byrd was effectively born again.

The transformation was impressive. Byrd immediately won the respect of the close-knit Virginia community; soon he was being called "Colonel Byrd." At twenty-one, he married Mary Horsmanden, the daughter of a highborn British colonel. (Her father, at odds with Oliver Cromwell and his lowborn Roundheads, had escaped to Virginia, as did many other blue-blooded English Cavaliers. He returned to England when Charles II ascended the throne, but his daughter stayed behind to get married.) In addition to a wife, Byrd also won a seat in the House of Burgesses, and later one on the Council of State. Furthermore, he secured the rich post of Receiver-General, for which he received a percentage of all taxes he collected.

Despite all the perquisites of his inheritance, Byrd was not content. He had two thousand prime acres; he wanted more, and slaves as well. To accomplish this end, Byrd capitalized on the business lessons learned from his merchant father. He began trading with the Indians, exchanging trinkets, rum, guns—whatever they would trade—for furs. Byrd, naturally, got the better end of the bargain. Eventually, he became a one-man department store, dealing in everything from tobacco to medicines to horse collars to slaves. At his death of gout in 1704, he was the President of the Council of State, a round table of twelve men who were, for the most part, the largest landowners in the colony. The twelve were appointed by the Crown for life, and functioned as Virginia's executive branch as well as its supreme court. Because royal governors were temporary and state councilors were not, Byrd I was the most powerful man in the colony. In effect, he was King of Virginia.

William Byrd II, who was born in 1674, was hustled off to England just as quickly as his father had been hustled off to America. Aside from

Jamestown, at that time the capital of the colony, and Williamsburg, with its incipient glitter, Virginia was a fertile but forbidding wilderness teeming with wild Indians. It was hardly the place for the education of a young aristocrat. William Byrd now had the means of providing his son with a squire's upbringing, and so, at age seven, William was enrolled in Felsted, an exclusive British public school.

Rather than sending him on to Oxford, William Byrd wanted his son to have practical as well as classical training. William was sent to Holland as a clerk and then back to England for more clerking at a firm that supplied many luxuries to his father in Virginia. Afterward, he decided to become a barrister and read law at the Middle Temple, one of the four great Inns of Court. The Inns were intellectually the liveliest spot in London and socially, the ne plus ultra. All the brightest young men seemed to be in attendance (Dickens, Disraeli, and Gladstone were among the luminaries who later were Innsmen). Their activities were hardly confined to law. Shakespearean plays and Restoration comedies were presented nightly. There were great feasts of roast beef and ale, "hostessed" by the prettiest wenches in fair London. How could young Byrd return to Virginia after all this?

He certainly didn't want to. While at the Middle Temple Byrd had become the protégé of Sir Robert Southwell, a leading diplomat and President of the Royal Society. Southwell had Byrd inducted into that scientific pantheon at a mere twenty-two. Also, through Southwell, Byrd became a valued fixture in London's most stately homes. He had even crossed the Channel to visit the glowing court of the *roi soleil,* Louis XIV. The Versailles trip was one of the highlights of his life. Byrd was dazzled, and committed himself to seek a similar existence. He became a gentleman of leisure, living on his father's largess—and doing no barristering whatsoever. The only activity that approximated responsibility was his appointment (obtained through his father) as Agent of Virginia. This was a gilt-edged lobbying job and perfectly suited Byrd's penchant for entertaining.

Although Byrd might have been content to transact all of his business with the colony by correspondence, his father's death in 1704 brought him home. At the age of thirty he inherited his father's fortune, 26,000 acres, and two hundred slaves and, in addition, was given his father's position as Virginia's Receiver-General. Moreover, no sooner had he stepped off the boat, resplendent in his curly black wig, than all the belles of the colony seemed to descend en masse on Westover, his estate. William Byrd II, with his lordly education and dandy's dress, was now the most-wanted man in Virginia. Within a scant nine months he was snared by Lucy Parke, daughter of Colonel Daniel Parke, the British Governor of the Leeward Islands. Parke himself was an immensely successful fortune hunter who had come to Virginia some years earlier to marry into a 70,000-acre estate. Having had extramarital affairs with one too many Cavalier wives, Parke was shamed back to England, but his reputation was restored in 1704 when he became a hero of the Battle of Blenheim. His royal governorship was one reward for the victory; another was rapprochement with the Virginians, who doted on war heroes.

With her father a royal governor, Lucy Parke's stock went sky-high. She was an elegant and classically beautiful young woman, whose English aquiline features were softened by a sensuous mouth and a voluptuous figure. She must have been formidable to capture William Byrd, since that young man fancied himself a connoisseur of lovely and willing women. The colonel, delighted at his daughter's match, promised a large dowry, but true to character, he never kept his promise.

Colonel Parke's profligacy proved to be an endless nightmare for his new son-in-law. Parke had another daughter, Frances, who had married one John Custis. (Their son became the first husband of Martha Custis Washington.) A shrewd woman, Frances Parke Custis had won a favored place in her father's will and, at his death, inherited all his land, while her sister, Lucy, inherited only £1,000. William Byrd, who had hoped he was marrying land as well as beauty, felt terribly slighted.

Frances was much less fortunate than she seemed. Along with the colonel's property, Frances also fell heir to the obligation of paying his debts. She soon came to the dismal realization that they were insurmountable. In her brother-in-law William Byrd, the crafty Frances found a way out. Knowing that Byrd was land crazy, she played to all his squirely instincts. She offered him all the land, as long as he took care of any debts, which she deliberately concealed. No buyer was ever more in need of a warning than Byrd, who leapt at the offer. It was the worst deal he ever made. Parke owed a fortune in England, and Byrd spent his entire life paying it off.

When he wasn't worrying about finances, Byrd occupied himself with politics. For all his fondness for things English, he was vehemently opposed to the attempts of the Crown to suppress Virginia's increasing self-government. He wasn't exactly Patrick Henry, but he was a vocal opponent of royal oppression, particularly in the form of taxation. Byrd's own fiscal worries provided him with a special empathy regarding taxes. As the best-trained barrister in the colony, Byrd was always deferred to by his fellow planters, who shared the growing dream of becoming masters of their fate. Byrd thus became the gadfly of the colony; the Governor of Virginia found him a royal pain.

Another of Byrd's occupations was medicine, inspired by his friendship with the preeminent British physician Sir Hans Sloan. Byrd devised a fitness regimen for himself, consisting of exercise or "dancing my dance," icy baths, and swims in the frigid James to ward off colds. He imported the ginseng root from the Orient as a life extender, though he discounted its aphrodisiac qualities. Believing that both nutritional and digestive harm ensued from multicourse repasts, Byrd ate only one dish per meal. Milk, boiled beef, and chocolate were his favorites; he rarely ate vegetables. Finally, he decided to share his medical theories with his slaves, whom he called "my people" and whom he frequently cured of sundry ills by the then-voguish practice of bleeding.

Byrd himself was being bled, financially, not only by the interminable Parke debt but also by the rising costs of running his plantations. In 1715, he decided to return to England to negotiate some sort of reduction of the Parke obligations, as well as of the power of the royal governor. His fellow planters were also sinking into debt morasses of their own, and they looked to Byrd to lead their case for tax relief and other financial incentive schemes from the Crown. Byrd had been in England for barely a year when tragedy struck. Lucy, who was with him, died of smallpox. Byrd sent his two daughters, Evelyn and Wilhelmina, to board at the country homes of friends.

To forget his sorrows, Byrd stayed in London and immersed himself in sex. While he would spend at least a few hours of each day attending to Virginia business, most of his time was devoted to various forms of sybaritism. Such sensual diversions were quite the order of the night for contemporary aristocrats; Byrd had no reason to feel guilty about indulging himself. He would typically spend the early evening drinking at a coffeehouse, then go gambling, then whoring, either in a brothel or al fresco in St. James's Park, a favorite cruising ground for ladies of the evening. Additionally, he kept several mistresses, whose usual fee was two guineas per hour, a rather princely sum in those times. In his secret *London Diary,* Byrd outlined the basics of his existence:

[*MAY 1, 1718*]

I rose about 8 o'clock and read a chapter in Hebrew and some Greek in Lucian. I said my prayers, and had boiled milk for breakfast. The weather was cold and cloudy. My tailor brought me some rich waistcoats but I liked none of them. About 11 o'clock I went to visit my cousins Horsmanden and drank tea with them. I sent for my daughters to see them, but about one o'clock I took my leave and went to Pontack's, where I dined and ate some boiled beef. After dinner, I went to Garraway's Coffeehouse and read the news, and about 4 o'clock went home, and about six went to Will's Coffeehouse, where I saw my Lord Dunkellen, who told me he left my mistress crying and had not eaten anything all day. I lost two guineas in betting to my Lord Orrery. Then I went to Mrs. Br-n who told me she had consulted Old Abram (a Society soothsayer) about me and he promised I should succeed. Then I went to Mrs. Fitz Herbert's and sat with her till 10 o'clock and then walked home but took a woman into a coach and committed uncleanness. Then I went home and prayed to God to forgive me.

[*OCTOBER 4, 1718*]

I rose about 7 o'clock and read a chapter in Hebrew and some Greek. I said my prayers and had boiled milk for breakfast. The weather was cold and clear, the wind west. About 11 o'clock came Mrs. Wilkinson and brought me some linen. Then I went into the City and dined with old Mr. Perry who gave me several letters from Virginia. I ate some cold roast beef. After dinner I received a hundred pounds and then went to visit Dick Perry who was exceedingly bad of the gout. Here I drank tea and about 4 o'clock went to Molly Cole's and sat with her half an hour. Then I went home and wrote a letter into the country and then looked in at the play. Then I went to visit Mrs. A-l-m and committed uncleanness with the maid because the mistress was not at home. However, when the mistress came I rogered her and about 12 o'clock went home and ate a plum cake for supper. I neglected my prayers, for which God forgive me.

–MARION TINLING and LOUIS B. WRIGHT, eds.,
William Byrd: The London Diary (1717–1721),
pp. 114–15, 180–81.

Not all Byrd's affairs were so ephemeral. He wanted, and needed, to marry another heiress. His plantations were netting him an income of nearly £2,000 a year, yet Colonel Parke's debts devoured half or more of that—and his own life-style required substantially more than the remainder. Besides, he needed a son in order to carry on the dynasty. He began going to parties at the Spanish ambassador's, which were attended by all the "right" young ladies in London.

Ultimately, at the age of forty-three, Byrd fell in love with the girl next door. From his chambers in the Strand, Byrd could look across the street to the Beaufort Houses, which contained some of London's most expensive flats. In one of the windows, he spied an exquisite girl in her early twenties. Upon further investigation, Byrd learned that she was Mary Smith, of an old Lincolnshire clan. Her father was very rich and on his last legs. Byrd went into a romantic frenzy, bombarding poor Mary with endless love letters and proposals. He called her "Sabina" (as in the rape of the beautiful Sabine women in Roman mythology) and signed his name "Veramour" (true love). He lost loads of sleep over her. "I dreamed that Miss Smith called me dear and was in bed with me," was a characteristic diary entry. Forced to sublimate his ardor during his pursuit, Byrd gave London's prostitutes a booming business.

While Mary's own response to Byrd was largely in his dreams, the father of the prospective bride, John Smith, also would not be moved. In spite of Byrd's promise to settle his entire Virginia estate (net worth over £30,000) on Mary, except for a £4,000 dowry reserved for his own daughters, Smith was not impressed. He thought Byrd was too poor, and rejected him as a husband for Mary in favor of Edward des Bouverie, a merchant-baronet with an income of £20,000 a year. Byrd consoled himself in the arms of Annie Wilkinson, his housekeeper.

After vainly combing the salons and masquerade balls for another heiress, Byrd gave up temporarily and in 1719 returned to Virginia to make sure that his properties there were properly being cared for. To satisfy his erotic longings, he took Annie Wilkinson with him. For his intellectual needs, he wrote a long treatise on the plague.

Once again, in 1721, Byrd responded to England's siren song. For three more years he continued the quest for his heiress, until he discovered Maria Taylor of Kensington, a wellborn young woman whose late father had left her a small estate. Not extraordinarily stunning, or extraordinarily rich, she was vivacious and, at twenty-six, quite young for her fifty-year-old pursuer. What's more, she could read Greek. Not wishing to hazard another parental veto, Byrd eloped with Maria in 1724. He told her mother of the fait accompli about two weeks later.

THE RENAISSANCE MAN

For the first time in his life, Byrd seemed to settle down. In 1726 he returned to Virginia, where he remained for the rest of his life. He went immediately to work on his line. By 1729, Maria had borne him three daughters and—at last—a son, William Byrd III. William II also brought home his two daughters by Lucy Parke. Byrd had quite a double standard where his children were concerned. His daughter Evelyn was much pursued in England, but Byrd was as harsh regarding Evelyn's suitors as the late Mr. Smith had been with him. The result was that Evelyn, whom Byrd proudly called his "Antick Virgin," never married at all. She pined away and died at thirty. Lucy's other daughter, Wilhelmina, was better adjusted to her father's strictures and married a wealthy neighboring planter in Virginia.

As for Byrd himself, he became Virginia's supersquire and doted on his patriarch role. He rebuilt and expanded Westover into the most glorious plantation in all Tidewater (the eastern area of Virginia). Others may have been larger; none were more elegant. His library of 3,600 volumes was surpassed in the colonies only by that of Harvard

College. His antiques were priceless and portraits of half the English peerage, all Byrd's friends, were proudly on display for the visitors to Westover's museumlike picture gallery. Nonetheless, Byrd was never able to relax about money. Colonel Parke's ghost still stalked the halls of Westover.

To continue his lifetime of debt payments, Byrd supplemented his tobacco sales with more political profiteering. While heading a commission to define the boundary line between Virginia and North Carolina, Byrd saw there was a fortune to be made in the wilderness along the border. He snapped up tens of thousands of acres and tried to induce Swiss colonists to come to America to settle it. This never worked out, but in selling off parts of this empire, Byrd was able to stay one genteel step ahead of his relentless creditors. One method of fiscal relief always avoided by Byrd was to resort to the fur business that had made William I rich. Trade, whatever its rewards, was simply beneath the dignity of this second-generation aristocrat.

Literarily, Byrd fared much better than he did financially. His accounts of his expedition, *History of the Dividing Line, Journey to the Land of Eden,* and *A Progress to the Mines,* were witty, delightful tales of the frontier and the Indians. No better picture exists of colonial America. William Byrd II lived to be seventy, remaining committed to his cold baths and ginseng to the end. The year before his death, he ascended to the presidency of the Council of State, as had his father. It was a splendid end to a splendid life.

END OF THE LINE

Byrd left 180,000 acres to his son, William III, who had all of his father's vices and none of his virtues. While in England at the Middle Temple, William gambled away several fortunes and squandered several more on racehorses. Since his unfertilized land was rapidly becoming exhausted, he couldn't even rely on tobacco to bail himself out. He was forced to concoct a massive lottery and auction off what later became the city of Richmond. Sharing his father's mating instincts, Byrd III had two wives and fifteen children. To support them all in a grand manner taxed his purse as well as his nerves. When the Revolution broke out, Byrd took the wrong side. Most of his fellow planters shared his Anglophilia, yet they still opted for independence. Cynics have suggested that the Revolution provided a golden opportunity to repudiate their debts. If so, Byrd should have been the first to take it. Instead, he took his own life, on New Year's Day, 1777, shooting himself in the head with his finest dueling pistol. He was forty-nine.

Byrd III's second wife brought further disgrace to the name. Mary (Molly) Willing Byrd was from a fine Philadelphia family; her sister, Anne Shippen Willing, married the glamorous General Benedict Arnold, whose own affinity for all things English crossed over the line into treason. Prevailing upon both family ties and Southern hospitality, Arnold established British headquarters at his sister-in-law's Westover, thus giving the Byrd name an indelible blot. The former Molly Willing became known as Willing Molly. She could have been tried and convicted, but she received a worse penalty: social ostracism. The old-line Virginians left her alone, quite literally. When she died, Westover was sold and the age of Byrd came to an end.

The Byrd family now went underground. William Byrd IV, who joined the British Army, died in France in 1771 in a fall from a carriage. Thomas Taylor Byrd, the oldest of William Byrd III's sons to have children, was also a Tory. After the war, he slunk off west to the obscurity of the Shenandoah Valley. There he became a small farmer, and there the family stayed for generations, until the Byrd brothers of the twentieth century—the one an Admiral, the other a Senator— brought the clan into the limelight once again.

Meanwhile, the only glory the Byrd family enjoyed was through its daughters and their alliance with another great Virginia dynasty. That family was Carter and it was Virginia's, and probably America's, wealthiest. Maria Byrd, one of the daughters of William Byrd II, married Colonel Landon Carter, whose father Robert was more than worthy of his nickname "King" Carter. Robert Carter was President of the Council of State in the 1720s and boasted 300,000 acres and 1,000 slaves. Maria's sister Anne also married a Carter, as did their brother, William III (his first wife). Their other sister, Jane, completed the tight circle by marrying John Page, whose mother was a Carter. The key to the Carter success was identical to that of the Byrds—early arrival plus assiduous land accumulation. Because the Carters remained one of the proudest stars in the galaxy of First Families of Virginia, the Byrds thereby eventually became related to everyone else of social significance.

THE RANDOLPHS

Throughout Virginia history, one family seems to have mattered more than any other. This was the Randolph clan. What made the Randolphs remarkable was that, unlike the Byrds, they managed to keep their tradition of prestige, power, and service unbroken through the centuries. Further, the Randolphs were married into every other important family in the state. Most Southerners feel that the Randolphs *are* Virginia.

The first member of Virginia's First Family was William Randolph of Turkey Island, an estate near that of William Byrd I. In fact, the two patriarchs, Colonel Byrd and Colonel Randolph, were great friends, and Randolph was the executor of Byrd's will. A native of Warwickshire, England, Colonel Randolph was from the same middle-class stock as Byrd. Beginning his career as a barn builder, Randolph moved up rapidly. He followed the Byrd pattern of land acquiring, slaveholding, and trading. His success was reflected in his election as Speaker of the House of Burgesses and his appointment as Virginia's Attorney General. (That he knew nothing about law was not considered an impediment.) The office became the Randolph hereditary fiefdom for three generations.

The next Attorney General was Sir John Randolph, the only colonial Virginian ever to be knighted. Two of Sir John's sons succeeded their father in the post. The first, John, was a Loyalist who fled to England on the eve of the Revolution. The second son, Peyton, more than compensated for his brother's lack of patriotism, as President of the American Continental Congress in 1774 and 1775. The leader of the fourth generation of these Randolphs, Edmund Randolph, was also Attorney General, but now on a national stage, serving his family friend, George Washington.

The Randolph line out of Turkey Island had many branches. The patriarch colonel had six other sons, identified by the estate he set each up with—Thomas of Tuckahoe, Isham of Dungeness, William II of Turkey Island, Richard of Curles, Henry of Chatsworth, Edward of Bremo. Sir John was of Tazewell Hall. These magnificent seven, plus their two sisters, enabled the Randolphs to establish a great dynasty. The family's genealogical tentacles reached out to include such men as President Thomas Jefferson, Chief Justice John Marshall, and General Robert E. Lee.

Of all the Randolph scions, by far the most interesting, the most brilliant, and the most eccentric was the grandson of Richard of Curles, John Randolph of Roanoke. This man, who boasted "I am an aristocrat. I love liberty. I hate equality" listed his loyalties as Virginia first and always, then England and, as a distant last, the thirteen colonies. The Demosthenes of Dixie, Randolph was rivaled as a speaker only by Daniel Webster. His acerbically eloquent defense of states' rights, especially the right of slavery, rallied the South into a hard-line position that decades later erupted into the War Between the States. John Randolph would not have objected, for he preferred war to compromise any time. As a politician and as perhaps the most violently proud of all Southerners, he left a legacy of extremism that has continued to color Southern statesmanship to the present day.

John Randolph's personal life was even more extreme than his politics. At his birth in 1773, to parents who were Randolph cousins, the hereditary Curles plantation had been replaced with a new one, with a new name, Bizarre. The name couldn't have been more appropriate. John's existence seemed to be a succession of traumas that formed his hysterical character. The shocks began at three, when his father died. His mother soon married Judge St. George Tucker, of a venerable Bermuda family that established an equally fine line in Virginia. Judge Tucker beat little John, as did his preparatory school headmaster. When John was fourteen, his mother died. Judge Tucker quickly remarried; his new bride was the widow of one of the powerful Carters. John described his stepmother as a "shrew and a vixen," and he detested her. Even John's classical education in the North proved wretched for him. At Princeton and Columbia, he accused his teachers of embezzling his tuition money. When he left college for Philadelphia to read law under his cousin, Edmund Randolph, the Attorney General completely ignored him.

Consequently, John dropped out of academe. He went on a drunken spree which lasted for months and dissipated the remainder of his funds. Empty-handed, he returned to his stepfather's home in Williamsburg, where he promptly contracted yellow fever. Then his real problem began, for his illness was said to have rendered him impotent. At nineteen, John had been a tall, very pretty boy, but he now matured into a shrill, shriveled, excitable eunuch. Whether John's emasculation actually stemmed from yellow fever or from birth has been a favorite subject of backroom debate among Virginia gossips. At any rate, he certainly ceased to be a ladies' man, and he was haunted by innuendos throughout his life. Luckily, the sharpness of his tongue more than compensated for his problems. His favorite reply to tormentors was: "You pride yourself upon an animal faculty, in respect to which the Negro is your equal and the jackass infinitely your superior."

BIZARRE

What John lacked in libido, his family did not. Witness the great Bizarre affair of 1792, the most notorious scandal in the history of the Randolphs, if not the entire South. No story better illustrates the perils of family inbreeding. It began, innocently enough, when John's older brother, Richard, invited his wife's sister Nancy to come and live with them after the girls' mother died and father remarried. The plot had already been thickened by the fact that Richard Randolph and his wife, Judith Randolph Randolph, were cousins. It was made totally viscous by the further facts, first, that Richard and Nancy became lovers and, second, that Nancy, then seventeen, became pregnant. Yet another wild card was that the baby did *not* belong to Richard but rather to his brother, Theodorick, who had passed away months before of tuberculosis and whom Nancy had seduced on his deathbed. A femme fatale indeed, Nancy was as coquettish and sexy as her sister Judith was plain. Even John Randolph had been tempted by her, but his condition prevented any consummation. His frustrations in this regard were to metamorphose into an utter loathing of Nancy. And no one in America could loathe with as much gusto as John Randolph.

The real fireworks began at a fall house party in October 1792 (almost nine months after Theodorick's death), near Bizarre at Glenlyvar, the country home of the Randolph Harrisons (the family of Presidents Benjamin and William Henry "Tippecanoe" Harrison and Randolph cousins, as well). In the neighborly tradition of American (and English) gentry, Richard, Judith, Nancy, and John all came as houseguests. Also present was Mrs. Harrison's brother, Archibald Randolph, who was still another of Nancy's lovers. Though the weather was nippy, it was not so cold as to prevent the Harrisons from noticing the enormous, heavy cape in which Nancy wrapped herself. During the night, she complained of a terrible stomachache and screamed for hours. The Harrisons were told it was a simple fit of hysteria, which was common in the Randolphs. Nancy was given laudanum, a form of opium, to calm her down, and everyone went to sleep.

Or so it seemed. There had been noise on the stairs, but it could have been a dog or a cat. The blood on Nancy's bed and on the stairs was harder to explain away. Even worse was the report from Old Esau, a Harrison slave, that he had found a dead fetus of a white baby in a backyard woodpile. All this combined with the Harrisons' perception that Richard and Nancy seemed more affectionate than mere kissing cousins. The gossip began to mushroom. The dead fetus was Richard's and Nancy's and together they had killed it, the whispers went. In Virginia, a bad name was even worse than a bad deed. Richard Randolph, counseled by John, decided that the best way to clear his name was to go public, before a court, and air the case.

Richard might not have been so eager to submit to justice had justice not been controlled by his family. For his counsel, he had not only the future Chief Justice, cousin John Marshall, but also Patrick Henry. Henry, who according to Thomas Jefferson loved money more than fame, at first refused a 250-guinea retainer to take the case, but he changed his mind when the fee was doubled. The Randolphs' solidarity was impressive. John Randolph testified to the wholesomeness of the family's relationships. Patsy Jefferson Randolph, Thomas Jefferson's daughter, who was married to Thomas Mann Randolph, Jr., another cousin, testified about Nancy's stomachache. And Judith Randolph, who knew all and could have ruined the couple with vindictive jealousy, said she saw nothing. Although it was assumed by virtually all insiders that Richard did either kill the baby or at least throw away a stillborn fetus, Judith claimed that Richard had slept by her side all night; she said he couldn't have gone to get the baby and dispose of it without her knowledge. Family honor transcended all other considerations.

Only one family member broke faith. This was Judith's and Nancy's Aunt Polly, Mrs. Carter Page, who reported having noticed Nancy gaining weight suspiciously. Polly had asked Nancy if she could see her without any clothes on to make sure she was still a virgin. Nancy indignantly refused. Not taking no for an answer, Polly perched herself by the keyhole until she saw Nancy nude and obviously expecting. When Aunt Polly poured out these revelations in court, her testimony was demolished by the expert Henry. "Which eye did you peep with?" he mocked, and sent the hushed courthouse into gales of laughter. "Great God," Henry continued in his best "give me liberty" histrionics, "deliver us from eavesdroppers." In addition to Henry's bravura performance, Richard and Nancy were aided by a Virginia law which said that slaves couldn't testify against their white masters. Old Esau was thus silenced. Further, there was no body, or corpus delicti, to serve as damning evidence. The Randolphs easily carried the day with a resounding "Not guilty."

There were other sentences, though, outside of court. Because of the unending colloquy, Richard Randolph brooded himself to death a few years later. According to John, however, Richard was poisoned by Nancy, who feared Richard might break down and reveal the truth, that she had murdered the baby and that he had disposed of the baby. Nancy herself denied any such thing. She cast the blame upon Judith, who allegedly gave poor Richard twenty times the prescribed dose of his medicine. Whoever did it, Richard died in 1793. Although John inherited Bizarre from his brother, he stayed as far away as possible. Building a new home at Roanoke, forty miles distant, John appended an "of Roanoke" to his name to distinguish himself from the many other John Randolphs.

As for Judith and Nancy, they continued to live together at Bizarre with Judith's two sons, St. George Randolph, a deaf-mute, and Tudor Randolph, a consumptive. With Richard's death, Judith's tolerance of her sister came to an abrupt end. Nancy was forbidden to stray into any rooms other than her bedroom and the kitchen. Only when Judith had gone to bed could Nancy mill about the house. Judith rarely spoke to her, and then only in snarls. When Judith suspected that Nancy had redirected her eroticism toward a handsome slave, she locked Nancy in her room until John came and banished Nancy from the premises. A few years after Nancy's exit, there was a fire at Bizarre, which destroyed it.

While Judith quietly lived out her days in modest circumstances, Nancy went north and struck gold. It was 1808, and Nancy, in her early thirties, was still most alluring. At a boardinghouse in Greenwich Village, she met Gouverneur Morris, the sixty-year-old rich Knicker-bocker who had just returned to America from a tour of duty as Minister to France. A friend of the Randolphs, Morris had remembered Nancy as a young girl, and like most men, he was unable to forget her. Although he initially signed her up as his housekeeper, they were married in less than a year.

Then greed set in. Morris's nephew, David Ogden, had hoped to get a share of his uncle's estate. Now Nancy would take all, and Ogden was insanely jealous. John Randolph was equally outraged at his cousin's good fortune. When Randolph was in New York, Ogden sought him out to share his venom. Randolph's was at a new high. Always sick, whether real or imaginary, Randolph had recently fallen down a flight of steps in Philadelphia and then smashed his leg in a stagecoach wreck. He felt awful, and the meeting with Ogden made him even worse. The result was two of the most hateful letters ever written, one to Nancy, and another to Morris to warn him that he, too, might meet an untimely death at his new bride's delicate hands. Re-garding Nancy's seduction of Morris as the final perfidy, John wrote:

Let me say that, when I heard of your living with Mr. Morris as his *housekeeper,* I was glad of it as a means of keeping you from worse company and courses. Considering him as a perfect man of the world, who, in courts and cities at home and abroad, had in vain been assailed by female blandish-ments, the idea of his marrying you never entered my head. Another connection did. My first intimation of the marriage was its announcement in the newspapers. I then thought, Mr. Morris, being a travelled man, might have formed his taste on a foreign model. Silence was my only course. Chance has again thrown you under my eye. What do I see? A vampire that, after sucking the best blood of my race, has flitted off to the North, and struck her harpy fangs into an infirm old man.

—WILLIAM CABELL BRUCE,
John Randolph of Roanoke,
Vol. II, p. 277.

John's final exhortation to Nancy was: "Repent before it is too late. May I hear of that repentance and never see you more." John didn't see Nancy, but his letter did not induce Gouverneur Morris to abandon her. He wrote off Randolph's missive as another of the Virginian's mad outbursts. Besides, Morris was in a second childhood, madly in love; the past was of no concern to him. He trusted Nancy so much that, partly to spite David Ogden and John Randolph, he drew up a will that left her a huge estate. Within two years, Judith Randolph Randolph was dead, Gouverneur Morris was dead, Nancy Randolph Morris was rich, and John Randolph of Roanoke was madder than ever.

THE GREATEST SOUTHERN POLITICIAN

Aside from the Bizarre affair, John had suffered another major romantic rejection. In 1800, when he was twenty-seven, he became engaged to Maria Ward, one of the prettiest girls in all Virginia. With the exception of his abortive crush on Nancy Randolph, this was the only time John had been in love. Sadly, he was jilted by Maria in favor of his cousin, Peyton, son of Edmund Randolph. Distraught, John now sublimated all his passions into horses, spending his days riding about the countryside and at one time making a marathon 1,800-mile circle from Roanoke to Savannah. It killed his horse, but it was the only activity that kept John exhilarated.

Whenever John wasn't in the saddle, he was on his deathbed. In fact, he claimed to be dying for nearly forty of his sixty years. A letter written at age thirty-five gives some idea of how he felt:

I can walk after a fashion, but the worst of my case is a general decay of the whole system. I am racked with pain and up the better part of every night from disordered stomach and bowels. My digestive faculties are absolutely worn out. When to all this you add spitting of blood from the lungs and a continual fever, you may have some idea of my situation. But, crazy as my constitution is, it will perhaps survive that of our country.

—John Randolph of Roanoke, p. 304.

Early on in his afflicted existence, John began easing his pain with opium. Since the drug was almost as easy to come by as tranquilizers are today, John became a habitual user, if not an addict. Consequently, when he wasn't low, he was high.

His hyperbolic personality was displayed in the House of Representatives, which he dominated from 1799 until 1829. John entered the House as a lieutenant of his cousin Thomas Jefferson and immediately outraged everyone by advocating the reduction of the size of the military. When he called American soldiers "ragamuffins," he was nearly beaten up by some insulted officers. Still, he put on such a good show that he quickly rose to the head of the all-powerful House Ways and Means Committee. Prancing around his domain, the House floor, in his boots and spurs, he punctuated his sentences with the horsewhip that became his trademark.

Despite his chronic illnesses, John Randolph looked and sounded like a little boy until he became an old man. When, with his beardless face and his soprano voice, he first presented his credentials to the House, the incredulous Speaker asked him if he were old enough to be qualified.

But though he looked young, he thought old. No Representative was ever as intransigently conservative. He opposed federal power in any of its forms—tariffs, military, taxes, anything that conflicted with his ultrastrict constructionist view of the Constitution. He even was opposed to government salaries, believing that the people's representatives should serve solely out of public concern. Still, he once broke with his parsimonious position to support a congressional pay raise from $6 a day during sessions to $1,500 a year. His rationale was that if members of Congress *had* to be paid, let them be paid as if they were gentlemen. Even if they were not of such status, the more lavish remuneration might inspire them to rise to the occasion, he said.

Randolph opposed the War of 1812, thinking it both too expensive as well as presumptuous for America to do battle with the Britain he worshiped. Because of this peculiar nonbelligerence, John suffered his only House electoral defeat in 1813, though he was reelected two years later. Eventually, John turned against Jefferson, whom he viewed as too liberal—just as he viewed almost everyone. Perhaps his most famous political statement is this: "Asking one of the States to surrender part of her Sovereignty is like asking a lady to surrender part of her chastity."

The greatest of John Randolph's legion of enemies was the "Great Compromiser," Henry Clay. As the Great Non-Compromiser, Randolph was fond of taunting Clay at every turn. "Clay's eye is on the Presidency," John said, "and my eye is on him." Eventually, after years of Randolph's catcalls, Clay had enough. When in 1826 Randolph characterized the alliance of John Quincy Adams and Clay as the combination "of the puritan with the blackleg," Clay challenged his tormentor to a duel. Clay shot first. His bullet missed the man, going through John's flowing cape. Now John, a crack shot, could have easily put an end to his old adversary. But he enjoyed harassing the man far too much to kill him. Instead, he graciously shot his pistol toward the heavens, declaring, "You owe me a coat, Mr. Clay." Clay, embracing his rival, replied, "I am glad the debt is no greater." When Randolph was dying, really dying, one of his last acts was to be carried into the Senate for a final handshake with Clay.

In keeping with his conservatism, John Randolph lived very frugally. He only splurged on slaves (he had 400), land (8,000 acres), and horses. His Roanoke plantation was a far cry from the mansions of Natchez. At Roanoke he lived in two small houses, one a log cabin. Randolph reveled in this modesty. The property had never belonged to anybody except the Indians and his ancestors, he always boasted, and that was what really mattered to him. Though he constantly pleaded poverty, his estate was estimated at his death to be worth half a million dollars.

John Randolph passed away in Philadelphia, whip in hand, in 1833, a victim of tuberculosis. He had contracted the disease in 1830, when he went to Russia as Andrew Jackson's minister to the czar at St. Petersburg. The mission had evidently proved too much for him, though a year of recuperation in England undoubtedly contributed to prolonging his life. John Randolph was buried at Roanoke. Normally, people were interred facing east, but Randolph—never one to follow convention—was laid out facing west, as legend has.it, so that he could keep his eye on Henry Clay, the Kentucky Westerner.

Randolph kept things exciting, even from the grave. In his will of 1821, Randolph, who had always opposed slavery but supported the right of the states to maintain the hated institution, had ordered his own slaves freed after his death. Land was to be purchased for them. However, in his will of 1832, he changed his mind. Now he directed that his slaves be sold, "down the river" as it was. The river was the Mississippi, where the slaves would be sent to work on the cotton plantations of the Deep South. There was little left to grow in exhausted Virginia. After more than a decade of legal contests, the 1832 will was declared null and void; Randolph was said to have been non compos mentis as the result of alcohol and opium. The slaves were freed and resettled in Ohio.

Stories about John Randolph of Roanoke still fill the South today. One of the most characteristic came from an executive at the United States Bank at Richmond who had the following encounter with Randolph in 1818:

I was passing along the street when Mr. Randolph hailed me in a louder voice than usual. The first question he asked me was whether I knew of a good ship in the James River in which he could get a passage for England. I told him there were no ships here fit for his accommodation, and that he had better go to New York and sail from that port. "Do you think," he said, "I would give my money to those who are ready to make my Negroes cut my throat—if I cannot go to England from a Southern port I will not go at all." I then endeavored to think of the best course for him to take and told him there was a ship in the river. He asked the name of the ship. I told him it was the *Henry Clay.* He threw up his arms and exclaimed: *"Henry Clay!"* No sir! I will never step on the planks of a ship of that name!" He then appointed to meet me at the bank at 9 o'clock. He came at the hour, drew several checks, exhausted his funds in the bank and asked me for a settlement of his account, saying he had no longer any confidence in the State Banks and not much in the Bank of the United States; and that he would draw all his funds out of the bank and put them in English guineas—that there was no danger of them.

—*John Randolph of Roanoke,* p. 344.

THE DECLINE OF VIRGINIA

John Randolph was indeed unique. So were the other Randolphs of his
generation. When they began to die off in the early 1800s, Virginia was
never again the same. The state lost not only its wealth, its tobacco, and
its slaves, but also lost the leadership of the South, which now shifted
to the cotton belt of the Deep South. Unlike John Randolph, most of
the rest of the Virginia dynasty died in extremely meager circumstances. Thomas Jefferson, for one, was virtually destitute. At his death
in 1826, his heirs were forced to auction Monticello for the distressing
sum of $3,000 in order to pay his debts. The estate was bought by Uriah
P. Levy, a Jewish admiral from Philadelphia, whose family ultimately
sold this most gracious of American homes for over $500,000. (The last
Levy to hold court on "the little mountain" was a New York congressman named Jefferson Monroe Levy. The veneration of the Virginia
dynasties, if nothing else, obviously continued in Charlottesville.)

By the mid-1800s, Virginia was becoming a ghost state, full of
decaying, mortgaged mansions and aging, bankrupt aristocrats. Those
who could often moved away. Edmund Randolph's grandson, also
named Edmund, became a forty-niner and one of the first great lawyers
of California. A cousin, John Randolph Grymes, went to Louisiana and
occupied an equally eminent position at the New Orleans bar. Still
another relation, John Hampden Randolph, also relocated to Louisiana
and became one of the lordliest of all sugar planters, with a fifty-room
mansion, tutors for his children, slaves and luxuries ad infinitum. Ellen
Jefferson Randolph, like her cousin Nancy, found salvation with a
Yankee marriage to Joseph Coolidge, Jr., a Boston Brahmin. But even
if they were broke, the Randolphs remained always smooth and charming—the perfect Southern aristocrats.

For those who remained in Virginia, life became increasingly difficult. Money, or lack thereof, was the root of all Virginian evil. Probably
the best illustration of the combination of decadence and desperation
that engulfed the state was the murder in 1806 of the eighty-year-old
chancellor, George Wythe, by his greedy nephew. Wythe, who had led

the Virginia delegation that signed the Declaration of Independence, was the foremost lawyer in America. The Socrates of the Old Dominion, he gave law classes at William and Mary, which attracted scores of FFV scions. Wythe's most famous disciple was Jefferson, who described his mentor as follows:

> No man ever left behind a character more venerated than George Wythe. His virtue was of the purest tint; his integrity inflexible, and his justice intact. . . . He was my ancient master, my earliest and best friend; and to him I am indebted for first impressions which have had the most salutary influence on the course of my life. . . . Such was George Wythe, the honor of his own, and the model of future times.
> —JULIAN BOYD, "The Murder of George Wythe,"
> *William and Mary Quarterly,*
> October 1955, p. 516.

The saintly Wythe, whose huge, round bald head made him look extraterrestrial, was certainly in advance of his times in his domestic habits. Having survived two wives, but having no children, he decided in his sixties to shed his upright, above-passion image. He took a mistress, and a black one at that. This was Lydia Broadnax, his maid. Not only did they live together openly, but they had one son, named Michael Brown. Proudly, Wythe made Michael the major heir to his estate. (Here, too, Wythe influenced Jefferson. The sage of Monticello also had a serious affair with his black maid, Sally Hemings, and the couple had many children, whom Jefferson freed.) Wythe was so august that no one dared question his living arrangements. Nonetheless, his ne'er-do-well grandnephew, George Wythe Sweeney, was outraged, partly by the concubinage, more so by Michael Brown's share in Wythe's will.

Previously, Sweeney had forged Wythe's name on several checks to pay gambling debts. He had also stolen rare volumes from the Wythe library and tried to auction them. This having failed, Sweeney resorted to more drastic measures. He came to visit his great-uncle before breakfast one morning and poured arsenic into the family coffeepot. Wythe and Michael Brown died gruesome slow deaths, marked by convulsions, hemorrhages, and paralysis. Lydia recovered but, because of her status (like that of Old Esau in the Bizarre case), she could not testify.

With Edmund Randolph as his attorney, Sweeney was acquitted. Wythe, though, delivered the final verdict, albeit posthumously. Just as he was about to die, he directed Randolph to disinherit Sweeney. The once-prodigal nephew left to live with the poor yeoman farmers of the western part of the state, together with so many other failed descendants of the Virginia aristocracy. He resigned himself to obscurity and entertained himself with remembrances of the glories of generations past.

III

The London of the Swamps: Charleston, South Carolina

THE BLACK GRIMKÉS

The nephews were black; the aunts were white. What was unusual about such bloodlines in mid-nineteenth-century America was not that they existed, but that the relatives acknowledged each other. What was more unusual was that these relatives bore one of the proudest names of Charleston, without doubt the nation's capital of proud names and fine families. The name of this fine family was Grimké. By 1868 it had become a name that Charleston wanted to erase.

As evangelical abolitionists, the aristocratic Grimké sisters, Sarah and Angelina, had done more than anyone in the South to bring the house of slavery to its fiery destruction. Now, by effectively adopting their plantation aristocrat brother's bastard offspring, they were compounding the felony, pouring salt into Charleston's wounds.

The war was over; Charleston was in ruins. Angelina Grimké, living in Massachusetts, had gone to visit Lincoln University, a black all-male college in Pennsylvania. There, two young men named Grimké were achieving outstanding academic records and giving impassioned speeches on black rights that were noted in the North's liberal journals. Since the name was so unusual, the Grimké sisters were curious. What Angelina found were two strikingly handsome boys with the patrician

[67]

features of their brother. Their hair was a bit more wavy, their skin tawnier, in an age where plantation white was a pallor that indicated indolence and, therefore, elegance. Otherwise, the boys were unmistakably Grimkés. Angelina embraced her long-lost kin.

The boys were named Archibáld and Francis. Their father was Henry Grimké, Sarah and Angelina's younger brother, a planter-*cum*-attorney. When Henry's wife died, the prettiest of his slaves, Nancy Weston, began doing more than light housekeeping on Caneacres, Henry's plantation twenty-five miles outside Charleston. Caneacres was far enough away from the mainstream of society for Henry to follow his instincts without fear of ostracism from the Charleson elite, for whom miscegenation was the ultimate sin. In the tradition of Thomas Jefferson, George Wythe, and other highborn Southerners, Henry Grimké made his servant his mistress. Henry already had three children, and Nancy quickly gave him three more. Because she was the plantation nurse, and the master's children's best friends were usually the slave children, it was not considered unseemly when Nancy raised the entire brood together.

Henry's affair with Nancy began in 1847, when she was in her late thirties, he in his late forties. Although as a younger man Henry had been expelled from South Carolina College for extreme rowdiness and had shown a penchant for brutalizing his slaves, he treated Nancy and their sons with enormous warmth and affection. He most certainly would have legally freed them, had a South Carolina statute not expressly forbidden such an act. Instead, he treated them as free and looked forward to the day when his mulatto sons could leave Charleston for the North and a better life.

Henry's plans, and Nancy's hopes, soon went astray. Henry died in a yellow fever epidemic in 1852. His white son, Montague, inherited Nancy and her sons Archie, Frank, and John. Despite Henry's deathbed exhortation to Montague that he continue to treat them as part of the family, Montague seethed with outrage that his half-brothers were half-black. Caneacres was sold, and the entire family moved to Henry's Charleston townhouse, where for a few years Montague contained his contempt for Nancy. Meanwhile, Nancy was able to build a tiny three-room cottage (bedroom, kitchen, hall) down the street with money she had inherited from Henry's estate.

Montague and his Aunt Eliza Grimké further enabled Nancy to live as semifree by employing her, for wages, as their laundress, and by recommending her shirt-cleaning skills to others in their Charleston circle and to the local hotels. Nancy charged a dollar for a dozen shirts. Her sons helped her by carrying buckets of water from the public pumps a quarter of a mile away, and by splitting wood to light the fire under the steam kettle.

Nancy invested her meager earnings in education for her boys. While the South Carolina slave code prohibited any education for slaves, in order to keep them ignorant, and hence docile, an underground schooling system did exist. Elderly black women (too old for manual labor and hence in quasi-"retirement"), for a dollar a month, would conduct clandestine tutorials on the alphabet and numbers. The young Grimkés thus learned to read and write, add and subtract, and to recite from memory famous American speeches on the order of the Patrick Henry "liberty or death" oration. In the process, the boys, too, learned to want to be free. They read by candlelight, the three of them and their mother in the one small bedroom, and talked and dreamed of their liberation.

The dichotomy between the white and black Grimkés was poignant. The white ones lived in huge porticoed mansions, catered to by dozens of servants—waiting maids, chambermaids, body servants, coachmen, footmen. They feasted on she-crab, quail, canvasback, and rare wines. They traveled to Newport and Europe for the summer. They read the classics. They had high teas, Haydn concerts, debutante balls. The black ones had almost nothing. They lived on a rice diet; "hoppin john," or rice and cowpeas, was their staple dish. Tea was a luxury, meat an impossibility. Aside from Sunday at the Zion Colored Church, endless work was all they could look forward to. Still, Nancy's lot was better than that of plantation slaves, who were under constant supervision. She and her sons were at least on their own, and this, to them, was a blessing.

This all changed in 1860, when Montague married a spoiled Alabama girl who had grown up with a retinue of slaves. She saw Archie and Frank and decided that they belonged, not with their mother, but in her house as her houseboys. They were tiny (well under five feet) and so handsome, just like Montague, but brown. In livery they would look divine. Of course, Nancy protested. But now Montague totally swept aside his late father's instructions. He gave his pent-up hatred full expression, locking up Nancy in the Charleston jail. She stayed there for a week without food, and would have died had the official physician not ordered Montague to consent to her release. A compromise was effected. Archie and Frank would work for Montague only by day. At night, they would sleep at their mother's house. Nonetheless, the boys, now reaching their teens, wanted out completely.

They hated their gray, brass-buttoned servants' uniforms, so much that they rolled downstairs and poured lye on them to show their contempt. In return, Montague showed his. He whipped the boys mercilessly. That failing to dampen their resistance, he tried other methods. Frank, the most recalcitrant, was locked in an attic. He picked the lock, made a face at Mrs. Grimké, and ran home. When Nancy forced Frank to return, Montague next locked him in a windowless room in the stables. Frank escaped through the chimney. Finally, Montague turned Frank over to a professional slave beater, who guaranteed to break anyone's spirits. But his regimen of starvation, beatings, and dressing Frank in rags failed to do the job.

Luckily for Frank, the Civil War erupted. Charleston was in turmoil from a fire that had destroyed much of the city, and Frank's taskmaster was distracted by the exigencies of war. Frank was able to escape once again. He got out of the city and went to a Confederate Army camp, where he hired himself out as a valet to one of Montague's unsuspecting cousins, Lieutenant Julius Moore Rhett. Being an officer's manservant was the height of status for blacks.

Archie felt his salvation lay not with the Confederates, but with the encircling Northern troops. In 1862 he, too, escaped from Montague's house. Yet he found it difficult to get out of Charleston and he spent the war years hiding out with a black family, leaving the house only occasionally under cover of dark, disguised as a girl, to visit his mother.

While Archie lay low, Frank's officer-master finally noted the family resemblance, and returned Frank to Montague, who had posted a reward for the boy. Montague threw Frank into jail for several months, then sold him outright to another soldier for three hundred dollars in Confederate money and twenty dollars in gold. When the Yankees took Charleston in 1865, Frank's officer-owner abandoned him. Safe behind Lincoln's Emancipation Proclamation, Archie and Frank returned to Nancy and their younger brother, John, who had remained at home. It was a joyous reunion.

One of the first acts of Reconstruction was to establish schools for black and white. In Charleston, a host of abolitionist Yankee schoolteachers, sponsored by the American Missionary Association, had come South to do just that. One of these teachers, Frances Pillsbury of Massachusetts, "discovered" Archie and Frank. Foreseeing a great future for both of them, Mrs. Pillsbury sent the boys north to Lincoln, which had originally been founded to educate freed blacks as missionaries who would go back to Africa to proselytize for Christianity. With Emancipation, the school realized that the blacks had even more important duties in America and revised its goals. Once the boys were discovered at Lincoln, Sarah and Angelina Grimké took over their guardianship. The sisters had been separated from Charleston, temporally and spiritually, for decades. The story of the black Grimkés touched them immensely. They felt it their duty to make up for the boys' suffering by steering them into careers worthy of their abilities. Under the tutelage of the Grimké sisters, Archie went on to Harvard and became a great lawyer, while Frank went on to Princeton Theological Seminary and became a great clergyman. Both of them were champions of women's rights, as well as those of blacks. Their aunts had taught them very well.

While the two black Grimkés made their mark, the white Grimkés who remained in Charleston simply faded away. So did most of the rest of the Charleston aristocracy. After the Civil War, the great families that had given America so many distinguished leaders and gracious livers ceased to give. They were still there, but their productivity was gone. The transplanted Grimké sisters, scorned by antebellum society as homely old maids and abject failures on Charleston's terms, were able to have the last laugh. Instead, they cried. Proud Charleston, the London of America, was paying heavily for its arrogance; the disintegration of this beautiful, cultured city was indeed a very tragic event.

THE WHITE GRIMKÉS—ROOTS

From their early youth, Sarah (born in 1792) and Angelina (born in 1805) sensed there was something they didn't like about Charleston. How could they? Of course, no American city was lovelier, with its soaring church steeples, its palmettos and orange trees, its grand pastel townhouses with sweeping verandas, its tropical breezes and sea vistas. There was a lovely theater, with all the best works from London coming on tour. There was the St. Cecilia Society, with its baroque chamber music and elaborate balls. There was the Charleston Library Society, with a wealth of literature to read. And there were charming people with beautifully ordered lives. This is what put the young women off. To have such ordered lives, and to afford all the luxuries, slaves were necessary. It was said that Charleston grandes dames spent half of their time preparing their toilettes, another fourth paying social calls, and a final quarter disciplining their slaves.

None of the above regimen appealed to the Grimké sisters. They watched in horror as their own servants were punished by having their teeth extracted, or by flogging, or by being forced to stand on one leg for hours, with a strap connecting the other leg to the neck. Nor did they appreciate the white woman's place as chief slave of the harem, as one English observer put it. Slave women did double duty as free prostitutes for master father as well as his sons, while the mother was expected to avert her eyes. The practice was, for the owners, both gratifying and lucrative. All the illegitimate children would become more slaves, and slaves were money. They could either work or be sold.

Naturally, the fine families took all this in stride, as an essential part of their gracious lives. Yet for the Grimké sisters, these families seemed less than fine, if not evil. And the stranglehold they had on Charleston made the prospect of reform impossible. No one understood this tyranny of ruling clans better than the sisters, for their family was one of the most powerful of all. Their father was Judge John Faucheraud

Grimké, former Speaker of the state House of Representatives and presiding Justice of the South Carolina Supreme Court. Their mother, née Mary Smith, was the daughter of Charleston's richest banker-planter and the descendant of a long line of blue bloods. The Smith family patriarch, Thomas Smith, was the first landgrave of the royal colony, a title deriving from the Crown, which gave the Smith family not only vaunted status but, more significantly, first grabs at the most valuable rice-growing land in the area. The family accordingly owned countless acres. The Smith family also gave the colony several royal governors and other privileged luminaries.

The Grimké-Smith nuptials in 1784 represented the Huguenot-Anglican amalgamation that characterized the local ruling class. Most of the Huguenots who settled in South Carolina had already been Anglicized, having fled to England from France after 1685, when the Edict of Nantes was revoked and a vicious persecution of Protestants began. Lured by lavish property grants and by the colony's promise of religious freedom, the ambitious, largely lower-middle class Huguenots crossed the Atlantic to start new lives. Despite the fact that this Promised Land was a wilderness of quicksand and poisonous snakes, deadly mosquitoes, and deadlier Indians, people like the Grimkés came nonetheless. They had left all they had in France and had nothing in England. There may have been little more in American than opportunity, but that was attraction enough. Better to be big fish in a swampy Eden than fishmongers in Billingsgate.

RUTLEDGE

Judge John Grimké was the third generation of his planting family, which had further shed its French background by numerous Anglicizing marriages. The best of these was when, in 1763, the judge's sister, and Sarah and Angelina's aunt, Elizabeth, wed John Rutledge, thereby forever establishing the Grimké family in the local Anglo elite. Rutledge, one of Charleston's stellar lawyer-statesmen, lent an invaluable helping hand to his brother-in-law John Grimké in the latter's ascent to his leadership of the local bar. Rutledge knew all about marital helping hands, since his family made a specialty of success through marriage. The Rutledge success story was typical of the Charleston-style pairings that made Sarah and Angelina Grimké delighted to remain spinsters.

The Rutledge family ancestor, Andrew Rutledge, came to America from Ireland in 1730, armed with a law degree from Trinity College, Dublin, and a burning desire to get rich quick in the New World. Eking out a law practice in a Charleston already closed to outsiders seemed too difficult; blackmail was quicker. Andrew had spent some time in London, mostly in pubs, where he had accumulated tidbits of gossip about various leaders of the colony where he would relocate. One was that Nicholas Trott, the Crown's sanctimonious attorney general and a pompous planter, was not the royalty he pretended to be, but the illegitimate son of Lord Shaftesbury. Once in Charleston, Andrew stopped by to see Trott and after a closed-door chat about genealogy, Trott took a beaming Andrew under his wing. For the price of silence, Trott referred a multitude of clients to attorney Andrew.

Within two years, Andrew Rutledge married the widow of his richest client, a British colonel who had amassed a wealth of land through his good service to the Crown. (Like him, Charleston's other early British settlers had not been landed aristocrats at home but rather upwardly mobile army men or land-hungry small shopkeepers.) Rutledge was chagrined that his bride, Sarah, had only a life interest in her late husband's great estate. When Sarah died, the estate would go not to Andrew but to her daughter, "little Sarah," then eleven years old.

Upon this sobering testamentary revelation, Andrew sent to Ireland for his brother John, a ship's doctor with questionable medical credentials. John moved in with Andrew, Sarah, and little Sarah, and hung out his shingle on Broad Street. Despite the prevalence of malaria and other swampy maladies, Dr. John's medical practice did not thrive, but then he didn't expect it to. After three years, in 1735, he married little Sarah, then fourteen and reputedly one of the wealthiest women in America. The couple produced two sons, John and Edward.

With their mother's unlimited dowry, John and Edward Rutledge were sent to London for a barrister's education. After being groomed in the best British manner, they returned (John in 1760, and Edward in 1773) as the most desirable young men in town. John Rutledge won a

Grimké for a wife; Edward married a Middleton. (The Middleton family had spawned a colonial governor, Arthur Middleton, and a President of the Continental Congress, Henry.) Not to be outdone by their in-laws, John and Edward Rutledge also took turns as Governor of South Carolina.

Through Elizabeth Grimké's marriage to John Rutledge the Grimkés were, therefore, keeping heavy company, but they held their own, both in terms of marriage and accomplishment. Like his new relations the Rutledges, Elizabeth's brother John Grimké was sent to England, graduating from Trinity College, Cambridge, and reading law in the Middle Temple. His wedding to Mary Smith completed his blue-chip portfolio. The colonials may have worshipped England, but they hated royal taxes and their status as subjects, even if their subjector was the king. Grimké thus joined his fellow grandees in the councils of state that organized the American Revolution.

Ever mindful of their dynastic obligations, John and Mary Grimké produced fourteen children. Because of her many social duties, Mary didn't have much time for any one of them. The offspring thus tended to pair off. Sarah, given her thirteen-year age difference with Angelina, became the latter's surrogate mother. In fact, Angelina even addressed Sarah as "Mother." No two sisters could have been closer.

The Grimkés spent the balmy winters on their vast rice plantation in Beaufort and the summers in their Charleston mansion. Because of mosquitoes and malaria after May, the rice fields were left to the slaves and the slave drivers, while the masters fled to the supposedly more salubrious climate of the city. Often, the health-conscious Grimkés and others would go north to Newport, Rhode Island, which became known as the "Carolina Hospital." Wherever they went, a whirl of parties followed, the object of which was to arrange suitable marriages for their children. Suitable meant, almost exclusively, an affiliation with another Charleston family. By the nineteenth century, nearly everyone who mattered was related to everyone else who did. Like Tinker to Evers to Chance, Grimké to Rutledge to Middleton was the kind of triple wedding play expected of Charleston families.

All of this was too close for Sarah's and Angelina's comfort. With their long horsy faces and slightly crossed eyes, they weren't the most ravishing of Charlestonians. Yet they were among the richest, and in a city where money preempted esthetics, they would have had no trouble finding swains; far less beautiful women had married well. But the sisters weren't interested. Their Yale-educated lawyer brother Thomas had just wed Sally Drayton, one of the most eligible local princesses, and they were less than entranced by the waterfalls of champagne and other pomp and ceremony surrounding the affair. These weren't weddings; they were mergers.

Instead, the sisters chafed that they couldn't go to Yale and become lawyers and doctors like their brothers. They wanted to read, to study, to *do* something more than simply exist as decorative objects. The sisters looked longingly back to the example of their relative, Eliza Lucas Pinckney, one of the most distinguished of all early American women.

PINCKNEY

The daughter of a British colonial administrator from Antigua, Eliza Lucas at sixteen was placed in charge of three Carolina plantations which her father had received as grants from the Crown. Colonel Lucas had to be on military duty in the West Indies, and in 1738 he left Eliza in command of his American holdings as well as with the duty of nursing her invalid mother. While she taught herself law and the classics, Eliza also began experimenting with seeds her father sent her from the various Caribbean islands. She was looking for a cash crop for the plantations. In indigo, she struck blue gold. England placed a handsome bounty on the crop, which it needed to color its Royal Navy blue. Having saved Britannia from having to import French dye, Eliza, at twenty, had become very rich.

This doyenne of dye was socially conscious, too. She held classes for her slaves, teaching them to read, a practice discontinued by later Charlestonians, who felt that the white man had no burden at all. Eliza also had time for love. At twenty-two, she married the Speaker of the colonial Assembly, Charles Pinckney, a widower who was nearly fifty. In view of the unhealthiness of the region, the marriage was inevitably short-lived. Pinckney died of malaria, and young widow Eliza was left in charge of their two sons, Thomas and Charles Cotesworth Pinckney. Again, she rose admirably to the occasion. She sent the boys to England for the best education at Christ Church, Oxford, and they repaid their mother with distinguished careers.

Thomas was a general in the Revolutionary War, American Minister to England and Spain, and Governor of South Carolina. Charles Cotesworth Pinckney was Minister to France during the XYZ affair, in which France demanded a bribe before entering into diplomatic negotiations with America. The slogan "Millions for defense but not one cent for tribute" was ascribed to Pinckney in this affair and made him a symbol of probity and dedication. Shifting from the symbolic to the tangible, Charles Cotesworth Pinckney married a rich Middleton (the sister of the wife of Edward Rutledge) thus bringing the Pinckneys into the tight Rutledge-Grimké family circle.

The Grimké sisters were dismayed that there were no more Eliza Pinckneys, a woman so respected that George Washington served as one of her pallbearers. Self-made women were not socially acceptable in the Charleston of their day. Contemporary progress for Charleston's grandes dames meant unlimited leisure time—time for new clothes, new recipes, new parties. But there was no time for intellectual diversions or unorthodox aspirations—those were considered unfeminine.

The Grimkés were also dismayed that among the men they were expected to consider as potential husbands, stalwarts like Charles Cotesworth Pinckney were rare. The generation that played such a vital role in founding the new nation had played itself out. The heirs had nothing to distinguish themselves, for with all the inherited money, slaves, power, and prestige, they had little incentive to accomplish anything.

HUGER

Of the younger generation, only one of the old Charlestonians stood out. This was Francis Kinloch Huger. Huger, the scion of a venerable Huguenot family, performed perhaps the most high-minded, patriotic act of any Charlestonian. In the 1790s, while in Vienna as a young man for his medical studies, Huger learned that his hero, the Marquis de Lafayette, had been imprisoned by the warring Austrians in the impregnable fortress of Olmutz. Meeting a like-minded young German aristo-crat in a Vienna coffeehouse, Huger became involved in a romantic plot to free their idol.

When Lafayette had come to America to aid in the Revolution in 1776, he had spent his first night ashore at the Huger plantation, then the greatest house on the Carolina coast. Inns were few and far between in the South, and the common practice was to house, lavishly and at no cost, any voyager who came knocking. There was plenty of room; the isolated planters loved the company. Such were the origins of Southern hospitality. Although Francis Huger was only three at the time, he never forgot his family's most famous guest.

The boys learned that Lafayette was taken for outings from the prison in a carriage from time to time. It was then that they vowed to liberate him. They hired horses, carriages, and servants and idled about the Inn of the Three Swans in Olmutz for days, pretending they were grand tourers en route to England. Finally, Lafayette's recreation day arrived. The boys sent their entourage ahead to the border town of Hoff. They planned to give Lafayette one of their horses and ride together on the other. Hiding in a forest, they saw Lafayette go for his constitutional, guarded by only two officers. The boys swept from their lair, knocked out the guards, and totally surprised poor Lafayette.

In the course of the confusion, one of their horses got away. They gave the other to Lafayette and went off on foot to Hoff. Unfor-tunately, Lafayette didn't understand Huger's directive "to Hoff." He thought his rescuer had told him to "be off," with no particular desti-nation in mind. They all got lost, and were all captured and taken to Olmutz. The worst part for the boys was that they were locked in separate cells. If at least they could have been confined with the mar-quis, their efforts wouldn't have seemed so fruitless.

After a year of solitary confinement in the wretched dungeon, the boys were finally released, through the good offices of none other than the Huger family's close friend, General Thomas Pinckney, then Amer-ica's Minister to England. Despite the fact that Huger only saw La-fayette for a few moments, his ordeal was not without compensation. Back in America, he became a hero himself. He was feted by George Washington and received not only a staff commission from General

Pinckney but his daughter's hand in marriage. And when Lafayette was finally liberated by Napoleon, he came to Charleston to pay Huger a special visit of gratitude. Although Francis Huger received his medical degree from the University of Pennsylvania, the patriotic episode got into his blood. He stayed in the Army and became Adjutant General before returning to his plantation and the state Senate.

Huger was the kind of energetic young man that the Grimkés might have been interested in, but he was already spoken for by a Pinckney. Of course, there were other attractive, interesting young men about, but each of them seemed to be occupied. For example, John Izard Middleton was a brilliant painter and delightful conversationalist, but he had no use for Charleston. After finishing at Cambridge, he took his share of the Middleton fortune to Italy, became a famous archeologist, and never came home. Those who did stay at home were described by a visiting theatrical producer eager to cater to these prospective patrons:

The South Carolina aristocracy of the present day is not exactly what it was fifty years ago: the living generation is indolent, and but little given to intellectual, or even plausible pursuits. They may, with great propriety, be called the unproductive classes; unless, indeed, like rice grown on their plantation, where they vegetate for a considerable portion of the year, may be taken as an equivalent for their want of personal industry. They generally flock into Charleston about this period (race week, a February horse festival), and may be distinguished from all the rest of mankind by their flowing locks, well-oiled, brushed, and curled-fantastic, goatish beards with whiskers and mustaches to match; all which forms their principal stock in trade. If the avocations of these "capillary Peripatetics" be not of a very ennobling kind, it must be confessed that they *dress* with unexceptionable taste, and are quite on a par with the most refined English gentlemen in external polish and address. Their propensity for aping European Continental manners renders them extremely obnoxious to the more sedate and sensible portion of the community; and as they lounge along the streets by fours and sixes, with that peculiar swagger which renders it impossible to conceive that the town is not their own, they are constantly calling forth remarks from their fellow-townsmen which are anything but flattering to their manhood.

—LOUIS FITZGERALD TASISTRO,
Random Shots and Southern Breezes.

[79]

THE ABOLITIONIST SISTERS

Small wonder then, that Sarah and Angelina had no desire to become female ornaments for these Charleston dandies. They decided that they wanted to get out of town. Sarah's chance came at twenty-four, in 1818, when her father contracted a rare disease that was beyond the capacity of the Charleston medical corps. Although most local physicians were better qualified than the first John Rutledge, Judge Grimké's ailment baffled everyone. It was decided to send him north to Philadelphia to be treated by America's leading medical man, Dr. Phillip Synge Physick.

Dr. Physick was renowned both as the father of American surgery and the inventor of soda water. He prescribed neither for his new patient, who was accompanied by Sarah. She had eagerly volunteered to play nurse, and her mother, busy with the summer social whirl, was happy to defer to her. Baffled by the malady, Dr. Physick sent Judge Grimké off for cool, fresh air at Long Branch, New Jersey, then a chic summer resort. The judge promptly died.

There was one benefit to Sarah's journey. In Philadelphia, she discovered the Quakers. The Society of Friends' philosophy of simple, modest living and its commitment to egalitarianism was a dramatic contrast to the Charlestonian belief in ostentatious elitism. Quaker nonviolence was contrasted with the slave-whipping that was an entrenched Charleston custom. Women were not suppressed; they could even be preachers. Sarah was a ready convert; before long, "thee" and "thou" became part of her language.

When Sarah returned to Charleston, she was considered odder than ever before. Not only was she not married, she wasn't even Episcopal any more. The only one Sarah appealed to was her younger sister, Angelina, who followed Sarah's Quaker footsteps. After a while, the colony's vaunted freedom of religion came to be viewed by the sisters as a sham. In the early 1830s the two women felt compelled to move to Philadelphia.

Soon, however, they decided that even the Society of Friends was too confining, too passive. That the Quakers had not taken a dynamic position on slavery distressed the women. They wanted to go all the way, to be activists. Angelina, the more intrepid of the two, broke the ice. She wrote a letter to William Lloyd Garrison, editor of *The Liberator,* that most inflammatory journal of abolitionism. In it, she urged Garrison, who had nearly been tarred and feathered even by Northern mobs for his antislavery agitation, to press on:

If persecution is the means which God has ordained for the accomplishment of this great end, EMANCIPATION, then . . . LET IT COME, for it is my deep, solemn deliberate conviction that this is a cause worth dying for.
                              —CATHERINE BIRNEY,
                              The Grimké Sisters, p. 126.

To the surprise of Angelina and everyone else, Garrison published the letter. The die was cast. She had betrayed her class, in print. Rather than recant, Angelina forged ahead. Her next writing in 1836 was her *Appeal to the Christian Women of the South,* a thirty-six-page pamphlet challenging her sisters not only to urge their husbands to free their slaves, but also to free the women's own personal servants, even if it meant sacrificing some of the comforts of their cotillion existence. She exhorted the women to educate the blacks, to pay them wages, and to petition their legislatures for emancipation. She closed with a thinly veiled threat of violence:

Slavery must be abolished. . . . Now there are only two ways in which it can be effected, by moral power or physical force, and it is for *you* to choose which of these you prefer. Slavery always has, and always will, produce insurrections wherever it exists because it is a violation of the natural order of things, and no human power can much longer perpetuate it.
                              —ANGELINA EMILY GRIMKÉ,
                              Appeal to the Christian Women of the South, p. 33.

Angelina's tract, published by the American Anti-Slavery Society of New York, was the talk of the country. Nowhere did the work create a bigger stir than Charleston, where it was publicly burned by local postal officials. Here was a Southern aristocrat, and a woman at that, who opposed slavery. It was revolutionary indeed and gave abolitionism the impetus it needed to become a major national movement. The police gave notice to Mrs. Grimké that her daughter Angelina would be thrown into jail like a vicious criminal should she ever venture into

Charleston again. Threats on Angelina's life were legion, but the sisters were undaunted. The only family member they had been close to was their brother Thomas, an eminent lawyer who had been swayed by his sisters' views and had become an influential speaker in the world peace movement. His death from cholera in 1834 had been the catalyst that brought Angelina out of the closet. Though they would have ordinarily paid obligatory periodic family visits, the sisters were not broken-hearted at being forbidden to do so. They never saw Charleston again.

Not to be outdone by Angelina, Sarah penned her own *Epistle to the Clergy of the Southern States.* The sisters became powerful stump speakers, attracting and swaying huge, curious crowds throughout the North. When certain proper New England ministers objected to their platform appearances as unfeminine, the Grimkés got so angry that they added women's rights to the growing list of grievances they spoke out on. In many ways, they railed, women were treated barely better than slaves. People began to listen. The sisters' influence was undeniable. Their 1839 tract, *American Slavery as It Is,* sold over 100,000 copies in its first year and was the best-selling antislavery treatise in history.

Though Sarah never married, the folks at home were further appalled when Angelina wed arch-abolitionist Theodore Weld, who had a wild appearance that presaged the Bolsheviks to come. The Southern outrage reached a climax with the 1852 publication of *Uncle Tom's Cabin,* written by Harriet Beecher Stowe, a close friend of the Grimkés. Indeed, Sarah and Angelina gave Mrs. Stowe much of her material. That most villainous character in American literature, the slave driver, Simon Legree, got his name and probably much more from a Charleston family that had once been among the Grimkés' closest friends, a slave-rich dynasty named Legare (pronounced in Charlestonese, Legree, just as Huger is pronounced You-gee).

CHARLESTON'S LAST STAND

While the Grimké sisters were on their Northern juggernaut, the city they left behind was not standing idly by. Charleston was the seat of

American privilege, and each new attack on it made the local aristocracy fiercer in its defense of its cherished status. By the 1830s, the founding families were over a century removed from their roots as land-hungry bourgeoisie. Now they fancied themselves royalty, with slaves as an inalienable prerequisite of their position. Charlestonians were princes of the earth; the Yankees, in their view, were peasant tradesmen, and bitterly jealous ones.

A typical example of this metamorphosis was the Manigault (pronounced Mani-goe) family. Gabriel and Pierre Manigault were two poor French Huguenot brothers who had emigrated from France to England in 1685 to escape the anti-Protestant reign of terror of Louis XIV. Finding it hard to succeed in London, the brothers came to South Carolina in 1695, armed with small land-grants for their pioneer efforts and with a small black slave named Sambo, who was to help them clear their land. Unfortunately, the land was mostly marsh and water, and was unclearable. Setting aside dreams of stately homes, the brothers moved to Charleston, where Gabriel became a carpenter, and Peter (who had Anglicized his name) set up a small pub with beds for lodgers.

Some years later, Gabriel died after falling from a scaffold. Peter, however, had a surer footing. To cut his overhead on imported spirits, he built a brandy still, which grew into a large distillery. Because of the colonists' insatiable demand for liquor, brandy enabled Peter to build warehouses and branch out into nonspiritous merchandise. Peter had married the widow of a fellow Huguenot émigré. Their son, Gabriel, named in memory of his late uncle, grew up and joined his father's thriving business, which soon included the buying and selling of slaves. This was the most lucrative line of all.

By the 1730s, Gabriel Manigault was the wealthiest merchant in the colony. But trade, like law, was to a would-be grandee only the means to an end. Land, and only land, meant respectability. Now Gabriel could buy all the respectability he ever dreamed of. He acquired a host of plantations, and became the toast of the colony, instead of merely being its bartender. Father Pierre had changed his name to Peter, a small measure, yet essential to assimilation. Gabriel went father one better by marrying the daughter of one of the original English

lords proprietor of the Carolinas. Their sons were sent to England for
schooling, then were married into the leading English-descended clans;
they built great plantation manses and townhouses and furnished them
with the best European furnishings. On the patriotic side, the family
furnished no great warriors, yet was just as useful to the cause; Gabriel
bankrolled the colony during the Revolution. By 1800, the Manigaults
were so rich, powerful, and revered that their humble beginnings had
become ancient history.

Dynasties like the Manigaults had worked hard for their plantations. Yet the fact that their elaborate lives depended on slavery made
them highly nervous. The Denmark Vesey slave insurrection of 1822
turned their worst anxieties into realities. Denmark Vesey was a free
black carpenter who had bought his freedom through winnings in a
lottery for which his master had given him tickets. A brilliant, literate,
angry man, Vesey organized a labyrinthine plot among the local slaves
that was nothing short of a revolution. They would seize the Charleston arsenal, kill *all* the local white men, rape the wealthiest white
women, torch the plantations, and loot the banks. Then they would sail
off into the sunset for Santo Domingo, whose own slave revolt under
Toussaint L'Ouverture had been Vesey's inspiration.

Vesey's fatal mistake was in trying to organize house servants as
well as field slaves. These wigged and liveried blacks were the elite of
the slave corps and revered their masters for their special position.
Predictably, one of them informed on Vesey. Vesey and thirty-four of
his co-conspirators were hanged in the middle of town, and all the area
slaves were herded by to be chastened by the carnage. More than thirty
others were tortured, then deported. The remaining slaves were terrified, though not as much as their masters. Whites were well outnumbered by blacks in the Charleston population of about 40,000.

Following Vesey's death, Charleston lived in an imagined state of
siege, greatly exacerbated by the Yankee abolitionist attacks spear-
headed by the Grimké sisters. The many witchdoctors, so popular with
the blacks, were put out of business. An early curfew was imposed.
Blacks were shackled and whipped for even a dirty look. Slaves were not
allowed to learn to read and write. No master could free his slaves
without the special consent of the legislature. All citizens had to take a
loyalty oath to South Carolina. All dissent was stifled.

WILLIAM BYRD II *(1674–1744).* The First Gentleman of Virginia and the prototypical Southern aristocrat, based on the English model.
To forget his own sorrows, Byrd stayed in London and immersed himself in sex. While he would spend at least a few hours of each day attending to Virginia business, Byrd would typically spend the early evening drinking at a coffeehouse, then go gambling, then whoring. Additionally, he kept several mistresses, whose usual fee was two guineas per hour.
(Courtesy Wilson Randolph Gathings)

WESTOVER. Stately home of William Byrd II.
The most glorious plantation in all Tidewater.
(Courtesy Wilson Randolph Gathings)

JOHN RANDOLPH of Roanoke *(1773–1833)*. The South's greatest orator, its most
dynamic politician, and its most fervent conservative.
I am an aristocrat. I love liberty. I hate equality.
(Courtesy Wilson Randolph Gathings)

NANCY RANDOLPH. The femme fatale of the incestuous scandal at Bizarre
that sundered the Randolph family. She later married
the distinguished Knickerbocker, Gouverneur Morris.
*A vampire that, after sucking the best blood of my race, has flitted off to the North,
and struck her harpy fangs into an infirm old man.*
(*Courtesy Wilson Randolph Gathings*)

GEORGE WYTHE *(1726–1806)*. Great Virginia lawyer and mentor
of Thomas Jefferson, Wythe was murdered by a jealous nephew outraged
over Wythe's black mistress.
Wythe was so august that no one dared question his living arrangements.
(Courtesy Wilson Randolph Gathings)

ANGELINA EMILY GRIMKÉ *(1805–1879)* and SARAH MOORE GRIMKÉ *(1792–1873)*.
Charleston aristocrats turned radical abolitionists/feminists.
Charleston grandes dames spent half their time preparing their toilettes, another fourth paying social calls, and a final quarter disciplining their slaves. None of the above regimen appealed to the Grimké sisters. They wanted to read, to study, to do something more than simply exist as decorative objects.
(New York Public Library)

ARCHIBALD HENRY GRIMKÉ *(1849–1930)* and REVEREND FRANCIS JAMES GRIMKÉ
(1850–1937). Illegitimate mulatto nephews of the Grimké sisters
and early leaders of the civil rights movement.
What Angelina found were two strikingly handsome boys with the patrician features of their brother. Their hair was a bit more wavy, their skin tawnier. Otherwise, the boys were unmistakably Grimkés.
(New York Public Library)

ROBERT BARNWELL RHETT *(1800–1876)*. First cousin of the Grimké sisters,
a champion of slavery, known as the Father of Secession.
What made Rhett so popular was that he spoke from the heart. His passion came from his roots,
which were the most aristocratic in the state. He evoked for the planters
a sense of patrician glory that was uniquely Charleston's.
(Courtesy Wilson Randolph Gathings)

JUDAH P. BENJAMIN *(1811–1884)*.
The Brains of the Confederacy.
Benjamin was a giant success on multiple
fronts. Socially, he was a gentleman sugar
planter and the toast of the Creole aristocracy.
Professionally, he was America's highest-
paid laywer. Politically, he served the United
States as Senator and the Confederate
States as Secretary of State. He was possibly
the most distinguished Jew
in American history.
(New York Historical Society)

NATALIE BENJAMIN, Creole wife of
Judah P. and one of the most spoiled
women in Southern history.
Oh, talk not to me of economy.
It is so fatiguing.
(Judah P. Benjamin Memorial Association)

JOHN SLIDELL *(1793–1871)*. Political overlord of Louisiana and the Confederate Minister to France. *Slidell helped elect James K. Polk president by his own fifth column of paid ruffians whom he herded onto two large steamboats. The voters sailed down the Mississippi casting votes at every stop along the bayous. Their quintuplicate ballots sealed a close election. In return for this ingenuity, Slidell quickly rose to a position of prominence in the Democratic Party.* (Courtesy Wilson Randolph Gathings)

MATHILDE SLIDELL. John Slidell's daughter, whom he married off in order to raise money for the South. *Slidell had a secret weapon—his ravishing young daughter. He unleased her on Frederic Erlanger, the shy son of Emil Erlanger, the most important banker in Europe after the Rothschilds. Tantalized by Slidell's bait of his Creole daughter, the Erlangers offered the Confederacy a giant loan of $25 million.* (Courtesy Wilson Randolph Gathings)

BERNARD DE MARIGNY *(1785–1868)*. Flamboyant Louisiana Creole who gambled away
the French Quarter, which he owned.
Bernard even established a Rue de l'Amour for his many kept women
and a Rue des Biens Enfants for his horde of illegitimate children.
(The Historic New Orleans Collection)

JEFFERSON DAVIS *(1808–1889)*,
President of the Confederacy, and
VARINA HOWELL DAVIS *(1826–1906)*,
his First Lady.
Despite the possible stigma of new wealth,
the Confederacy had to be led by hard-liners.
Of all the fire-eaters, as the rabid
secessionists were known, the Jefferson Davises
were the most polished,
most social of the lot.
(Courtesy Wilson Randolph Gathings)

JAMES MURRAY MASON *(1798–1871)*. Confederate Minister to England.
Despite Mason's disconcerting habits, such as chewing tobacco, and spitting on the floor of the
House of Commons, the English upper classes were crazy about him.
(Courtesy Wilson Randolph Gathings)

FRANKLIN J. MOSES, JR. *(1838–1906)*.
Dissolute scalawag Reconstruction
Governor of South Carolina.
*Moses had bacchanals almost every night,
surrounding himself with black prostitutes
whom he dressed in diamonds, furs, and Paris
finery, all paid for by the state treasury.*
(Courtesy Wilson Randolph Gathings)

GENERAL PIERRE G. T. BEAUREGARD
(1818–1893). The most elegant general of
the Confederacy, who sold his
"image" to the corrupt Louisiana lottery.
*Jungles of flowers were sent to him.
Racehorses, children, even women's corsets were
named Beauregard. On his campaigns, the
suave Creole always carried a trunk full of
love letters, for inspiration.*
(Courtesy Wilson Randolph Gathings)

GENERAL NATHAN BEDFORD FORREST *(1821–1877).* Confederate cavalry hero
and first Imperial Wizard of the Ku Klux Klan.
He loved to fight, loved to kill, and he believed in fear as a vital weapon. Frequently wounded
in the midst of a fray, he had twenty-nine horses shot out from under him.
(New York Historical Society)

GENERAL WADE HAMPTON *(1818–
1902)*. Old-guard, powerful South
Carolina Governor and Senator who
rallied the Southern aristocracy and
brought Reconstruction to an end.
*He went stalking into the woods with his
 ounds, armed with only a huge knife. When
he found one of the black bears, he would
stab it to death; then, hoisting the four-
 hundred-pound beast onto a waiting horse,
he would ride back to the plantation
in triumph.*
(Courtesy Wilson Randolph Gathings)

LUCIUS Q. C. LAMAR *(1825–1893)*.
Leader of postbellum reconciliation and
Supreme Court Justice.
*Lamar became known as the Great
 acificator. He secured his own election to the
Senate and, with it, an impregnable
position as America's favorite
token Southerner.*
(New York Historical Society)

WARD MCALLISTER *(1827–1895)*.
Savannahian bon vivant, who was
America's foremost social arbiter and
creator of the "400." MRS. WILLIAM
BACKHOUSE ASTOR—Ward McAllister's
"Mystic Rose," the queen
of New York society.
New York's elite thought it was an
outrage that Ward was spilling their secrets
to the masses. But the book was more than
a primer on how to be socially acceptable. It
was a paean to Southern social superiority
and a satire of the rich Yankee as
parvenu tradesman.
(Courtesy Wilson Randolph Gathings)

While most of the wealthy local youth were too preoccupied with their London tailors and other dandyisms, the more intellectually adept devoted themselves to the politics of defending their state and its planter plutocracy. Most of the statesmen who spoke for South Carolina, though, were not old-line at all. Rather, they were a new breed who found power at the polls, not the plantations. Their secret was that they said exactly what the old families wanted to hear.

The foremost of these champions was John C. Calhoun. Calhoun began life as anything but an aristocrat. His Scotch-Irish parents lived in the inland, up-country piney woods and owned a small farm. The family was thrifty and ambitious, and sent young Calhoun to Yale. Nevertheless, a Yale diploma alone was not enough to insinuate him into the inner sancta of the Grimkés and Pinckneys. Brains, charm, looks were all irrelevant unless one had land. Calhoun got his land by romancing a wealthy distant cousin who owned a rice plantation outside of Charleston. This gave him both the entrée and the financial independence to enter South Carolina politics.

Calhoun did almost everything in American government except become President, which he narrowly missed on several occasions. He was a Senator, Jackson's Vice President, Tyler's Secretary of State, Monroe's Secretary of War, and a third of the Calhoun-Clay-Webster great triumvirate which dominated national politics. But where South Carolina was concerned, Calhoun's greatest role was as defender of the theory of states' rights. According to this theory, if a state believed that an act of Congress was unconstitutional, the state did not have to obey it. The first such act that aroused Charleston's ire and that of Calhoun was the tariff that protected developing Northern industry. Its heavy duty penalized Charleston, which manufactured nothing and bought all its luxuries from abroad.

THE SECESSIONIST COUSIN

The 1828 "Tariff of Abominations," as the South denounced it, was merely a prelude to further Yankee interferences, the worst of which was the mounting effort to abolish slavery, that most pivotal of all Southern institutions. To the Southern aristocracy, this was the last straw. They cringed at the prospect that their fabled life-style might be legislated out of existence. Taking states' rights to its logical end, the elite felt it might be better to be outside the Union than not to be rich within it. On the Washington scene, Calhoun was their champion, but an even greater force was Charleston's own aristocrat, Robert Barnwell Rhett, "Father of Secession." And curiously enough, Rhett was the first cousin of the notorious Grimkés, whose treacherous agitation was causing so much of the trouble. A diverse family, to be sure, that could accommodate all extremes.

Rhett's father was the brother of Sarah and Angelina's mother, Mary Smith Grimké. Rhett had a host of noble antecedents going all the way back to Sir John Yeamans, a legitimate knight of the realm, the original founder of the colony, and its royal governor. Rhett's original name was Robert Barnwell Smith, but he changed it to one borne by the ancestor he venerated most. This was Colonel William Rhett, a dashing soldier who became admiral of a Charleston fleet assembled by the colony in the early 1700s in defense against the pirates who preyed on its commerce. The predators were so bold that they once sailed into the harbor with Blackbeard at their helm, seized eight ships, and demanded a treasure trunk of medicines from local doctors as a going-away present.

The swashbuckling Colonel Rhett drove the pirates out of business by winning a nine-hour pistol duel with their leader, the Barbadian buccaneer, Stede Bonnet. The fact that Bonnet was educated, courtly, and English appealed to the local gentry, but they hanged him anyway. The colonel became a hero and was rewarded with the post of customs collector, potentially the most lucrative in the colony. Realizing this potential to the fullest, he was eventually charged with smuggling, extortion, larceny, and all the other opportunities attendant to his position, and he died in prison.

Robert Barnwell Rhett prided himself on having all his ancestor's good points, and none of the bad. Accordingly, he was in debt most of his life. Although, like his aunt Mary Smith Grimké, he descended from Landgrave Smith, his father, James Smith, had made a mess of his great inheritance. Given the best childhood Europe could offer and educated at London's Inns of Court, James should have stayed at the

Middle Temple. Instead, he fell prey to the lure of the plantation. Too interested in books to supervise his slaves, James was an abject failure in the rice fields. He couldn't even afford to send his son, Robert Barnwell, to England for his education. The boy, born in 1800, was shuttled around to the private tutors who lived with various members of the extended family.

At one point, he and cousin Sarah Grimké spent several months together on one of the Smith plantations. They were both in their twenties and Sarah had come for a long visit to forget the trauma of her father's death. Robert Barnwell Smith, now Rhett, was extremely handsome, with a splendid sense of humor, and extremely well-read. Sarah was supposedly taken with him. Had it not been for their close consanguinity, he might have lured her out of spinsterhood. At that point in their lives, he hadn't developed his political philosophy but was busy reading law, which Sarah herself yearned to do. Because Sarah was still not married, the relatives contemplated matching her up with Rhett, but first cousins were just too close. Had they been second cousins, the history of the South might have been different.

As it turned out, Sarah Grimké went off to the Quakers, where all her antislavery, anti-Southern sentiments were crystallized. Barnwell Rhett, on the other hand, went off to study law with Sarah's brother, Thomas. There all Rhett's proslavery, pro-Southern feelings came into clear focus. Upon his admission to the bar, Rhett immediately distinguished himself as the best young speaker in the state. Southerners loved to talk, but Rhett talked better than anyone. He was such a smash in court that he quickly built up a major practice, especially with cousin Thomas Grimké steering him clients. Another major aid was his marriage in 1827 to Elizabeth Burnet, a highborn young woman whose guardian, her uncle, was Henry de Saussure, chancellor of the state court of appeals and founder of South Carolina College, at the time the Harvard of the South. Now in the state's legal and social vanguard, Rhett solidified his position by buying plantations (on easy credit) and winning election to the state legislature. By age thirty-two, he was South Carolina's Attorney General.

What made Rhett so popular was that he spoke from the heart. Calhoun, the poor up-country outsider, was an eloquent champion of the South, but Rhett was far more fervent. His passion came from his roots, which were the most aristocratic in the state. No one could have been prouder of his heritage and no interest could have been more vested than his. Rhett spoke as if his life depended on it. Better than anyone else, he evoked for the planters a sense of patrician glory that was uniquely Charleston's.

Rhett was the crown prince of nostalgia, and nostalgia was, increasingly, all that Charleston had left. Denmark Vesey and the Grimké sisters weren't the only hostile forces at work. The steamboat had spelled doom for Charleston as an important port, for it made shipping a much more independent industry. The city could no longer count on the trade winds blowing unpowered sailing vessels to her balmy harbor. Instead, the steamships focused on New York, which was closer to Europe, and on New Orleans, which was closer to the Mississippi Cotton Kingdom that had vanquished the rice fields as the South's chief money producer. At the same time Charleston was being eclipsed as a port, New England was growing rich on its factories. It seemed that neither North nor South *needed* Charleston any more. Even South Carolina didn't need her. The cotton-growing, up-country small farmers greatly resented Charleston's hegemony as far out of proportion to her actual population.

In truth, Charleston was becoming increasingly isolated, a beleaguered city-state, rather than the national city it had been at the time of the Revolution. As the original Pinckneys and Rutledges began to die off, Charleston treasured a native son like Barnwell Rhett, who could speak for it. The rest of the state disliked him intensely for his highborn arrogance. But nothing fazed him. For him, Charleston *was* the South.

In the 1830s Rhett turned on his old mentor, Thomas Grimké, a supporter of the Union, whom Rhett saw as a victim of his sisters' heresies. When Grimké supported the efforts of the American Colonization Society to free the blacks and send them back to Africa, Rhett scorned the notion as an abolitionist plot. And when Grimké, an educational reformer, suggested before the Yale Phi Beta Kappa Society that students should not be expected to learn the classics by rote, but instead be taught to think for themselves and use their minds to better mankind, Rhett was aghast. He didn't believe that mankind could be improved, by education or otherwise. Self-help, in Rhett's view, did not exist.

Rhett was not ashamed to articulate what his fellow patricians believed. Blacks were inferior, he claimed. Their lot in life was to do the world's dirty work, while the white aristocracy could enjoy the higher pursuits of civilization. In return, the whites could care for blacks better than the blacks could care for themselves.

Unless capital forgets its instinct, overworking, starvation and cold . . . and the heart-sickening fears which often make life one long agony, cannot be the fate of the laborer. An enlightened self-interest will ever dictate that all the virtues which lead to happiness and contentment should be cultivated. In such a form of society, there is no collision between capital and labor, and a free Government may exist so long as the intelligence and virtue of the most enlightened and cultivated portion of the population will permit.

In this speech to Congress in 1852 Rhett was preaching benevolent despotism. For years, he boldly urged the South to get out of the Union. He urged it in the House of Representatives, in the Senate, and all over the South. By 1861, this most indefatigable force of states' rights had won the South to his position. Rhett and his elegant constituency were truly shocked when he did not become the most benevolent despot of all, the President of the Confederacy. But, despite his distinguished lineage, Rhett was at a disadvantage. His realm was rice, while Jefferson Davis was the voice of the land of cotton, now the keystone of the Southern economy. Because money was power, whatever cotton wanted, cotton got. In addition, Rhett was seen as a man who was more concerned about South Carolina and specifically Charleston than about the Confederate States as a whole. As it turned out, the sole representative of Charleston in the Confederate cabinet was a poor German immigrant named Gustavus Memminger, who grew up not on a baronial plantation, but in a Charleston orphanage. Memminger made a name as a lawyer, but it wasn't a name like Rhett.

How the mighty had fallen! Yet Charleston could still find beauty in her own demise. Hugh Swinton Legare, whose family inspired Si-

mon Legree, was a local planter-lawyer-litterateur, who had roman-
tically compared decaying Charleston to sinking Venice:

When we read . . . of the prostrate and torpid conditions of Venice, certain
resemblances in her situation and history, with those of this once flourish-
ing city, bring them home to us with a sharp adaptation. Having their
origin in common from religious intolerance and persecution, the colonists
who took refuge . . . amidst the Lagunes of Venice, and the Huguenots
who fled to these shores, have other points of assimilation in the site,
fortunes and look of the cities they respectively founded. Beneath a south-
erly clime and sunny skies, in a champain country, and with a choice
harbor, the structures of their sanctuaries, as you approach from the water
of Sullivan's Island, corresponding to the Lido, forcibly induce a mutal
recollection—and when the moon has thrown its light around, as the solitary passenger, through the deserted and sepulchral streets of Charleston,
meditates upon her time-worn, rusty, and mouldering edifices, he is gloom-
ily reminded of the blank, icy and desolate aspect of that other city afar;
now manifestly expiring before the eyes of her inhabitants, and fast sinking
into the slime of her own canals. —*Southern Review*, Vol. I, 1828.

The beginning of the Civil War was Charleston's final moment of
glory. Barnwell Rhett triumphantly led the signing of the Ordinance
of Secession before a tearfully cheering assemblage at, appropriately,
Charleston's and America's most aristocratic affair, the St. Cecilia Ball.
This was sponsored by the St. Cecilia Society, originally a music appreciation circle that had become the supreme arbiter of "us" and "them,"
old and new. Its influence extended far beyond its lavish annual full-
dress ball. The society was all-male: the members planned the ball,
invited wives and daughters, and arranged dancing partners, who
would, frequently, end up marrying each other. This was the way
Charlestonians ordered their lives, and the society was the absolute
preserver of the status quo. To be a member, one's father had to have
been one, and his father, and his. Membership was assured for eternity,
except for some outrageous scandal or below-station marriage, which
rarely happened in that proper city.

The night of the secession, December 20, 1860, was Barnwell
Rhett's night, and the Old Guard drank and danced as if there would
be no tomorrow. In fact, there wasn't. After the attack on Fort Sumter

in April 1861, it was all downhill, for Charleston, for the Confederacy, and for Rhett. Spurned by the Confederate cotton leadership, Rhett retreated to his paper, the *Charleston Mercury,* to lash out against the South's military and diplomatic failures. No one listened. By the time the war was lost, Charleston was sacked and burned, and Rhett was forced to escape to an unfurnished Alabama plantation named Castle Dismal.

Because he had devoted his entire efforts to his secessionist cause, Rhett's neglected finances were as dismal as his new home. He couldn't even afford books for the library. Worse, he had developed skin cancer on his face. The burning treatment used at the time had mutilated his distinguished features, with the result that this most public of public men was now too embarrassed to appear before anyone except his immediate family. After the war, the Rhett clan moved to another plantation near New Orleans. There, Rhett's son edited the *Picayune,* his son-in-law wrote the biography of General Beauregard, and Rhett himself, while closeted because of his deformed visage, wrote and reigned as the aging sage of the Southern aristocracy. He died in 1876.

Although Sarah and Angelina had won the war, the rest of the family refused to admit defeat. On his deathbed, Barnwell Rhett—who had not communicated with his two cousins in many years—maintained that the Southern way of life was noble and right. And the Charleston Grimkés wrote the sisters that though their slaves, home, and land had been taken from them, and they were living on grits and water, they would still be happy "to die for slavery and the Confederacy."

Still, family was family. Sarah and Angelina were treated as equals in their mother's will. Though they promptly freed the slaves they inherited, the rest of their inheritance enabled them to live quite comfortably. In return, they never forgot their kin, differences notwithstanding. The sisters supported an invalid brother, a staunch slavery man, in Charleston until his death in 1864. They even insisted that their proslavery sisters come to live with them to ease the blight of Reconstruction and to give them some decent food. Reluctantly, two of the Grimké women came north, but the ideological differences proved insurmountable. Preferring the ravages of Charleston to Yankee comfort, and wanting to be with their "own people," they returned South.

The ones who really thrived on Sarah's and Angelina's care were the black nephews. Frank became the pastor of a major Presbyterian Church in Washington, D.C., and a trustee of Howard University. Archie practiced law in Boston, was the leader of the NAACP, wrote books about William Lloyd Garrison and Charles Sumner, and was American consul in Santo Domingo, whose 1791 slave insurrection had inspired Denmark Vesey.

The sisters kept on marching. When they died—Sarah in 1873, Angelina in 1879—Charleston, a city of eulogies, refused to recognize them at all. Yet the sisters had changed the city, as they had changed the South. Haughty, aristocratic Charleston, now wasting away as an elegant slum, refused to remember; but Charleston, deep inside, could never forget.

IV

Sybaris on the Delta: New Orleans

In 1828 a cherubic, sixteen-year-old Jewish Charlestonian, fresh out of Yale, arrived in New Orleans to seek his fortune. At first blush, the city seemed anything but inviting. It had a few fairly imposing government buildings from the Spanish and French regimes, the charming town-houses of the French Quarter with their ornate wrought-iron balconies, and an occasional columned plantation manor on the outskirts. But the rest of the city was a swampy slum. Wooden houses were built on stilts above the quicksand-muddy thoroughfares to avoid the alligators and snakes. The steambath air was a cacophony of vicious mosquitoes. Malaria and yellow fever were everywhere. The main artery, Canal Street, was a vast open sewage ditch. The stench was overpowering. Venice it was not.

Nevertheless, despite its Amazonian ambience, New Orleans was hardly torpid. The city of 50,000 was already becoming one of the world's great ports. There were steamboats from the Mississippi, banana boats from Central America, luxury cargo boats from Europe, slave boats from Africa. The city was cosmopolitan, and it was booming. The young boy could not help being excited. Like hordes of similarly inclined fortune hunters from all over America, he regarded the burgeoning metropolis at the mouth of the Mississippi River as the fiscal Promised Land. His instincts were impeccable. In the golden age of the Cotton Kingdom, New Orleans became the greatest city in the South. The boy became arguably the greatest of all Southerners. His name was Judah Philip Benjamin.

Benjamin was a giant success on multiple fronts. Socially, he was a gentleman sugar planter and the toast of the Creole aristocracy. Professionally, he was America's highest-paid lawyer, with clients from all over the world, and wealth enough to enable him to turn down an appointment to the U.S. Supreme Court. Politically, he served the United States as Senator, and the Confederate States as, successively, Attorney General, Secretary of War, and Secretary of State (hence his nickname "the Brains of the Confederacy"). And, after the Civil War, he escaped to England, where he forged still another brilliant career as one of the greatest barristers who ever served the Queen. Considered the American Disraeli, Benjamin was one of the most distinguished Jews in American history.

All this in a Louisiana where, only short decades before his arrival, Jews were declared non grata by the French region's infamous Code Noir, which kept blacks in bondage and kept Jews out. Nor was Judah's religion his only stigma. He had been disgraced in Charleston by the bankruptcy of his poor merchant father. He was even more disgraced in New Haven, where he had been stripped of his Old Blues on account of thievery, a nasty blot on his brilliant academic record. Judah was a golden boy, but a badly tarnished one. New Orleans was his last resort.

OPEN CITY

In the 1820s, New Orleans was the last resort of many scoundrels and geniuses. Blots of all sorts were stock features on the records of ambitious new arrivals. Judah may have been inspired by Edward Livingston, Hudson River grandee and mayor of New York. Livingston fled to New Orleans in 1803 after being implicated in a municipal fiscal scandal on a far grander scale than Judah's New Haven folly. One of Livingston's lieutenants had absconded with one hundred thousand dollars' worth of bonds, and Livingston assumed the blame for his subordinate. His past associations did not impede his career in Louisiana, though. Livingston immediately was lionized by the locals as a great lawyer-politician. They were proud to have him. Judah felt that he, too, could find a fresh start.

After all, New Orleans was America's open city, both in commerce and in its notoriously decadent night life. Judah Benjamin had every reason to hope to make money, lots of money, and to have a good time in the process. But socially? How could a poor Jew, old school ties notwithstanding, hope to crash the formidable, seemingly impenetrable, French aristocracy? Easy. Unlike the rest of the stratified South, New Orleans had an elite that possessed no Old World antecedents. Or, at least, none that they wanted to talk about. Here skeletons outnumbered closets.

The members of the ruling class of the city were known as Creoles, a term denoting the white descendants of the original French colonists. The term colonist normally has active connotations, conjuring up images of intrepid adventurers carving out a new frontier. In Louisiana things were different. In contrast to the upwardly mobile Virginians and South Carolinians, who could trace their roots to the lesser English gentry or at least the bourgeoisie, the heritage of the Creoles was decidely embedded in the French lower depths. The first families of Louisiana were largely composed of thieves and prostitutes, rounded up from French prisons and shipped to the New World. No colonists could have been more passive.

From the time of La Salle's explorations in 1682, the French had been eager to establish an empire in the Louisiana territory. Unfortunately, a coalition of Indians, heat, insects, and reptiles thwarted all ambitions. Then in 1717 a remarkable Scottish huckster named John Law talked Louis XIV into granting him a monopoly on the colony. Law's promise in exchange was that he would populate the empty region for the Sun King. Immediately Law plastered the walls of Paris with posters extolling the territory as a paradise of gold and silver, fountains of youth, and the like. When the savvy Frenchmen failed to nibble at the bait, Law panicked. He had been selling a fortune in stock in his Mississippi Company. Now he had to have people, any people, in his El Dorado, or his fraudulent scheme would be uncovered.

Hence the sweep of jails and mental hospitals. Vagabond peasants straying into Paris would be collared and given the hard sell. By 1718 Law's ships were packed; Louisiana was launched. Still, the catch was the population. Never paragons of initiative to begin with, the passengers' indolent instincts were reinforced by Law's promise of African slaves to do all the work—mining that gold and silver and scooping up pearls from the Gulf. When the riches never materialized, the settlers (or at least those who hadn't died of assorted jungle diseases) simply reverted to their Parisian routine of stealing, wenching, and drinking. By 1731 almost anyone who could returned to France. There were barely one thousand inhabitants left, clustered in the swamp that would become New Orleans. Law's Mississippi bubble burst. The king revoked his charter and again assumed the responsibility to civilize the endless Louisiana wilderness.

The Crown's first effort was to upgrade the population. An attempt to recruit the black sheep scions of aristocratic families came to naught. More successful was a convent of Ursuline nuns, established to convert the joyless *filles de joie* into something vaguely resembling ladies. Additionally, a shipload of well-behaved girls from orphanages and poor farming communities was dispatched to provide more stable conjugality than that offered by the prostitutes. These young women were known as *filles à la cassette,* or casket girls, because of the little trousseau box each of them carried. To be descended from a casket girl and a French soldier (these poor conscripts constituted the flower of local manhood) is thus the height of New Orleans lineage.

Louisiana's first taste of elegance came with the appointment in 1743 of the new royal governor, the Marquis de Vaudreuil. This foppish courtier was intent on making the most of his American tour of duty. Seeing himself as the Sun King of the bayous, the marquis built a governor's mansion, amid the huts of New Orleans. It was his "petit Versailles," where he gave lavish balls, established a theater, and upgraded the city's dress code. However, he was chagrined that his only guests were soldiers, casket girls, and other functionaries.

Desperately longing for some more fashionable compatriots, the marquis turned to the pork barrel. Trade monopolies, inflated government positions, and kickbacks of all sorts lured a number of his relatives and friends to the Delta. New Orleans' brief era of elegance ended abruptly in 1753 when the marquis was replaced by a puritanical governor. Still, the seeds of pretension had been planted among the locals. As one generation succeeded another, the sordid past became increasingly romanticized.

The French at home were never, however, enchanted with Louisiana. In fact, they were delighted, in 1762, to unload the territory on Spain as a reward for Spanish assistance during the French and Indian War, and to redeem Spain's loss of Florida to the English in that conflict. The Spanish administration, under the mercenary Irish General Alexander O'Reilly, was singularly corrupt. Bribes, graft, and the sale of political offices were commonplace, though few Spanish other than the administrators actually settled in Louisiana. In 1800 Napoleon took the territory back for France, but his need for empire was less urgent than his need for cash. Besides, the territory was still quite an albatross; the French remained loath to become settlers. Because President Jefferson sensed the strategic importance of the port of New Orleans, he was quick to conclude a $15-million deal. Americans, who were apparently much more intrepid colonists than the French, began to pour into the new territory.

By the time of the Louisiana Purchase in 1803, Creole society had clearly emerged, less a matter of grand tradition than as a xenophobic reaction to the rough-and-ready Americans. The roughest of the lot, and the group with which all Americans were equated, were the "Kaintucks," backwoods fur traders from Kentucky, descending like a Mongol horde on their flatboats down the Mississippi. It became a question of old versus new, of European versus "Americain," a word always pronounced with a disdainful slur. During the interlude of Spanish occupation, the fellow Latin Catholic conquistadors were not regarded by the French with a fraction of the antipathy that was directed at the Americans. Regardless of how they got to New Orleans, the Creoles had gotten there first. That, and that alone, made them the city's aristocrats.

No sooner had the Americans taken over the Louisiana Territory than New Orleans was divided in two. The Creoles had their Vieux Carré, now known as the French Quarter, bordered by the Mississippi levees and Canal Street, which became a great line of demarcation. The "other" side of Canal, where the Americans lived, became known as the

Garden District. At first this was merely a euphemism but later became an elegant, verdant reality as the Americans made their fortunes in cotton, cane, and shipping-related trades.

There were fewer than 8,000 people in New Orleans in 1803. By the time Judah Benjamin arrived in 1828 the population had grown to 50,000. Ten years later it was up to 100,000. The Creoles were a rapidly shrinking minority, yet the smaller they became the more their social mystique grew. The fact that they owned most of the land in the city didn't hurt them either. All out of proportion to their numbers and shady past, Creoles became synonymous with all that was good in New Orleans.

When Judah reached New Orleans, the richest Creole of all, and the one most shrouded in mystery, was Bernard de Marigny, actually named Bernard Xavier Philippe de Marigny de Mandeville at the time of his birth in 1785. His claim to being an aristocrat was founded on his grandfather Pierre, who had been a French infantryman fighting the Indians in Canada and was subsequently transferred to Louisiana as a commandant of troops. If not quite the duc de Richelieu, Pierre's status was at least better than the run of thieves, murderers, and miscreants who populated the area at this time. Pierre bought up most of the swamps for a pittance. By the time Bernard arrived, the swamps had become the city.

Bernard was sent to Paris and London for refinement and education. But the only thing he seemed to learn, aside from very broken English, was a new French game of chance called hazard, which had become the rage at Almack's, London's great coffeehouse. Bernard, more at home in the raffish French Quarter than in Mayfair, brought hazard to Louisiana, where the dice game became known as craps (after "Johnny Crapaud"—French for frog—the American put-down for Creole). Bernard himself had a run of very bad luck. He gambled away his entire fortune, and paid his enormous debts with tracts of land in his vast Faubourg Marigny. One of the main thoroughfares that he wagered away was for decades known as the Rue de Craps until its name was changed to the more respectable Burgundy. The flamboyant Bernard even established a Rue de l'Amour for his many kept women and a Rue des Biens [sic] Enfants, for his horde of illegitimate children.

Love and Good Children streets are still so named. Bernard died a pauper—the flashiest pauper in the South.

Bernard de Marigny was an exemplar for other high-rolling Frenchmen, whose self-indulgence may have shocked the new American arrivals. The de Marignys were perhaps the most colorful of the Creole families that dominated French New Orleans. There were others equally influential: the Villeres, the de la Vergnes, the de la Rondes, the de la Houssayes, the de Verges, the de St. Pauls, the Toutant Beauregards. Many of these families intermarried, thus creating a local aristocracy sharing not only the same tastes but also the same blood. Almost all the families liked to trace their roots to the French nobility, when actually the French military might have been more realistic. Whatever, their pedigrees seemed more august than most of the new "Americains." Unlike the Virginia and Charleston elites, the Creoles, by and large, did not involve themselves in politics. They left that to the Americans. Consequently, few acquired names that were known outside their tight orbit, but this low visibility, too, was as they liked it.

Most of the Creoles were planters, with townhouses in New Orleans and plantation manors outside the city, on the River Road flanking the Mississippi. They split their time between the two locales much as the Charlestonians did, but their cash crop was sugar instead of rice, and their inspiration Paris instead of London. While in the city, the emphasis was on fun. The Creoles had their own theaters, restaurants, gaming houses, and brothels. The men kept their black mistresses. Their shops were open on Sunday. The Creoles ate, drank, and made love with unconcealed enthusiasm. True to their French heritage, the Creoles reveled in their own sensuality. They were decadent, yet their decadence had panache.

Things were very different on the American side of Canal Street. Only the Kaintucks were decadent, and in the worst drunken, brawling way. As for the rest of the Americans, they weren't much fun at all. Most were there to make money, which the carefree Creoles already had. The Americans, then, devoted their efforts to trade, which the Creole planters considered vulgar. Brokerage offices, small shops, shipping activities, and the like were the American concerns. The Puritan ethic reigned. There was little time for amusement; moreover, the

Americans were clearly not welcome in the Creole pleasure dens. As they grew richer, the Americans gradually began to cross Canal, but the process was a slow one. Of course, not all the Americans who came to the Delta were déclassé by Creole standards. A good number of high-born Virginians and other Southerners were lured to the Gulf by the cotton siren. Nevertheless, for the most part they avoided New Orleans like the plagues that afflicted it. Big cities weren't for the Southerners. They wanted what they were used to–country plantations with plenty of space. They thus left the field wide open for Judah Benjamin, whose brains and drive were coated with a Southern accent and an Ivy League veneer. He was a rarity, an American with class. New Orleans was his for the taking.

UPWARD MOBILITY, À LA CREOLE

Judah's road to the Delta was circuitous. Born in the Virgin Islands, he was a Sephardic Jew of noble stock that had fallen on hard times. Judah's ancestors were of a high-caste family associated with the Spanish court. These Sephardim, as they were called, were prominent in Iberia for many centuries. The philosopher Maimonides was a Sephardic Jew, as were many other intellectual, religious, and political figures. The Sephardic hegemony ended with the Jews' expulsion, instituted in 1492 by Ferdinand (himself part Jewish) and Isabella, who financed the voyages of Columbus. Judah's ancestors on both paternal and maternal sides fled to Holland, then to England. His father Philip was born in the British colony of Nevis, in the Caribbean, but returned to London's Cheapside ghetto to open a dried-fruit shop. There he met Judah's mother, Rebecca de Mendes, whose father was also a merchant.

Judah's father failed to find the success he sought in Cheapside; apparently the market for dried fruit had dried up. In 1810 the Benjamins emigrated to the British island of St. Croix, where there was a sizable Sephardic community. The weather there was better, though business was not. In 1813, two years after Judah's birth, the gypsy Benjamins threw themselves on the mercy of a great-uncle, Jacob Levy, in the port of Wilmington, North Carolina. Although Levy had a fairly prosperous general store, the added pressure of his poor relations forced him to close up shop and seek wider opportunity. He moved inland to the pioneer Scots-Irish town of Fayetteville, opened a new store with Philip Benjamin as his clerk, and hoped the lack of competition would augur well for him.

It didn't. Fiscally, the Benjamin brood was the kiss of death. In 1822, Jacob Levy's Fayetteville venture folded, and he returned to Wilmington. Philip Benjamin, with his wife and five children, set off for Charleston, hoping for a turn for the better. He opened a small dry-goods store on King Street, which, though it did not become the local Macy's, did at least break even. In haughty Charleston, the local Jewish community, with a beautiful synagogue, Beth Elohim (still standing), was isolated from the rest of the city.

Young Judah, however, was one of the first of the congregation to cross Broad Street, a thoroughfare that separated the mansions of Pinckney-Rutledge Charleston from the shops and homes of the plain people who served the ruling class. He did it chiefly by brains, through the aid of Moses Lopez, the philanthropist president of the Hebrew Orphan Society. Lopez did not want the brilliant boy to waste his mind at the inferior public school; he enrolled Judah in an exclusive Anglican private academy and paid his tuition there. Before long Judah was reciting Shakespeare while waiting his turn at marbles with his friends.

By the time he was fourteen, Judah had completed his preparatory studies. No one in Charleston could recall a more prodigious intellect. All his instructors agreed that he had to go to the best college. For Charlestonians, the best meant Yale. Southerners comprised almost a third of Yale's student body, and only New York, New Haven, and Hartford sent more men there than Charleston. Now the city's golden boy, Judah was expected to surpass the New Haven record of that other great South Carolinian John C. Calhoun.

Things began splendidly, according to schedule. By his junior year, Judah was at the head of his class and had won several glittering prizes for scholarship. He was too tiny (barely five feet) for sports, but was popular nonetheless and was inducted into several fraternal societies that tapped the most promising undergraduates. Then his world fell apart. The old ghost of insolvency returned to haunt his father, making tuition payments virtually impossible. Worse, Judah was accused of stealing various items belonging to his friends—watches, fraternity pins, pencil cases, pocketknives, and worst of all, money. A trap was baited by suspicious classmates, and apparently Judah was found to have amassed such a cache of goods that he could have opened a store of his own. Quietly and ignominiously, the brightest boy in New Haven withdrew from the college at midyear, and beat a hasty retreat to the South.

While he never publicly admitted his guilt, the incident was to haunt Judah the rest of his life. Before the outbreak of the Civil War, when he was being blamed as the evil genius behind secession, several Yankee Yale alumni brought up the episode in the national press. Despite the imminent conflict, Judah had many powerful Northern friends who would have gladly assisted him in a libel suit. Yet he never responded to the charges. Furthermore, throughout his life, he displayed a distinct paranoia concerning his background. He destroyed all his correspondence and urged his friends to do likewise. He could talk and loved to talk about anything, but he never talked about his past. He might have claimed to have been framed, or he might have written off his error to sixteen-year-old callowness, or even financial desperation to continue his studies. Instead, he built a wall of silence.

Whatever the explanation, Judah was too disgraced to show his face in Charleston. The town expected him to return summa cum laude, not in shame. After a brief, clandestine visit to his family, he proceeded to that haven for tarnished heroes—New Orleans.

When Judah arrived, penniless, he took his first job in the shop of a Jewish merchant. Realizing his hereditary indisposition toward such endeavors, he vowed to break the mercantile curse of the Benjamins. He quickly found a totally different job with a notary public named Greenbury R. Stringer. Meanwhile, he began studying for the bar and, more important, for the altar. Judah noted the dominance of the Creole elite and saw that any upward mobility here would require that he be fluent in French. Cleverly, he proffered his services as a private tutor of English to prominent Creoles, who in turn would help him learn their own language. Because Greenbury R. Stringer handled forms for an exclusive clientele, Judah began moonlighting for all the right people.

His favorite pupils were the Auguste St. Martins. No family in New Orleans was better qualified to initiate Judah into the ways of the Creoles. Unlike most Creoles, the St. Martins were not descended from Parisian jailbirds. Rather, they came from Santo Domingo, a lush tropical isle that had been something of a playground for French country gentlemen. In 1791, their gentility had been interrupted by a turbulent slave uprising and massacre of the rich planters, causing the St. Martins and other fortunate survivors to flee to New Orleans, where they gave the city a long-needed touch of class. Auguste St. Martin became a prominent landowner and marine insurance broker. Judah was impressed by the St. Martins' European life-style—and by their beautiful teenage daughter Natalie.

Both parties seemed to have learned their respective new languages, and more. Within a few years, Judah was admitted both to the bar and into the Creole inner sancta. In early 1833, when he was twenty-one, he wed Natalie, who was only sixteen. In addition to his new social status, he enjoyed Natalie's dowry, two mulatto slave girls and a handsome sum of cash. Both Judah and Natalie kept their own faiths. (Though Judah was not actively religious, he never renounced his Judaism.) The couple moved into the St. Martins' mansion on Bourbon Street in the French Quarter. It was quite a step up from Judah's rooming house, and it was only the beginning. Judah was launched on his way to becoming a grand seigneur.

Immediately, all the right doors began opening for him. In a city full of glib lawyers, Judah built up the most lucrative practice of them all. Nor did he do it by Creole connections alone. He prepared exhaustive digests of all the Louisiana court cases, which made him the authority on Napoleonic Code jurisprudence. Despite his preeminence in the legal field by age thirty, law for Judah wasn't enough. First and foremost, he was a Southerner, and he was not content just to be a lawyer or even *the* lawyer. Judah wanted his own plantation, replete with linen suit, mint julep, and, of course, slaves.

He got just what he wanted—Bellechasse, an elegant white-columned mansion on the River Road, the plantation-lined Creole "Gold Coast" overlooking the Mississippi. Bellechasse began as a weekend retreat, but it turned into a high-profit venture. On one of his annual

holidays in France, Judah developed an interest in sugar planting and
refining. Back at home, as a respite from the law, he began tinkering
with a new refining machine. It was such a successful invention that
Bellechasse became one of the most productive sugar plantations in the
Delta and "Massa Judah," as his slaves called him, became something of
a plant wizard, the Luther Burbank of cane.

LOVE AND MARRIAGE

The only area in which Judah lacked the Midas touch was at home. His
wife, Natalie, was splendid for connections, abysmal as a wife. She was
spoiled beyond belief. When Judah cautioned her to stop spending
money so indiscriminately, she replied in a rare letter, "Oh, talk not to
me of economy. It is so fatiguing." Eventually, Natalie was fatigued by
more than just economy. Plantation luxuries notwithstanding, she
came to the conclusion that Louisiana was too barbaric for her.

In 1845, twelve years after her marriage, Natalie left Judah for Paris
and civilization. With her she took their only child, Ninette, who
shared her mother's Creole beauty—petite, with jet-black hair and eyes,
fine cheekbones, and ivory skin. This was not a divorce. Natalie's de-
vout Catholicism, plus daughter Ninette's "image" prevented that,
though, otherwise, it might have been the wisest course. Few women,
even Creole women, were as selfish as Natalie. She loved herself far
more than Judah ever could.

Judah went to see his wife and daughter each summer and continued to support them in the high style to which they had become
accustomed. For his wife to leave him was a severe embarrassment to
Judah, who did his best to maintain some illusion of a union. He
continued as the best of friends with his St. Martin in-laws, but even
after he moved to London after the war, Natalie and daughter never
joined him. Natalie remained an absentee wife for the rest of his life,
refusing to return to Louisiana even to visit her parents. Her place as
mistress of Bellechasse was taken by Judah's older sister Rebecca, whom
he called Penny.

Natalie's departure was probably more a reflection on her own
nature than on any limitations on Judah's part. He was known

throughout the country as a bon vivant, if not a rake. It is possible that in Natalie's absence he engaged in the discreet pleasures for which New Orleans was renowned. The most hallowed tradition of all among the elite of Creole men was the keeping of a quadroon mistress. (Such a quadroon was a mulatto: the offspring of a white man and a half-white woman – thus one quarter black.) Creole women had a great reputation for chastity. After all, most upper-crust marriages were not love matches but were arranged. Their repressions did not extend to their black servants, who were far more pliable. Master and servant thus got to know each other intimately, if not well. The upshot of this was lots of quadroons and lots of mistresses.

The mistress system was elaborately organized by a powerful matriarchy. These mothers were well used to serving the elite, for their own fathers had been Creoles, as had the fathers of their daughters. The mothers were not slaves, but rather "free persons of color." The varying degrees of white and black genes gave Louisiana blacks a complicated caste structure of their own. The daughters were "presented" to society at great balls, held almost weekly. For the steep price of two dollars, finely dressed white men could gain admission to what was, in effect, a sexual slave market. The teenaged quadroon girls, escorted by their mothers and resplendent in Parisian fashions, were put on display in a ballroom processional. The daughter's clothes represented a major investment, often a mother's life savings. All the girls were guaranteed to be virgins.

Once a man made his selection, he approached the mother and requested her daughter's hand, so to speak. If the mother approved, and she always did if the price were right, the man would install the girl in a pristine white cottage in a special quarter with hundreds of such houses, on the outskirts of the Vieux Carré. There the man would come to call, usually each evening after work, as a sort of aperitif, en route to dinner with his family. The man paid not only a handsome settlement for the mother but also for his mistress's upkeep and for the care and education of their children, who were frequently sent to France for their schooling. These octaroon offspring generally did not go into the mistress trade. They could pass for white, and most of them moved north or to Europe and did exactly that.

As for the mistress herself, she was faithful to her Creole lover as long as she lived, or as long as he found her desirable. Whichever, his code of honor required him to take full responsibility for his mistress's social security even after her beauty had faded. Discarded mistresses usually did not marry. To wed a black man would be beneath their station. Only a rich white would do, but rich whites would only deal with such women in back-street affairs, never in public. The quadroon mistress system was never discussed by the Creoles. These lovely, tragic, tainted ladies thus formed a unique caste. The older ones developed a near-monopoly on New Orleans men's boardinghouses (for visitors and bachelors). The trade was a natural; no one knew better how to cater to male needs.

POWER POLITICS

In Natalie's absence, Judah found another absorbing activity in politics which, in addition to law and the plantation, composed the Southern trinity of "musts" for the gentleman-for-all-seasons. Here again, Judah rose to the top. The key element in political advancement was connections, and Judah had the best. His biggest helping hand came from John Slidell, a transplanted Yankee lawyer whose brother Thomas had been a Yale classmate of Judah's. Because of the Old Blue tie the two Slidells took young Judah into their law practice and gave his early career an important boost. His obvious genius enabled them to overlook his alleged Yale improprieties.

John Slidell was a remarkable character. He was the role model for many a Southern power broker to follow. Like Judah, Slidell had come to New Orleans as a gilded youth with a black mark on his record. The son of a rich, self-made New York banker who had started life as a ship's chandler and soapmaker, Slidell enjoyed a privileged adolescence and entree into the best of Knickerbocker society. He attended Columbia College, did a grand tour of Europe and, with his resemblance to Lord Byron, was one of the most-wanted men on the New York party circuit. Then, as abruptly as Judah fell from grace at Yale, Slidell's world also collapsed. First, his father went bankrupt. Then, seeking solace with a succession of gorgeous actresses, Slidell got into a duel with a theater manager over one of their mutual conquests. Slidell won, though not in the eyes of the law, which did not sanction such bouts of honor. Hounded by the police as well as by saloon keepers, haberdashers, and gamblers, to all of whom he owed money, Slidell took off for New Orleans in 1819.

Slidell's father gave his fleeing son one name to contact in the South. That was Edward Livingston, who had reconstructed himself splendidly after his own scandals had driven him south. Through his influential Creole wife, Livingston had rebuilt his fortune, his law practice, and his political standing. He would become Minister to France and Secretary of State. Slidell's father urged his son to use Livingston both as inspiration and as a vehicle for advancement.

John Slidell listened carefully. He read law and, through Livingston, was appointed U.S. District Attorney. He also wooed and wed one of the most desirable of Creole belles, Mathilde Deslondes, whose sister was the wife of the dashing General Pierre G. T. Beauregard. Slidell was now in a perfect position to put his electoral skills to work. For all his carousing, he had always been interested in politics and was fascinated by the workings of New York's Tammany Hall.

Now he brought Tammany to the Delta. In one of the most celebrated of all electoral sleights of hand, Slidell helped elect James K. Polk President in 1844 by "swinging" Louisiana into Polk's column. He did so by his own fifth column, a gang of paid ruffians whom he herded onto two large steamboats. The voters sailed down the Mississippi casting votes at every stop along the bayous. Their quintuplicate ballots sealed what would have otherwise been a close election. In return for this ingenuity, Slidell quickly rose to a position of prominence in the Democratic Party, a king-maker if there ever was one.

In Judah Benjamin, Slidell saw a valuable lieutenant. Unlike many men of his time, Slidell was happy to work with Jews, especially when they were as brilliant as Judah, or August Belmont, who had been Slidell's protégé up north. Belmont, an apostate (in contrast to Judah, who was proud of his Jewish heritage), had married a niece of Slidell's and wielded considerable power throughout the North. He had come to American from Germany as agent for the house of Rothschild, an esteemed and powerful Jewish family who were neighbors of the Belmonts on Frankfurt's Judengasse. Proving himself as adept at social climbing as at high finance, August Belmont won the heart of Caroline Slidell Perry, daughter of the commodore and of John Slidell's sister. To Slidell, Judah was a Southern August. Slidell got them both into Manhattan's ultraexclusive Union Club, where they began to hatch their plans to conquer the world.

Through Slidell, Judah became a favorite of the Louisiana political bosses, who appreciated his legal acumen and cleverness. Faced with a scandal over land fraud or other rip-offs, they could always get Judah to find them a legal precedent for their behavior. After all, lawyers, then and now, are hired guns, and Judah was the fastest draw in the nation.

In the legal-political arena, another of Judah's mentors, whom he met through Slidell, was John Randolph Grymes, the dean of the Louisiana bar. As his middle name indicates, Grymes was of fine Virginia stock. However, not being the first son, there was no estate for him to inherit. (Virginia's primogeniture laws allowed the eldest son of a family to take all when the father died.) Grymes forlornly left the Old Dominion for the Delta's horn of plenty. The oratorical skills that seem to be the birthright of Virginians helped Grymes make his mark, as did his Cavalier social heritage in a sea of rabble. Virginia Randolphs were welcome anywhere. Edward Livingston took in Grymes as his law partner. Their first case together was the defense of the pirate Jean Lafitte.

Grymes had been serving as the district attorney in charge of prosecuting Lafitte, known as the "Scourge of the Gulf." However, Lafitte, more than anyone, knew the value of a dollar. He offered Livingston $40,000 to get him off, and to free his brother Pierre, who was being held as a legal hostage. Livingston in turn offered to split the take with Grymes, who resigned from public service on the spot. As sensitive about his honor as he was avaricious, Grymes couldn't bear to be accused of corruption by the outraged new district attorney. In order to silence him, Grymes challenged his successor to a duel and crippled him for life. No one else said a word. When Grymes went to Lafitte's island pirate's den to collect his booty, Lafitte invited him to spend a few days in the sun. Grymes was seduced. A compulsive gambler, he began playing cards with Lafitte, and soon lost his share of the retainer as well as that of Livingston.

Grymes continued to get huge fees. He lived as flamboyantly as any man in the South, with the possible exception of the gambler Bernard de Marigny, into whose family Grymes married. He dressed in red, white, and blue and gave twenty-course dinner parties almost every evening, proving that an Anglo could outdo the Creoles in haute cuisine. Grymes's daughter Medora married Sam Ward of New York, a man who had reigned over the Manhattan social scene in the 1830s through his late wife, Emily Astor. Now the Grymes connection gave him New Orleans. Under John Randolph Grymes's tutelage, Ward became America's leading gourmet and Washington lobbyist, plying Congress, the President, and the Supreme Court with food and drink. Sam had one other important nexus with the Southern elite. This was his first cousin, America's foremost arbiter of taste, Ward McAllister of Savannah, who went to New York, latched on to an Astor of his own, and invented the "400." Through Grymes and Slidell, who together founded their own drinking club, the Elkin, Judah Benjamin was initiated into this tight circle that dominated the country's social and political life. And Judah held his own in this winner's circle because he was acknowledged to be the brains of the outfit.

In 1853, after paying his dues in the Slidell machine, Judah was "elected" to the U.S. Senate at the age of forty-two. In those days, senatorial selection was not open to the public. Instead, Judah was chosen by the upper house of the Louisiana legislature, where the dominant planter class was assured that Judah would safeguard their interests.

Not everyone was enamored of Judah. The New Orleans *Delta,* for example, had mixed feelings about him, partly because of his looks.

His appearance in that body [the Senate] would startle the gossips at Washington. His boyish figure and girlish face . . . would render him decidedly the most unsenatorial figure in that body of grey beards and full grown men.

Yet even the *Delta* had to concede Judah's talent:

But when he should arise in the Senate and . . . proceed to pour forth a strain of the most fluent and beautifully expressed ideas . . . carrying all minds and hearts with him by his resistless logic and insinuating elocution—then would the old Senators stretch their eyes and mouths with won-

der, whispering to one another "That's a devilish smart little fellow"–then would all the ladies declare "What a love of a man!–what a perfect Admirable Crichton,–so beautiful, yet so wise,–so gentle, yet so terrible in sarcasm,–so soft-toned, and yet so vigorous in logic."
–New Orleans *Delta,* October 10, 1851.

Just before Judah took his seat in the Senate, he received another honor–a nomination to the Supreme Court by President Millard Fillmore. He was the first Jew ever to be called to the high court, but he declined. He preferred a more active political career and, more pressing, he had to support his wife and child in Paris. Supreme Court Justices received smaller salaries than Senators, and while Judah may have been America's most highly paid legal mind, he needed every cent to keep Natalie in her high style. After Judah turned down the appointment, the President nominated, in turn, two of Judah's young law partners, Edward Bradford and William Micou. Though neither of them was confirmed by the Senate, which was openly hostile to Fillmore, no other firm ever made such a sweep.

When Judah went to Washington, there was nothing in the day's moral code to prevent him from continuing his law practice. During his term, he traveled around the country and the world handling big cases and big deals–to California to settle the title of the nation's largest silver mine, to Ecuador to secure a guano concession on the Galapagos Islands, to Mexico to try to build a railroad across the Isthmus of Tehuantepec, and to Europe to raise money for the vast Mexican project, later aborted by the Civil War. In the Senate, Judah Benjamin was the most reasoned and articulate spokesman for states' rights, worthy of the mantle of his Yale predecessor, John C. Calhoun. He was perhaps the most intellectual Senator, North or South. On one occasion he broke up a filibuster to deliver a paean to Tennyson, his favorite poet. All of his orations were peppered with classical or literary references.

Near the end of his first term, Judah was offered the post of Minister to Spain by President Buchanan, the virtual pawn of John Slidell, now Judah's fellow Senator from Louisiana. It was another great feather in Judah's cap; his return to Iberia in glory would have been a symbolic triumph for all Sephardic Jews. However, again Natalie came first. Judah had to keep working on his cases. Paris fashions were evidently becoming more expensive.

In 1859, after his reelection, Judah was both surprised and thrilled when Natalie decided to grace America with a visit. To receive her properly, he rented the most elegant mansion in Washington, the Stephen Decatur house, and filled it with rare antiques and fine carpets. Natalie would be in illustrious company, for the French, English, and Russian ministers had all lived in the Decatur house at one time, as had Henry Clay, John Quincy Adams, and Edward Livingston.

None of this was enough for Natalie. Although Judah was proud of his pretty wife and made every effort to introduce her to Washington society, Natalie sullenly refused to get involved. Instead, she made vicious remarks about her husband's appearance and religion to the few luminaries she deigned to meet. With the haughtiest elitism she limited her socializing to the French embassy set, except on one occasion that broke Judah's heart. This was her affair with a German officer attached to his legation in the capital. Natalie not only eloped with her Teutonic lover; she also arranged for all the objets d'art in the Decatur house to be auctioned, and the proceeds sent to her in France. Disgraced, Judah left Washington for California for many months, immersing himself in his mining case until the scandal subsided. If only out of affection for his daughter, he continued sending money to Natalie in France, though he did not see her again until after the Civil War.

THE BRAINS OF THE CONFEDERACY

By the time Judah returned to Washington in 1861 his marital problems had been obscured by those of secession. While Judah was hardly one of the fire-eaters who swept the South into the Civil War, he was a conservative gentleman slave owner who was loyal to his class and to his region. Truly believing that he and his peers afforded their slaves far better treatment than they would receive if on their own, he saw the North-South antagonism less as one of idealism and human dignity than one of competitive economics, states' rights, and sectional honor.

When Lincoln's election rendered further compromise impossible, Judah had no choice but to acquiesce in the South's walkout. Anything less would have branded him as a traitor.

It was only natural for Judah to be appointed the Confederacy's Attorney General. Jefferson Davis knew him and admired him from the Senate as well as from the Natchez-New Orleans social circuit. He quickly became Davis's most important adviser, and as the sundry ineptitudes of the Confederate cabinet became apparent, Davis moved him up to Secretary of War. But despite his many-faceted capabilities, the distinctly nonbellicose Judah didn't stand a chance amid the likes of Lee and Jackson. As a civilian, he did not have the respect of the generals. And when the Southern forces fared poorly during his seven months in office, he became a convenient scapegoat, even though this losing streak was not in his control. When Davis's second Secretary of State resigned, he shuffled Judah into that post to get him off the military firing line.

The State Department was the Confederacy's last hope. Only by securing European recognition and assistance could the South have any chance of overcoming the massive odds against it. Judah did his best. With John Slidell as his man in Paris, the crafty duo would have turned the tide, had it not been for some terrible luck at the diplomatic gaming tables (as will be seen). Judah's efforts were respected by friend and foe, not the least of whom was Abraham Lincoln, who viewed Judah as the "smartest" man in the South.

Whatever the tide of war, Judah never lost his sunny disposition. His beatific smile won him still another superlative as "the happiest Confederate." The undisputed favorite of all government wives in the Richmond capital, Judah was even rumored to have had an affair with Dixie's First Lady, Varina Howell Davis. That they were very close is not disputed; certainly Judah, with his rapier wit and international anecdotes, was more amusing than the somber President. In addition to balls and belles, Judah never lost his New Orleans-acquired penchant for gambling, and was a regular at many of the illegal casinos that sprang up to distract the harried politicians.

Judah headed the invitation list at Richmond socials; he was even more desired by the federal authorities after Appomattox. With Lee's surrender there, the Davis cabinet began retreating south from Richmond with no intention of giving up, but instead hoping to reestablish the government in another location. By the time they reached Greensboro, North Carolina, their circumstances had been so reduced that the statesmen were billeted in a leaky boxcar. The Northern troops were closing in on all sides. Now the only cabinet member to continue to back the unsinkable Jefferson Davis in his resolve to continue fighting was Judah, who tried to keep everyone's spirits up by reciting verse, such as Tennyson's "Ode on the Death of the Duke of Wellington."

Eventually, it was apparent even to Judah that the cause was lost. Now self-preservation was the first priority. Everyone feared that Judah would be the least likely to succeed. He was decidedly nonathletic, had grown very fat, and barely could ride a horse. Yet he vowed never to be taken alive. His hatred of "Yankees" had been fanned by a group of his Yale classmates who taunted him for his dismissal throughout the Northern press. The North wanted the head of the South's "evil genius" even more than that of Jefferson Davis. Judah was not about to give them any satisfaction.

His escape was a combination of high adventure and high camp. Setting off through the Georgia swamps, Judah disguised himself as a visiting Frenchman named Monsieur Bonfals, who spoke English with a very broken accent. He hired a horse and cart, put on dark goggles and a slouch hat covering his face, and wrapped himself in a Dracula cape. The Civil War wasn't exactly prime holiday time for jaunty French tourists, but Judah was forced into certain poetic license. When he crossed the border into Florida, he changed costume, donning some overalls and pretending he was a dirt farmer looking for a new plot to call home.

Judah then compromised in his aversion to horseback riding by acquiring an old mule and riding about the central Florida underbrush in search of a way to Europe. He finally found an expatriate French sailor whose specialty was navigating the marshy Everglades and who promised to take Judah to the Florida Keys and freedom. The men lived a Robinson Crusoe existence for weeks, living on coconut milk, fish, and turtle eggs, sailing by night, sleeping in swamps by day. Several times they were almost captured by Northern gunboats that policed the coast, and once their sloop was actually apprehended by a Yankee search party. The ingenious Judah foiled them, however, by disguising himself as the Frenchman's cook. He donned an apron and a white hat, covered his face with cooking grease, and set about filleting a fish, a task his own chefs had always done for him. Meanwhile, the Frenchman explained that he and his faithful servant were merely out on a fishing trip. The Northerners bought the story and left.

After finally reaching the Keys, Judah transferred to another small boat and set sail for Bimini, then changed ships for Nassau, Havana, and, at last, Southampton, England. The journey was anything but placid. First waterspouts off Bimini nearly sank Judah. He had to bail water out of the little boat with his hat. Leaving Nassau, Judah's next ship actually did sink. He returned to Nassau in a tiny skiff, with three black sailors, one bowl of rice, and one oar. And between Havana and St. Thomas, his next vessel caught on fire and barely made it back to port. London couldn't have looked more inviting.

In the British capital, Judah arranged for the sale of a hundred bales of his cotton that had been shipped to him there through the blockade. This netted him over $20,000, not what he was used to but enough for a fresh start. His temporary financial security assured, he left for Paris and a long-overdue reunion with Natalie and Ninette. Despite Natalie's cruelty, Judah never ceased to be devoted to her. Why he could not say no to her is a mystery that has eluded all Benjamin scholars. Yale and his family were two subjects on which Benjamin refused to comment.

Even gladder to see Judah than his family was John Slidell, completely unravaged by the war. Slidell's daughter had married a d'Erlanger, the scion of a powerful Jewish family second only to the Rothschilds in European finance. Slidell had become an intimate of Emperor Napoleon III and his court and, through him, Judah could have had any position he wanted in Paris.

Instead, he went back to London and his first love, the law. Why he didn't stay to practice law in France is unclear, since he was an expert on the Napoleonic Code. Maybe being around Natalie was too painful for him. Or, more likely, for her. She had made it clear in America that she and Judah were married in name only. Living apart in Paris would be too embarrassing to her. The social mores of the day did not sanction an admission of incompatibility. Divorce meant disgrace. An ocean, or at least the English Channel, made Natalie's separation from Judah more respectable. She could always claim that his career came first. Wherever he was, Judah kept sending money, both to Natalie and Ninette and to his sisters back in New Orleans, whom he loved dearly and was homesick for.

Like a young law clerk fresh from Oxford, Judah, at age fifty-five, entered Lincoln's Inn to serve a three years' apprenticeship prerequisite to becoming a barrister. (In England's bifurcated legal system, only barristers appear in court. The other half, solicitors, confine their practice to contracts and other paper work.) Judah's clerkship, though, was unusually privileged, for he was not only America's leading commercial lawyer, but also a famous statesman who was greatly respected by the pro-Southern English upper classes. One stately home after another was opened to him, and his acquaintances ranged from his counterpart Disraeli, to his idol Tennyson. He prepared for the bar under Charles Pollock, one of London's more prestigious and prosperous lawyers and the son of the Chancellor of the Exchequer.

This red carpet proved to be essential, for the bank where he was keeping his funds failed. There was no deposit insurance in those days, and Judah could not start earning fees until his three-year qualifying period was up. With Natalie harassing him from Paris, he took a position with the *Daily Telegraph,* writing a column on international affairs. The epicure who had been used to feasting on canvasback and caviar was now reduced to subsisting on cheap pub lunches. Every cent he made now went to Natalie and Ninette. Luckily, the moment the three years were up, Judah shot to the top of his profession. His stature was enchanced by his treatise *Benjamin on Sales* which he had written while awaiting the call to the bar. The book immediately became *the* authority on the subject, both in England and America, and Judah Benjamin became *the* commercial lawyer of the British Empire.

For the next two decades, Judah was a dominant figure of the British bar, punctuating his busy case schedule with visits to Paris. He was especially worried that his daughter Ninette at age thirty had not yet married. Finally, in 1874, following her mother's predilection for soldiers, she wed a dashing French artillery captain, Henri de Bousig-nac, in a Catholic ceremony. The highest cost of the ceremony was that Judah, at sixty-three, was unable to retire as he had been planning. Ninette required a yearly dowry and Natalie still demanded her own large annuity. Even though he was earning nearly $100,000 a year, his family's demands ate up his savings and forced him back to law prac-tice. Moreover, he was building Natalie a mansion on the Avenue d'Iena (later to be a Rothschild palace).

In 1881, the chipper Judah received a terrible blow to his health when he fell off a Paris streetcar. In addition he began having heart trouble. He kept trying cases before the House of Lords, until a major heart attack forced him to retire for good and, at last, back to Natalie and their Paris home. Natalie, aging and ill, seems to have permitted a reconciliation in their old age. Judah was the quickest to forgive and forget. When Natalie had to have surgery, he went to her side at the operating table and held her hand through the entire ordeal. His dearest dream, that of grandchildren and a dynasty of his own, was an impossible one. Ninette, being her mother's daughter, spent much more time with Natalie than with her captain, living at her mother's home most of the year. She never had children. In 1884, after a year with Natalie, Judah, age seventy-three, had a final heart attack. As he was slipping away, Natalie called a priest to administer final rites. It was the last thing in the world Judah wanted, the unkindest cut of all. Yet he was too weak to protest. He died and was buried with a Catholic service and in a Catholic cemetery. Natalie always got her way.

V

Cotton Crusade: Southern Aristocrats in the Civil War

THE NEW ARISTOCRATS

For the South, the Civil War was one conflict that was, figuratively, decided on the playing fields of Eton, not on the battlefields of Gettysburg. Romantic images notwithstanding, it was as much Judah P. Benjamin's war as that of Robert E. Lee. Lords Palmerston and Russell were just as strategic enemies as President Lincoln and General Grant. The war of Southern secession was at the same time a war of European recognition. If Europe had intervened on the side of the Confederacy, it is likely that America would now be two nations instead of one. And the Southerners always felt that the English would lead the other European nations to their support. To them, it seemed natural that an alliance would be forged between the aristocrats of the Old World and those of the New. Faced with popular revolutions in their own lands, the ruling classes of Europe felt threatened by the success of the American democratic experiment. Their own elite position would be vindicated by the triumph of the aristocratic South.

Or so it seemed. The irony was that the architects of secession and war were not really the original Southern aristocrats. They were no Byrds or Randolphs, Pinckneys or Rutledges. They were the new generation of self-made planters, nouveaux riches of their time. Not a fraction as nouveau as the rulers of the South after Reconstruction, but definitely upstarts compared with the Virginia-Charleston elite that had drafted the Constitution and given America so many of its distinguished founding fathers. But the James River tobacco lands and the Charleston rice fields were no longer agricultural gold mines. By the 1820s Eli Whitney's cotton gin of 1794 had changed that. Cotton had become king, and the black belt of Mississippi, Alabama, and Louisiana, the Deep South, was where the money, and hence the power, was concentrated. The lords of the region required slavery for their plantation existence, so much so that they were willing to go to war for it. With them, they swept along the old aristocracy, now on the verge of destitution but still retaining its sense of honor and pride in being "Southern." The members of the new aristocracy legitimized themselves by this coalition with the old, though there was no doubt that the newcomers were really in control. They felt old Europe would admit them as equals. When it didn't, their world ended.

Just who were the members of this new ruling class? We have met Judah Benjamin and John Slidell. These two were bourgeois lawyers, outsiders who used their brains to become insiders in an urban setting. More typical of the new planter class was Mississippi's Jefferson Davis, who, like Lincoln, was born in a log cabin. Davis rose to prominence as a soldier-cotton-planter-politician, with the additional help of two brilliant marriages. Unlike the stereotypical landed Southern gentleman of the original Virginia order Davis grew up in a world devoid of privilege and pretense. The son of an itinerant Welsh subsistence farmer, Davis was born in Kentucky in 1808. Luckily he had a highly motivated brother, Joseph, twenty-four years his senior, who went south and became a lawyer in Natchez at the beginning of the cottom boom in the early 1800s. The time and place were right for self-made men, and Joseph Davis seized the moment by using his legal fees to buy thousands of the best acres along the Mississippi River. Soon he was a millionaire in the same league as the founding Natchez families, the Surgets and the Minors. He had a noble plantation, Hurricane, and thousands of slaves. However, Joseph was more interested in raising cotton than in raising a great family. The latter he would leave to his brother, Jefferson, whom he sent through college at Transylvania, back in Kentucky, and for whom he acquired an appointment to West Point in 1824. Joseph may have felt ill at ease among the New England Brahmins who were making Natchez an outpost of Boston, and he was too coarse to make himself over. Jefferson, more patrician in appearance, could be molded to give the Davis clan its own stature.

Everything proceeded according to Joseph's plan. Following his graduation from West Point in 1828, Jefferson served as a lieutenant at a Wisconsin fort commanded by Zachary Taylor, later to be President of the United States. Taylor's nickname, "rough and ready," belied his background, which was pure First Families of Virginia. Thus, the most eligible young woman at the fort was his beautiful daughter, Sarah. In 1835 Jefferson married her. Now Joseph could boast that his brother's new bride was a direct descendant of the illustrious Lees, while his brother himself had attended West Point with Robert E. Lee. If one could be a Southern aristocrat by association, Jefferson Davis certainly had achieved that status.

Joseph was so proud of Jefferson that he built him and his new bride a plantation of their own on his estate. Unfortunately, despite the servants and fine furniture, the delicate Sarah was completely overwhelmed by the malarial environment, and within three months of the wedding she was dead of a tropical fever. Jefferson went into a silent depression that lasted for nearly a decade. During this protracted period of mourning, he sat in Joseph's study immersing himself in political theory. He saw no women, went to no parties, had no friends other than his brother. His only companions were his slaves, to whom he grew quite close. Eventually, Joseph became concerned with his brother's monasticism. In 1844, Jefferson was thirty-seven and still alone with his books. It was high time for another wife.

Now Joseph played matchmaker with a vivacious Natchez girl, Varina Howell, gorgeous, regal, and nearly six feet tall. Only she could bring Jefferson out of his shell. Her lineage easily passed muster with Joseph. Her mother was an FFV; her father was a planter, and his father had been Governor of New Jersey for eight terms. Varina at seventeen was pretty and voluptuous, smart and smooth, having enjoyed a Harvard-trained private tutor as well as a fancy Philadelphia finishing school. With Joseph playing an insistent Cupid, an unsuspecting

Varina was brought to Hurricane as a Christmas guest. When Jefferson rode up on his horse, Varina was smitten. "Would you believe it, he is refined and cultivated and yet he is a democrat," she wrote after their first meeting. Though initially phlegmatic, Jefferson came around. They married in 1845 after a brief courtship.

With Varina at his side, Jefferson Davis blossomed politically, as well as socially. The year of the wedding, he was elected to the U.S. House of Representatives. His term was interrupted in 1846 by the Mexican War, for which he volunteered to fight under his former father-in-law, General Taylor. They both became heroes, Davis for the V formation he devised, which observers—including the Duke of Wellington—lauded as responsible for the great American triumph at Buena Vista. All this, plus a bullet in his foot. On crutches, he returned to Mississippi as that state's favorite son. When one of Mississippi's Senators died, the governor appointed Davis to his place. He was elected in his own right for another term.

Davis's own lionization as hero, his pivotal role in the annexation of Texas, and his family's giant plantation interests combined to make him the Deep South's leading advocate. Davis was worried that the soil of the black belt might some day be depleted, like the tobacco land along the James. Thus, he championed the right of Southerners to take their slaves with them as they expanded their Cotton Kingdom to the new lands of the West. The planters had to have the Western escape valve and could not be stymied by antislavery laws; without slaves, there could be no Cotton Kingdom. As early as 1850, Davis was ready to lead the Deep South out of the Union, and divide America into two nations stretching from Atlantic to Pacific, one slave and one free.

The Davis-dominated 1850 Nashville Secession Convention did not achieve this separation, but it did establish the battle lines that would lead to the Civil War. Interestingly enough, at this point Davis was more concerned with secession than Mississippi was, so that when he resigned from the Senate to run for governor in 1851, he was defeated by a pro-Union man. At this point he might have faded from the political scene, and the Civil War might have been averted, had he not been appointed Secretary of War by his old friend, President Franklin Pierce, one Yankee who bought the Davis line on the economic and humanitarian "necessity" of slavery. Davis became the major power broker in the Pierce cabinet, redeemed his stature in Mississippi, and was subsequently reelected to the Senate. At the same time, Varina Howell Davis became acting First Lady, standing in for Pierce's sickly, antisocial wife, Jane. Varina was perfectly suited to the role.

By 1861, when the North-South tensions had reached their outer limit, Jefferson and Varina Davis were, if not the Deep South's liveliest couple, certainly the most "presidential." At the presidential sweepstakes of the Montgomery Secession Convention, the Old Guard FFVs were not included, since Virginia was still wavering about leaving the Union. Despite the possible stigma of new wealth, the Confederacy had to be led by hard-liners. Of all the fire-eaters, as the rabid secessionists were known, the Jefferson Davises were the most polished, most social of the lot. Accordingly, they were chosen for the top slot in the rebel government. Robert E. Lee, Joseph E. Johnston, J.E.B. Stuart, and the other aristocratic Virginia generals only joined the fray after the die had been cast.

These Virginians were only the warriors; the intellectual leader of the secession movement was hardly an aristocrat. While Robert Barnwell Rhett had quite a pedigree, he was eclipsed, due to Charleston's loss of influence, by that most influential of all secessionists, Alabama's William Lowndes Yancey, a rabble-rousing, full-time politician and newspaperman, a brilliant writer and orator and also one of the hottest of heads. He had won a reputation for his duel with another congressman who had challenged his proslavery views, for killing his wife's uncle in a street brawl, and for stalking out of Congress when he concluded that the whole governmental process was a sham and a waste of time.

As for the political leaders of secession, there was little blue blood in Davis's cabinet. Gustavus Memminger was Secretary of the Treasury. Stephen Mallory, Secretary of the Navy, had no education whatsoever; his widowed Irish mother ran a boardinghouse in Key West, Florida. The Vice President, Alexander T. Stephens, was from yeoman-farmer stock. Except for the Secretary of State, Robert Toombs, the son of a rich Georgia planter, none had begun life with any privileged head start. This speaks well for upward mobility in the South. The war may have been waged for the benefit of planter plutocracy; it was being orchestrated by a distinctly nonaristocratic corps of politicians, whose constituents considered them aristocratic by virtue of simply being Southern.

INNOCENTS ABROAD

This illusion was shattered by their first effort to secure European recognition and thereby intimidate the North out of attempting any major conflict. Half the United States would be no match for mighty England, it was assumed. More important, the South felt that in cotton she held the ultimate trump. Cotton made the mills of England and France go round; how could they live without it? The North had put up a blockade (albeit permeable) around the Southern coast; Europe literally couldn't afford to allow it to continue, for fear of an economic cataclysm.

Davis therefore dispatched three of his stalwarts to the Continent to meet with the foreign leaders. All got the cold shoulder. One of the diplomats was the distinguished Judge Pierre Rost of Louisiana, who had studied law in Natchez under Joseph Davis, Jefferson's brother, and was a close friend of the entire Davis clan. Rost had been born in France, spoke fluent French, had served under Napoleon in the artillery, and seemed like a logical appointee. The French did not see it that way. They were insulted that they were being sent a Frenchman who, they felt, had not succeeded in the mother country. To the French, any emigrant, by definition, was a failure. Why not a native American, they complained? The second envoy was a Virginian, A. Dudley Mann, a former Assistant Secretary of State and U.S. Consul in Europe. This time, the English were insulted that Mann wasn't the "right" kind of Virginian. He was ridiculed for being the son of a bankrupt grocer, as well as for dropping out of West Point in his last term to avoid military service. The third was the firebrand William Yancey, whose very existence symbolized the slavery that England and France were on record as detesting. He was regarded as a slave driver not worthy of an audience with the sheriff, much less with the Crown. Consequently, the welcome was hardly what had been expected. Yancey and Rost returned to America, where the excitable Yancey, frustrated at the English stone wall, soon died, at only forty-nine years of age. Mann went on to Belgium to propagandize for the South.

Davis tried again. With Judah Benjamin plotting the action, Davis appointed Benjamin's ally, John Slidell, as Minister to France. Slidell, the smoothest talker in America, would be a perfect foil for Napoleon III, a crafty wheeler-dealer himself. Furthermore, unlike poor Judge Rost, Slidell was an American and he spoke lovely French, without an accent. His wife was the queen of Creole society, his daughters beautiful. If Slidell couldn't succeed in Paris, no one could.

England was a tougher assignment. Robert E. Lee had the Cavalier mystique that the English would have loved, but he was indispensable on the battlefield. After pouring through the genealogical registers, Davis and Benjamin came up with an alternative in James Murray Mason, long-time chairman of the U.S. Senate Committee on Foreign Relations, and a man with an impeccable pedigree. His grandfather, George Mason of Gunston Hall in northern Virginia, was a great landowner and perhaps the most influential founding father, though he worked behind the scenes. Known as the fourth George Mason (since there had been three in Virginia before him), he was the author of the Virginia Declaration of Rights, upon which his fellow Virginian Thomas Jefferson based the Declaration of Independence, and which was the basis for the U.S. Constitution's Bill of Rights. Ironically, Mason had refused to sign the Constitution because of his implacable opposition to slavery.

James Murray Mason, son of the fifth George, who was a lordly tobacco planter, was so proslavery that his grandfather must have been turning in his grave. Because Mason wasn't even a planter, his support of the institution was based on Southern pride, rather than self-interest. Both Virginians, the proudest Americans of all, and the Deep Southerners, for whom self-interest was the rule, counted themselves lucky to have such noble support for the odious system of bondage that made them the country's richest class.

For such a doctrinaire Southern states' rights advocate, Mason's background was not at all parochial. He had been educated in private schools in nearby Washington and at the University of Pennsylvania. There he met his wife, a Philadelphia Chew, one of the Quaker City's leading clans. Breaking with family tradition because of their nearly exhausted tobacco soil, Mason moved to Winchester, Virginia, in the Blue Ridge Mountains, and became a country lawyer. Of course, Virginia country lawyers rarely confined themselves to pleading cases. Soon, Mason was trading on his family's position. Before he was thirty, he was serving in the state legislature. In 1837, at thirty-six, he went to Congress, and in 1847, to the Senate, where he earned his reputation as slavery's great apologist.

Actually, apologies weren't Mason's style. He always took the initiative, as in drafting the 1850 Fugitive Slave Law, which required runaway slaves to be returned to their masters. Less tangible, but surely Mason's most despised act on behalf of slavery, was his warm support of Preston "Bully" Brooks in his near-murder of Charles Sumner, Senator from Massachusetts. The dean of abolitionists in the Senate, Sumner was a rabid Dixie-baiter, and Brooks, the congressman from South Carolina, felt that no words could respond to Sumner's vicious put-downs. Accordingly, he nearly bludgeoned Sumner to death with his walking stick. Mason served as the chief defender of Brooks's vigilantism. All the North was aghast, particularly at Mason. The South loved the entire episode. By going to bat for Brooks in his felony trial, the august Mason shed his image as an aloof, imperial Virginian. Now he was among the best of the "good-old-boys."

In 1861, Slidell and Mason sailed for Europe, confident of a royal reception. But before the Europeans could embrace them, the Yankees did, at least temporarily. The British ship *Trent,* on which the two envoys were traveling, was seized by a bold U.S. Navy captain, Charles Wilkes, who had been a childhood friend of Slidell in New York. Old school ties now bore no weight, and the Southern diplomats were carted off to a Boston prison. Although most Yankees wanted the pair to be drawn and quartered, especially Mason for his role in the Sumner caning, American fear of a war with England over the incident resulted in a speedy apology. Mason and Slidell were freed and went on across the Atlantic.

Despite Mason's disconcerting habits, such as chewing tobacco and spitting on the floor of the House of Commons, the English upper classes were crazy about the large, courtly, broodingly distinguished American. He was feted by a host of luminaries, such as the Marquis of Bath and Lord (later Prime Minister) Robert Cecil. Most of Parliament ignored his slavery position. There was a great deal of glee among the British ruling class at the prospect of the upstart American democracy going down the drain. The British Empire would triumph at last! Even William Gladstone was for recognizing the Confederacy. Yet all this popular support was for naught. The two men Mason needed most— Lord Palmerston, the Prime Minister, and Lord Russell, the Foreign Secretary—treated him no better than they had William Lowndes Yancey. The majestic threat of war over his capture was the closest thing to formal recognition the English government ever accorded to Mason.

Palmerston and Russell were the Mutt and Jeff of British diplomacy, Palmerston a giant, Russell a dwarf. Queen Victoria didn't like either one, for they paid scant attention to her. Of the two, Palmerston was the South's real enemy. He couldn't have cared less about America. He was more worried about Europe, especially about Napoleon III, and was wary of any alliance with the Emperor on the South's behalf. Besides, Britain did not immediately need cotton, the South's trump card. The British had a supply of cotton which Palmerston hoped would last until the conflict was over, and they were trying to develop their own cotton fields in India. So, Palmerston was willing to ignore all admiralty law in recognizing the federal blockade of the Southern coast. Judah Benjamin penned one elaborate opinion after another explaining why the blockade was ineffective and illegal; he wanted British ships to enter Southern ports with much needed cargoes. He also wanted the federal navy to interfere with these ships, thus forcing England into the war. Palmerston wouldn't budge. England didn't need anything in the South, not yet, so he saw no call for entangling alliances—principles be damned.

Poor Mason, who had naïvely assumed that the England of his forefathers would act on principle rather than politics, simply sat in

London gnashing his teeth. All his attempts to get a fair hearing went unanswered. He was incredulous that the Prime Minister of England could have such bad manners. In the end, he had to settle, not for arms, but merely for recognition of the Confederacy as a nation. For Lord Palmerston, even that acknowledgment was too much.

Things in France went far better for Slidell, who became a court favorite. Napoleon III, a pale shadow of his uncle and namesake, had grand ambitions nonetheless. He dreamed of an empire in Mexico and counted on a Southern victory to keep the Monroe Doctrine at bay. Slidell, a consummate politician, was willing to countenance what that doctrine forbade—foreign interference in the hemisphere—if it would help the Southern cause. He played up to Napoleon and to his beautiful Empress Eugénie, flattering her incessantly in Spanish, her native tongue. Slidell was also a favorite of the royal bastards, the decadent Duke de Morny (the illegitimate son of Napoleon III's mother) and of the scheming Count de Persigny, architect of the coup d'état that had placed Napoleon III on the French throne. Morny and Persigny liked to play cards with Slidell at the Tuileries. They found him *sympathique,* a man after their own hearts.

Yet for Slidell's friends, France still would not come out and recognize the Confederacy. For one thing, France had an understanding with England that it would follow the latter in such recognition, and England wasn't budging. For another, since the days of Lafayette, the French people had identified very closely with the American Republic. And they had more contempt for slavery than for English cooking. Even though Napoleon III was the least democratic man on earth, he couldn't lead a unilateral action that might stir up another revolution. Benjamin and Slidell offered Napoleon massive cotton bribes, promises of free trade with the Confederacy, whatever he wanted, but Napoleon's timidity outweighed his cupidity.

Slidell was never one to give up. The Confederacy desperately needed help, if not English and French military might, then at least their pounds and francs. The Confederacy was no great credit risk, but Slidell had a secret weapon—his ravishing young daughter, Mathilde. He unleashed her on Frederic Erlanger, the shy son of Emil Erlanger, the most important banker in Europe after the Rothschilds. Tantalized by Slidell's bait of his Creole daughter, the Erlangers offered the Confederacy a giant loan of $25 million through a bond issue they would manage.

The loan was not without other benefits to the house of Erlanger. It was secured by Confederate cotton, which the Erlangers would be able to acquire at one-fifth its actual value, a transaction that would net them millions. Millions more would come from commissions and discounts they arranged for themselves. It took the shrewd Judah Benjamin to spot the one-sidedness of the contract. Benjamin knew how much the Confederacy needed the loan, but he didn't want money on these terms. Only the Erlangers' agreement to scale down their booty, coupled with Slidell's appeal to Benjamin's friendship, got Benjamin and Davis to agree to the transaction.

The sale of the bonds began auspiciously, kicked off by the gala Erlanger-Slidell nuptials. At first, the price skyrocketed. Then the Yankee propaganda machine went to work, scaring investors with tales of imminent Southern collapse. The market was further depressed by federal front men who bought large blocs of bonds at low rates. Lee's defeat at Gettysburg in 1863 was the final blow. The price of the bonds plummeted.

The Erlangers counseled the Confederates to buy the bonds themselves, in order to prop up the issue. Mason authorized over $6 million in dwindling Confederate funds to be so used. It was a further fiasco, with the Confederates—and only the Confederates—buying the bonds. The sole party to come out ahead was the Erlangers, who earned nearly $3 million in commissions for executing the Confederate purchases. Slidell may have gained a son, but his government had lost a fortune.

The remaining Southern diplomatic efforts were akin to grasping at straws. The next brainstorm came from A. Dudley Mann, who had earlier been rebuffed by the English for being a bankrupt grocer's son. Mann now decided that the one man who could save the South was the Pope. If the spiritual leader of all Christendom endorsed the rebel cause, the temporal leaders of the world would have to follow suit. Because Mann had been one of America's leading diplomats before the war, serving as consul to Germany, Switzerland, Hungary, and elsewhere, the Confederate leaders tended to listen to him—even if his plans seemed out of this world. Together, Mann, an agnostic, Davis, a Pres-byterian, and Benjamin, a Jew, drafted a letter to the Catholic pontiff.

Lo and behold, the Pope agreed to an audience. Mann scurried off to the Vatican. Almost the first question Pius X asked was whether Jefferson Davis was a Catholic. Disappointed by the negative, the Pope then asked Mann if he were a Catholic. No, again. At this point, Mann was forced to take the offensive. Sensing the Pope's unease about slav-ery, Mann extolled the benevolent Southern masters and assured the Pope that Southern blacks had neither the inclination nor the ability to be free men. Lincoln's Emancipation, Mann asserted, was the most inhumane approach of all. These people needed care, not liberty. The Pope's only reply was a beatific smile.

Mann struck a more responsive chord when he revealed to the Pope how poor Irishmen were being lured to America as mercenary soldiers by Protestant ministers in the North. The Pope was shocked that his fellow Catholics were serving as Yankee cannon fodder, with false illusions of twenty acres and a mule, as a reward for their military service. Mann left, all smiles, at the Pope's promise to write a letter to Davis. But the letter Davis received was little more than a sympathy note. Like London and Paris, Rome was staying distinctly out of the fray. Even religion had failed the Confederacy. A final effort by Ben-jamin to sway world opinion—a proposal to draft blacks into the Con-federate Army in return for their freedom—was too late. There was no money, no supplies, no allies, only the courage of a crippled Army. The war was over.

THE DEFEATED

The frustrations on the European front were nothing like the frustra-tions at home. Almost all the prominent Southern families sent their able-bodied sons and husbands off to war. Many died. The wives stayed on the plantations, whose basic life-style was not disturbed by the war nearly as much as that of the cities. Of course, the women had to learn to live without their European wines and finery, excluded by the federal blockade. But the slaves usually remained loyal, even after the Emancipation Proclamation. Because the plantations grew their own food and were basically self-sufficient, the worst part of wartime life there was in learning the bad news from the front.

The cities were far harder hit. Terrible inflation sent prices soaring beyond the reach of the poorer families. Many commodities were in short supply. Bread riots were widespread, and mob violence and looting were commonplace. For instance, in the Confederate capital of Richmond in 1863, over a thousand women staged a food riot. It took a soothing speech by Jefferson Davis to quell the revolt. Of course, as various areas began to fall to federal troops, the situation grew much worse. Most planters deserted their townhouses for their country estates, though even these were frequently looted and pillaged by marauding Union soldiers. Some Northern generals, the most extreme of whom was William T. Sherman, felt that the entire South, civilian as well as military, needed to be taught a lesson. Accordingly, such commanders burned everything in their path. It was just a taste of how awful Reconstruction would be. For all their bad luck, the Confederate statesmen in Europe were fortunate indeed in being abroad with their families.

The fate of the Confederate diplomats after the war was no better than that of the Confederacy. The exceptions here were Benjamin, who had a brilliant rebirth in England, and Slidell, who became a fixture of the French aristocracy until his death in 1871 at seventy-eight. His other daughter, Roseann, became a countess, marrying the Comte de Saint-Romain. Mathilde became a baroness, as the Erlangers fled even further from Judaism by adding a titled *d'* to their name. Eventually, the family ended up in a grand castle in Sidi Bou Said, Tunisia, where one of the heirs became the world's leading authority on Arabic music—a far cry from the Frankfurt ghetto where the family began. The one tragedy in the Slidell dynasty was Slidell's wife, Mathilde Deslondes, who went into a fatal depression at fifty-one over the fall of her beloved New Orleans and the Creole life-style, for which all the titles in France couldn't compensate her. When Slidell died, he was, curiously enough, buried at the Villejuif (Jewish Village) cemetery in Paris—while his best friend, Judah Benjamin, was interred at Père La Chaise, a Catholic cemetery.

James Murray Mason stayed in England until President Andrew Johnson pardoned him in 1868. He then came home to Virginia, where he died broken-hearted two years later. Perhaps the most traumatized of all was A. Dudley Mann, who couldn't bear to return to a ravaged South ruled by the Yankees he so despised. He stayed in Europe preaching the rightness of the Southern cause, though he could find few listeners. He kept the most meticulous records of all Davis's lieutenants, but when he wrote his expansive memoirs, no one would publish them. Wandering aimlessly alone along the boulevards of Paris, Mann died a forgotten, bitter old man in 1889.

The saddest lot of all was that of the symbol of the Confederacy, Jefferson Davis. Benjamin, Mason, and Slidell were more hateful to the North, but they were beyond the law's long arm. Davis had to bear the brunt of Yankee wrath—which included becoming the scapegoat for the assassination of Lincoln. The popular song with the refrain "We'll hang Jeff Davis from a sour apple tree" was almost euphemistic; the most horrible forms of Oriental water torture were what the South's enemies had in mind.

The indignities began when Davis was captured by federal troops. Judah Benjamin had gotten away by disguising himself as a French tourist. Varina Davis had the well-intentioned idea of going Benjamin one better—she tried to disguise her husband as a woman. He was still wearing her shawl and bonnet when he was apprehended in Georgia, and his costume brought on a tremendous amount of ridicule in the Northern press. Yankee cartoonists depicted him in a hoop skirt, reducing the King of Cotton to its Drag Queen.

Still, the humiliation was no worse than the physical rigors that followed. The Davises were thrown into a dark prison van. Their belongings, from gold to baby clothes, were looted and Northern troops snatched away food intended for the Davis children. The soldiers exposed themselves to Varina Davis. En route to prison, the Davises received one touching gesture while locked in a hotel room in Savannah. The black waiter who brought their food tray hid, under the cover, a bunch of beautiful red roses and tearfully expressed his sorrow at what had happened to the Davises and to the South.

While the family remained in the hotel, Davis was taken incommunicado to Fort Monroe in Virginia, a stronghold known as the Gibraltar of the Chesapeake. Not wanting to take any chances, the federal commander there surrounded Davis with an entire garrison of troops and locked him in heavy chains in a viewless, tiny cell. His only furniture was an iron cot, his only utensil a wooden spoon, his only rations unchewable boiled beef, stale bread, and water. Squeaky-shoed soldiers marched around him twenty-four hours a day; he was never allowed a private moment. Guards even stood around him when he used the portable toilet that was brought into his cell. Davis's only company was a mouse he made his pet. If the North wanted to design a hell that was the antithesis of the plantation life Davis stood for, Fort Monroe was it. Davis, always a sick man, nearly wasted away. He had been indicted for treason, but was never brought to a trial. Habeas corpus and all other basic rights were denied, and he was left to languish in the darkness.

Davis was the only Confederate leader who remained incarcerated— he was doing penance for the whole South. In 1868, after even Northern sentiment was outraged at his unusual punishment, he was freed and reunited with his family. For his dignity under the most horrid of conditions, he won a martyr's reputation throughout the South, giving inspiration to the thousands suffering through the abject poverty of the postbellum period; any stigma of having lost the war was forgotten. But Davis needed money for himself and his family. His plantation was now in the hands of his former slaves. With several young children to educate, Davis, for the first time in his life, needed a job.

Dazed, he went to Europe, where the more fortunate Confederate leaders had fled. There he was a hero and a celebrity. Everyone wanted to meet him, from Lord Cecil, who had had a nervous collapse when the Confederacy failed, to Napoleon III, who was too cowardly to aid the "lost cause." Benjamin and Slidell embraced their leader emotionally and rolled out the red carpet. All Europe offered Davis hospitality; no one offered him work.

Almost penniless, Davis concluded his grand tour and returned to Memphis, to become the president of a small insurance company. Unfortunately, postbellum Southerners didn't live as long as the actuarial tables predicted they would; unable to pay all the claims, the company failed, a victim of Dixie's unexpectedly high mortality rate. Davis went back to England to try again for a job with a British company with American operations, but the story was the same: many interviews, many dinners, no offers. It was believed that Davis was bad for any company's image in the North. Since no one was about to invest in the ravaged South, Davis's figurehead mystique was not bankable.

Luckily, Davis found a patron, Mrs. Sarah Dorsey, a wealthy Southern widow who had moved to England and still had her money. Davis was her idol. She encouraged him to come with her to Beauvoir, her gracious estate in Biloxi, Mississippi, on the Gulf, and write his memoirs. Varina, in Germany overseeing her daughter's education, was jealous at first, but Mrs. Dorsey moved away from her home so that Varina could return and be alone with her husband. That Mrs. Dorsey was dying of cancer at the time is some measure of her devotion to Davis. She left him Beauvoir and all her other property.

Another disappointment was the commercial failure of Davis's memoirs. Southerners couldn't afford to buy the two-volume set; still-prejudiced Northerners wouldn't even consider a purchase. But as one of the great stoics in American history, Davis never despaired. He still enjoyed great prestige abroad and was visited at Beauvoir by several foreign dignitaries, including Oscar Wilde.

Still further tragedy kept the Davises from establishing a Southern dynasty. Their sons all died, the first in an accidental fall from a balcony, another of diphtheria, and the third of yellow fever. Their daughter, Varina Anne, or "Winnie," had been crowned by Southern war veterans as the "daughter of the Confederacy." However, she alienated the entire South when she fell in love with a Harvard-trained Syracuse attorney whose grandfather had been a prominent abolitionist. The affair killed her father in 1889, and nearly 150,000 thronged to his funeral. Davis had outlived nearly all his enemies and had become a symbol of heroism to both North and South. Out of respect, Winnie called the marriage off and never wed. She became a novelist and was on the verge of success when she died of gastritis at age thirty-four, in 1898.

Varina Howell Davis lived until she was eighty. When Jefferson died, her own dire poverty forced her to make an extreme compromise.

Unable to afford the upkeep of Beauvoir, she moved to New York to try to earn a living as a writer. She wrote a lengthy biography of her husband, but it didn't sell. Only a staunch Davis admirer, Joseph Pulitzer, could keep her from the poorhouse. Pulitzer gave her a $1,500 annual salary for a column in his *New York Sunday World.* Aside from this, she spent her entire last years writing in defense of her husband. She wanted so much to die in Natchez, but she couldn't afford it. All she had left were memories of King Cotton's glory days. In 1906, Varina Davis was given a heroine's military funeral and was buried beside her husband in Richmond, the former capital of the Confederacy.

VI

From Champagne to Chitlins: The Aristocracy During Reconstruction

THE SPOILS

The tragedy of Jefferson Davis mirrored the postbellum plight of the rest of the Southern aristocracy. Stripped of their slaves, their cotton confiscated, their currency worthless, their mansions sacked, the planter elite was rendered powerless, in most cases for all time. Further, the aristocrats were blamed by the North for the Civil War; consequently, they were singled out for special punishment during the Reconstruction period in the decade or so following the war. The Radical Republicans who controlled Congress were led by Thaddeus Stevens (whose great Pennsylvania iron foundry had been leveled by Confederate soldiers and who was goaded into South-hatred by his mulatto mistress), and by Charles Sumner, finally recovered from his near-fatal Southern caning. These two had special scores to settle with Dixie's patricians. The most detested of all Yankees, they wanted nothing less than to reduce the aristocracy to the standard of living formerly endured only by their slaves.

To this end, no amnesty was granted to any of the Confederacy's high officeholders, nor to anyone worth over $20,000. This group was prevented by Congress from voting and holding office, while the blacks were fully enfranchised. The South was divided into military districts to ensure that the new civil rights laws would be honored. The freed blacks became the new ruling class. In effect, the South's code of white supremacy was completely reversed. White officeholders were removed whenever the Stevens-Sumner leadership deemed them too sympathetic to the old order. They were replaced with inexperienced, usually illiterate, blacks, or with unscrupulous white outsiders known as carpetbaggers. What was once government became anarchy. No mercy was shown to the ravaged South. For example, state laws providing artificial limbs for crippled Confederate soldiers were set aside by a vindictive Congress.

Still, there were survivors. And there were some prosperous survivors, though the price for prosperity was almost invariably the loss of honor. The most notorious survivor of all was Franklin J. Moses, Jr., of South Carolina. Moses is generally regarded as the worst of all scalawags. (The term scalawag was, before the war, used only to describe scaly pigs or diseased sheep. Now it became the most opprobrious of appellations for turncoat Southerners. Carpetbaggers was the term for Yankee interlopers who came South with all their possessions in carpetbags. They left, however, with trainloads of spoils.)

The Moseses were one of South Carolina's first families. Meyer Moses had come to Charleston in the mid-1700s from Barbados and was a minor hero in the Revolutionary War. Meyer had a son named Meyer, who was a prominent local banker and represented Charleston in the state legislature. Also an author, the younger Meyer wrote books on politics, including a treatise on the French Revolution, and was a leader of the Beth Elohim Congregation, of which Judah Benjamin's family were also members. Meyer's son, Israel Franklin Moses, dropped the Israel and added a J as a middle initial. (The J was merely an initial; it didn't stand for anything, until Franklin's son, Franklin J., Jr., adopted it. Then locals supplied Judas to end the enigma.)

Born in 1804, Franklin J., Sr., was one of the most brilliant young men in the state of South Carolina. He was graduated at seventeen from South Carolina College with highest honors and studied law under James L. Pettigru, one of America's foremost attorneys. While traveling across the state, Moses lodged one evening at the Sumter estate of Judge J.S.G. Richardson, who convinced the young man of the golden opportunities in the hills of the up-country. The judge set up Moses in what became one of the state's most profitable legal practices. Moses subsequently served in the state House and Senate and culminated a brilliant career as Chief Justice of the South Carolina Supreme Court.

His son, Franklin J. Moses, Jr., who was born in 1838 and raised as a Methodist, his mother's faith, was brilliant, too, but in all the wrong ways. Although he dropped out of South Carolina College, he was adept at utilizing his father's contacts. First, in 1859, he married Judge Richardson's daughter, Emma. Then he secured a prestigious appointment as secretary to South Carolina Governor Francis Pickens, which gave him instant political stature. Joining Robert Barnwell Rhett as one of the state's staunchest advocates of secession, Moses in 1861 personally assisted in ripping down the American flag from Fort Sumter and single-handedly raised the rebel banner. Archly handsome, with wavy hair and a luxuriant mustache, Moses was a spellbinding orator. Among political insiders, he was at the top of the list of young men most likely to succeed.

When the South was defeated, Moses couldn't bear to be taken off the list. Accordingly, he became a reborn Republican. As editor of the *Sumter News,* this former desecrator of the Stars and Stripes now became the state's leading advocate of cooperation with the Yankee conquerors. He even joined the Union League, an organization primarily composed of occupation troops and other Northerners. While South Carolinians stood back aghast, the Stevens-Sumner people smiled their approval. Moses played unashamedly to the black voting majority, making unlimited promises no one could keep. The naïve electorate loved him, making him Speaker of the largely black state House of Representatives. In fact, they loved him so much that when he lost a thousand dollars at the horse races, the House voted to assume all his betting debts.

By 1872, the thirty-four-year-old Moses was Governor of South Carolina. One of the most flagrantly dishonest politicians anywhere, he took countless bribes for pardons, for patronage positions, for pushing through legislation. The only vestige of the Old South that he retained was his penchant for lavish entertaining. Appropriating the grandest house in Columbia as the governor's mansion (rechristened by resentful whites the Château de Plunderville), Moses had bacchanals almost every night, surrounding himself with black prostitutes whom he dressed in diamonds, furs, and Paris finery, all paid for by the state treasury. The orgies were not confined to the château. Often, Moses would pack four of his bejeweled concubines into his landau, along with a champagne-pouring houseboy, and go for joyrides along the streets of Columbia. As he stuffed bunches of grapes into his mouth and bathed his girlfriends in rare wines, this hero of Dixie blithely admitted to spending ten times his salary on "living expenses."

For all his derelictions, Franklin J. Moses, Jr., never forgot his relatives. The Moseses had the dubious honor of being the First Family of South Carolina during Reconstruction. Moses's father was kept on as Chief Justice. As chairman of the board of trustees at South Carolina College, Moses, Jr., proudly gave his father an honorary Doctor of Laws degree. He selected uncles Montgomery Moses and Meyer B. Moses for high judgeships. He helped his cousin, Altamont Moses, gain election to the legislature. He appointed cousin Zalegman Moses general of the state militia, and still another cousin, Henry Clay Moses, as a major. (Patriotic surnames were popular with the family, as with other Southerners. Another uncle, Andrew Jackson Moses, ran a leading Sumter general store.)

Eventually, Moses's behavior grew too outrageous even for the worst scalawags. His satanic appearance, all pointed ears, was given new emphasis in the press. In 1874, the state was convinced he was the devil reincarnate. He was not renominated, and his law practice in Columbia fizzled. In 1878, his wife divorced him. Soon thereafter, when he declared bankruptcy, he owed nearly $100,000. He quickly fled the state.

The hero's welcome he expected in the North didn't materialize. Used to a champagne existence, Moses now couldn't even afford beer. He became a small-time swindler, drifting from city to city and bilking the local elites through his still-smooth Southern gentleman routine. The nadir of his new career came when he spent six months in the Boston House of Correction for cheating one of the Brahmin Higginsons out of thirty-four dollars. Moses died by asphyxiating himself in a bleak Massachusetts boardinghouse.

Despite his own Methodist upbringing, Moses was still regarded as a Jew. Moreover, his outrageous actions provided fodder for the anti-Semitism throughout the South. The hatred of carpetbaggers who happened to be poor Jewish peddlers was grossly magnified because of his legendary corruption. Added to this was the born-again Christian evangelism sweeping the South. "Jews killed Christ. Jews killed the South." This was the new litany that overshadowed the achievements of Southern Jews like Judah Benjamin and Moses's own forebears. As a result, many decades passed—decades of threats, abuse, and lynchings—before Jews could hope to be better than second-class citizens in a region where, before the war, they had suffered no disabilities at all. Things got so bad that many of Moses's kinfolk, whom he had so graciously pork-barreled, dropped the once-powerful name in favor of the more Christian maiden names of their mothers.

Though Moses was the most profligate of the Southern survivors, he was by no means alone. Another highborn opportunist who escaped the specter of Reconstruction was General Pierre Gustave Toutant Beauregard, who started the Civil War with his attack on Fort Sumter. A descendant of one of the oldest Creole families in Louisiana, Beauregard could boast ancestors who were not the typical convicts or derelicts who peopled New Orleans. Rather, they were fairly high-level civil servants under Louis XIV, who were sent to administer the new Louisiana territory. This not only allowed the family to claim extensive and choice sugar lands, but also gave it as valid a claim to aristocracy as one could have in the Delta. Beauregard's lineage was reinforced by two exalted Creole marriages. The first was to Laure Villere, granddaughter of the first native-born French Governor of Louisiana. Because Governer Villere had been murdered by the Spanish when they took over the territory, the family acquired a martyr mystique which further enhanced its social standing. When Laure Villere died, Beauregard married Caroline Deslonde, another sugar heiress and the sister of the wife of John Slidell.

Beauregard's educational and military credentials were as impressive as his social ones. He had been second in his class at West Point in 1838 and had been appointed superintendent of the Military Academy just before the Civil War erupted. At a time when West Point far eclipsed Harvard in prestige and power, this position was the pinnacle of American academe. Beauregard also won several citations for bravery in the Mexican War and was a brilliant engineer, having supervised the herculean task of draining the New Orleans swamps in the 1850s. Widely regarded as perhaps the bravest of Confederate generals, Beauregard definitely had the greatest sex appeal. Short (five feet seven), dark, and handsome, with an intense Gallic fire, he wore specially tailored uniforms and flowing capes. When he galloped along on his white steed, his dark eyes blazing, Beauregard foreshadowed Valentino. Women, North and South, went wild about him. After the Confederate victory at Manassas, a new dance, the Beauregard Manassas Quick Step, became a brief rage. Countless bouquets of flowers were sent to him. Racehorses, children, even women's corsets were named Beauregard. On his campaigns, the suave Creole always carried a trunk full of love letters, for inspiration.

Beauregard's military campaigns belied the notion that war was total hell. When Prince Jerome Bonaparte came to visit him on the battlefield, Beauregard toasted his honored French guest with roast canvasback and mint juleps served by a retinue of slaves and treated the prince to such amenities as a private barber and masseur. Frequently, members of the general's female fan club would come behind the lines and spend several nights in a special tent protected by an honor guard, where Beauregard entertained them. When he was assigned the defense of Charleston, the city gave him more parties and parades than any other celebrity who had ever been there, including Lafayette.

This was the hero of Fort Sumter, Manassas, and Shiloh, this general who kept leading the charge at Bull Run even as his horse was shot dead from under him. No one in the South would have expected him to sell out. He did. Not that he was in danger of starving. This most *soigné* soldier of all had turned down postwar offers to command the armies of Rumania, Egypt, Brazil, Argentina, and even Japan. He would have taken a similar post in France to fight in the land of his ancestors had his brother-in-law, Slidell—who had played cat-and-mouse with Napoleon III—been able to get the job for him. Instead, he became president-chief engineer of the New Orleans, Jackson and Great Northern Railroad. Then, in 1877, real opportunity knocked.

The Louisiana state lottery, an institution as venal as Franklin

Moses and controlled by carpetbaggers of the worst order, needed a front man. The lottery organizers, who were Northerners, wanted to dress Beauregard up in his battle grays and have him draw the winning tickets out of a great revolving drum. As a beloved military figure and a highborn Creole, he would lure the masses to the lottery and give it respectability as well. For several hoopla-filled drawings a year, Beauregard would receive an annual salary of $30,000, renewable until the lottery's charter expired in 1893. Since the Khedive of Egypt had offered him only $12,000 to lead the camel corps, the offer was irresistible, especially when he observed his fellow aristocrats virtually starving to death around him. Beauregard admitted that he was motivated by the money; while not destitute, he wanted to provide for his family as well as he could. At sixty-two, he didn't see the market for old rebel soldiers as holding great promise. Besides, he rationalized, Louisianians—who were born gamblers—were bound to get bilked in some get-rich-quick scheme anyway. High-rolling was an essential element of the Creole character. Perhaps he could have a sobering influence or at least keep things as honest as possible. Beauregard far overestimated himself, or at least underestimated the lottery. In terms of unconscionable profits it was the biggest rip-off the South would ever see.

Each drawing was a veritable sideshow. First, General Jubal Early of Virginia mounted the stage in full regalia and stood at attention before the huge ticket drum. Next, to a rousing ovation, Beauregard marched in. Having decided that mourning clothes were more in order for the event, he had stood firm in refusing to sully his uniform. No one minded. He was still the general, no matter what he wore. With his flowing white hair, he lent an incongruous dignity to the prize wheel he stood beside. Two black boys spun Early's drum containing the lucky numbers. Early drew a ticket and announced the winner. Then Beauregard spun his own wheel. When it landed on the amount of the prize money, Beauregard boomed out the result. Pandemonium followed. The procedure would be repeated several hundred times during the long day of the drawing.

The best deal of all was for the owners of the lottery. Their gross annual revenues were nearly $30 million, but they paid out in prizes only half that amount. The lottery company was tax-exempt and only had to pay the state a donation of less than $100,000 to assorted charities as the price for its monopoly. Its only other expenses were salaries and bait advertising, which promised everything from wealth to health to sexual potency, for the price of a ticket. In all, the lottery leaders had well over $10 million in net profits each year to spend on revels and bribes that rivaled those of Franklin Moses. Through contributions the lottery controlled all of Louisiana—the legislature, the hospitals, the French opera house. Such institutions depended upon the lottery for their financial survival.

The founder of the lottery was a rough operator from Baltimore named Charles Howard, who was said to have forged papers indicating service in the Confederate Army, and the Navy as well. When he tried to polish himself by seeking membership in an old-Creole social club, he was flatly refused. In return, he bought the club, razed it, and turned it into a cemetery, all with Northern capital. This surly, brutal man was considered the ideal carpetbag agent. He was able to ram the lottery through the venal legislature by unashamedly handing out over $300,000 in payoffs. Then again, this was the Louisiana of John Slidell, with his steamboats full of quadruplicate voters. Howard was simply following ancient traditions of chicanery. Eventually, he joined his face man, Beauregard, in the local aristocracy.

In 1893, Congress effectively outlawed the lottery, which relocated in Honduras, under the management of Charles Villere, Beauregard's elegant but equally ambitious brother-in-law. Beauregard himself died the same year, 1893, leaving an estate of close to half a million dollars. In an age when other Confederate generals had no skills other than fighting to fall back on and died proud paupers, the Creole Napoleon again stood out conspicuously. Nevertheless, as Louisiana's favorite son and most gallant figure, he was given a hero's funeral.

IN DEFENSE
OF SOUTHERN HONOR

The other generals and Confederate leaders took a less charitable view. Although Beauregard wasn't actually a scalawag, his complicity had put more millions in the hands of the Yankees who controlled the lottery. Where was that honor upon which the Old South prided itself? To the hard-core rebel elite, any type of collaboration with the North was evil. This extreme view manifested itself most vividly in the Ku Klux Klan. The organization that became one of the fascist nightmares of the twentieth century began, sophomorically, as a Greek-letter social group for wellborn Confederate junior officers. (The Klan thus began as an aristocratic group. The poor whites normally associated with it joined only in later years.) The young men took the name from *kuklos,* Greek for circle. Fraternities and their arcane rituals were always popular in the South and, in the postwar era, there was no money for other amusements; good fellowship had to suffice. Thus, from the humblest beginnings in Pulaski, Tennessee, in 1865, chapters of the Klan spread all over Dixie.

The Klansmen soon realized that their uniform of flowing robes and pointed hoods was a secret weapon, and perhaps their only weapon, against the indignities visited on them by Yankee Reconstruction. Southern blacks were very superstitious. Terrified of the dark and by the apocalyptic garb, the were placed in a new kind of thrall by these night-riding ghosts. To blacks, the Klan's monstrous rebel yells and pounding horses' hooves came to signify the approach of Satan. The Klansmen milked this devilish mystique to its outer limit, terrorizing blacks into believing that they were dead Confederates returned from hell. "Don't cause trouble, don't vote, don't rock the boat, revere your old masters"—all this constituted the devil's message, as solemnly proclaimed to blacks by the Klansmen on their midnight rides.

The costumes of these galloping ghosts had been the brainchild of a once-wealthy charter member who had traveled in Spain before the war. There he had seen the pre-Easter Holy Week ceremonies in Granada and Seville, where penitent Catholics dressed in identical attire with pointed hoods and marched in endless nighttime processions, holding candles, singing dirges, and mourning the death of Christ. The Klansmen transmuted the impressive Spanish traditions into their own Unholy Week, and celebrated it every week of the year. They also developed a new geography of the South, turning it into an Invisible Empire divided into realms, dominions, provinces, and dens. The em-

pire was headed by an Imperial Wizard who was aided by Grand Drag-
ons, Titans, Giants, and Cyclopses. Members were called Ghouls.
Within a mere two years, there were over 500,000 of them.

The first Imperial Wizard couldn't have been a better choice, for
shock value alone. He was General Nathan Bedford Forrest, perhaps
the greatest of all cavalrymen. General Forrest was famous for his
analysis of his military success: get there "fustest with the mostest." By
the close of the Civil War, the untutored, though brilliant, Forrest had
ascended from poverty to the pantheon of Dixie gentility. It seemed as
though the sword could create a Southern aristocrat just as well as the
plowshare (wielded by slaves). Actually, Forrest made it both ways. The
son of a blacksmith, he was a self-made millionaire slave trader and
cotton planter who also rose in the Confederate Army, from private to
general, by means of his swashbuckling horse soldiery.

Like the similarly heroic Davy Crockett, Forrest was born on a
mountaintop in Tennessee. He was evidently also born to be wild. He
spent his childhood in such wilderness pastimes as strangling snakes
and splitting logs. His greatest frustration came when as a boy he went
all the way to Texas to fight in an anticipated Mexican War (as Davy
Crockett had), but was turned away when the war didn't materialize.
The prototype of rugged masculinity, Forrest returned to Tennessee
and met his wife by lifting her buggy out of a mud hole.

Although he had less than six months of formal education, Forrest
was shrewd enough to see the golden opportunities in the cotton belt.
In order to buy land, he was forced to amass capital in the dangerous
slave trade. Well over six feet tall and fearless, Forrest outmuscled all
his competition and built a four-story markethouse, Memphis's largest.
There he sold, to black belt planters, humans whom he had acquired at
discount prices from Virginians whose land would not grow any more.
Soon Forrest was able to join the plantation parade, acquiring thousands of rich acres along the Mississippi. His powerful image was further burnished when he single-handedly dispersed a vigilante lynch
mob. Just as the rope was about to be hoisted, Forrest, who was passing
by, charged through the crowd, whipped out his huge hunting knife,
cut the noose, and brought the victim to the safety of jail. Memphis
loved it and elected Forrest an alderman.

During the war, Forrest's reputation grew still more. He was considered by many the South's most intrepid officer. He was also one of its handsomest. With Hollywood-perfect features, highlighted by battle scars and a piercing stare, he was what a warrior was supposed to look like, even more so than the slightly effete Beauregard.

Forrest's guerrilla-style battle exploits were epic. He loved to fight, loved to kill, and he believed in fear as a vital weapon. Frequently wounded in the midst of a fray, he had twenty-nine horses shot out from under him. What made him the darling of the Klan was his role in the infamous Fort Pillow massacre. In taking the Union fort, Forrest's troops hanged, crucified, burned, and otherwise gruesomely murdered most of the Fort's black soldiers, former slaves whom Union forces had freed and inducted into the Army. The North called him a butcher; the South called him a hero. General William T. Sherman, who modeled his equally shocking march to the sea on Fort Pillow, regarded the fearless Forrest with unabashed admiration, calling him "the most remarkable man produced by either side—North or South."

In selecting its first Imperial Wizard, the Klan's inevitable nominee was Robert E. Lee. When the Virginian general politely declined, in an effort to avoid becoming the object of undue attention, Forrest was everyone's favorite second choice, including Lee's. At the Klan conclave at Memphis's Maxwell House in 1867, Forrest was formally inaugurated with the greatest fanfare. In trying its best to live up to Forrest's bloodstained record, the Klan began doing more than merely *scaring* blacks to death. Burnings, shootings, and lynchings, in the worst Fort Pillow tradition, became its new modus operandi. More federal troops were sent South to quell the violence. Forrest, whose massacre days were behind him, and who had actually become a voice for moderation, tried to call off the dogs. In 1870, he ordered the Klan disbanded and resigned his Wizardry. Nonetheless, the Klan and its violence continued, ultimately being instrumental in scaring blacks back "into their place" and scaring federal troops out of the South.

As for Forrest himself, the former cotton king became a pauper. After declaring bankruptcy, he followed Beauregard into the railroad business, with much less success. His greatest accomplishment was as a rabble-rousing speaker at benefits for Confederate war veterans.

Though Memphis and the South never stopped idolizing him, Forrest's end was tragic. During the war, he had contracted a virulent form of chronic dysentery, known as the "Confederate disease," since it felled so many rebels. The once-giant general literally wasted away. When he died, at age fifty-five in 1877, with Jefferson Davis at his bedside, Forrest weighed under one hundred pounds. Still, for generations afterward, the Forrest name maintained its magic.

Another hallowed Tennessee name which came through the war un-sullied was that of Overton. John Overton had come from a poor English family to Nashville in 1789. While apprenticing as a lawyer, he bunked in a local boardinghouse with the young Andrew Jackson. Neither could have asked for a better roommate. Property in the then-virgin territory was ripe for the taking. Overton and Jackson took it. Their greatest land speculation came when they purchased a huge tract of land for the price of cottonseed and named it Memphis. The Over-ton-Jackson real estate empire was aided significantly by Overton's succeeding Jackson as Chief Justice of the Tennessee Supreme Court in 1804. There the men shaped the amorphous land laws to their own benefit. The last word on land legislation, Judge Overton was, not surprisingly, Tennessee's largest landholder. He was also the architect of Old Hickory's political campaigns, and the Svengali behind the scenes of Jackson's presidency.

The South had been good to the Overtons. The judge's son, Colo-nel John, was good to the South. The richest man in Tennessee, he gave most of his fortune to the Confederate war effort. Symbolically, his finest hour came in 1864, when he feted eight Confederate generals, including his friend, Bedford Forrest, at his huge plantation, Traveller's Rest. It was the rebel version of the Last Supper. During the war, federal troops confiscated property of Overton's worth millions. After spending years seeking reparations, Overton got the grand total of $8,000. Nevertheless, he not only refused to declare bankruptcy, but also insisted on paying off every cent of his debts of nearly $2 million. His immense remaining acreage enabled him to do just that and more. He finished his great Maxwell House Hotel (for which the coffee was named), a beautiful Confederate veterans' home, churches, and war memorials throughout Tennessee. While other old Tennessee families survived by such ploys as converting their cotton bales into gold bars at the outset of the war and burying them, the Overtons refused to resort to subterfuge. They were just too land rich to have to. These pharaohs of the Mississippi Delta continued their dynasty, with Colonel Overton's son and grandson both serving as mayors of Memphis. It was virtually their birthright.

For old-line Southerners, the choice was not necessarily one of dishonorable scalawagging or dignified penury. There was one other way out—the fine art of Southern politics, that honey-tongued oratory indigenous to the American southland. The two postbellum masters here were, on one hand, impeccable aristocrats whose motives were above reproach. On the other hand, they were sly foxes who milked their aristocratic credentials for all they were worth. These were Mississippi's Lucius Lamar and South Carolina's Wade Hampton.

First Lucius. Or, to be complete, Lucius Quintus Cincinnatus Lamar, one of the heroes cited by President John F. Kennedy in his book, *Profiles in Courage.* By one magnanimous gesture—a tear-jerking 1874 eulogy of the South's most despised enemy, Charles Sumner— Lamar totally distracted the North from his once-rabid secessionism and Southern superpatriotism. His magic words, when read between the lines, were a paean to states' rights. Yet his syrupy tone fooled the Yankees; Lamar's rise to the top of the councils of state in Washington culminated with an appointment to the Supreme Court.

The Lamars were one of the leading families of Georgia. French Huguenots, they had come to Maryland in the late 1600s, when most of their confreres were going to Charleston. A century later the Lamars, too, heeded the call of the Deep South and moved to the then-uninhabited Georgia frontier, acquiring a lot of land for a little money, and becoming rich slave-owning planters. No one can accuse the South of not being good to its pioneers. Lucius Lamar's father, also named Lucius Quintus Cincinnatus, was one of Georgia's top judges. His uncle, Mirabeau Buonaparte Lamar, was a poet-adventurer who had gone to Texas to fight beside Sam Houston as a cavalry commander at San Jacinto and stayed on to become the second president of the Texas republic.

Back in Georgia, Lucius's father, Judge Lamar, fared less well. A chronic depressive, he committed suicide in 1834 when Lucius was only nine. Lucius was similarly affected and suffered from fainting spells and paralyzing anxiety attacks throughout his entire life. (One occurred during the Civil War, just as he was about to lead his troops into a battle. He never fought again.) As a young man, Lucius was sent to the Methodist Emory College at Oxford, Georgia. Although he was a mediocre student, socially he was summa cum laude and won as a bride Virginia Longstreet, the daughter of Emory's president, Judge and Reverend Augustus Baldwin Longstreet. A Yale-trained lawyer who got religion when his only son died, Longstreet became a Methodist minister as well as one of the nation's leading educators. While preaching and teaching, Longstreet wrote *Georgia Scenes,* precursor to the tales of Uncle Remus and Huckleberry Finn. This Southern Aesop was also a fierce advocate of Southern separatism and black inferiority. His attitudes had an indelible effect on his son-in-law.

When Longstreet went to the University of Mississippi to become its president, he took Lucius Lamar along and made him a math professor. Lucius practiced law on the side. Longstreet pushed his son-in-law into Mississippi politics and helped him draft numerous fire-eating speeches advocating states' rights. By age thirty-two, under Longstreet's strict tutelage, Lucious was the compleat Southern gentleman — a successful lawyer, planter, and member of the House of Representatives. A close friend of Jefferson Davis, Lamar was appointed Minister to Russia during the Civil War. However, he had such a good time in England and France being "briefed" by Mason and Slidell that he never went on to see the czar. Eventually, the Confederate government recalled him and made him a judge advocate and a colonel for General Lee in Virginia.

Returning to Mississippi after Appomattox, Lamar, whose tall, gaunt, white-bearded figure resembled that of the later George Bernard Shaw, became a professor of ethics and metaphysics at the University. This was basically a law post. In it, Lamar engaged his students in

Socratic dialogue, posing hypothetical legal quagmires for them to extricate themselves from. His success inspired Harvard's C. C. Langdell to abandon dry textbook lectures and imitate this lively "case method," which became the hallmark of the Harvard Law School. When the Radical Republicans took over the University of Mississippi in 1870 and instituted their version of black studies, Lamar quit and returned to law practice.

Eventually, though, Mississippi's whites regained control. Lamar, like most other old Confederates, was finally pardoned and became eligible to hold public office. With the invaluable support of the Klan, he was returned to the House of Representatives in 1873. However, confronted with impermeable Northern resistance, Lamar was totally frustrated in securing benefits for the South. He realized that his only asset was his tongue. When Charles Sumner died in 1874, he got his chance to unleash it. His speech is one of the most famous in the annals of the House.

Basically, the only thing for which Lamar praised Sumner was not Sumner's intellect and scholarship, which Lamar glossed over, but the "peculiar and strongly marked moral traits of his character, which gave the coloring to the whole tenor of his singularly dramatic public career; traits which made him for a long period to a large portion of his countrymen the object of as deep and passionate a hostility as to another he was one of enthusiastic admiration." In short, Lamar admired Sumner for being an extremist in adhering to his principles. Like himself.

To forestall any possible charges that he had gone over to the Yankees, Lamar devoted most of his speech to refuting Sumner's staunch defense of black rights:

It matters not that the slave might be contented with his lot; that his actual condition might be immeasurably more desirable than that from which [slavery] had transplanted him; that it gave him physical comfort, mental and moral elevation and religious culture not possessed by his race in any other condition; that his bonds had not been placed upon his hands by the living generation; that the mixed social system of which he formed an element had been regarded by the fathers of the Republic, and by the ablest statesmen who had risen up after them, as too complicated to be broken up without danger to society itself, or even to civilization; or finally, that the actual state of things had been recognized and explicitly sanctioned by the very organic law of the Republic. Weighty as these considerations might be, formidable as were the difficulties in the way of the practical enforcement of his great principle, [Sumner] held none the less that it must sooner or later be enforced, though institutions and constitutions should have to give way alike before it.   —*Congressional Record,* April 27, 1874, 3410.

Noting that Sumner had expressed forgiveness to the South toward the end of his life, Lamar challenged Sumner's Northern colleagues to match his "spirit of magnanimity." This depicting of the intransigent Sumner as a friend of the South was a brilliant bit of revisionism. Through Sumner's ghost, Lamar was appealing to Northern guilt:

The South—prostrate, exhausted, drained of her life-blood as well as of her material resources, yet still honorable and true—accepts the bitter award of the bloody arbitrament without reservation, resolutely determined to abide the result with chivalrous fidelity; yet, as if struck dumb by the magnitude of her reverses, she suffers on in silence.

The North, exultant in her triumph and elated by success, still cherishes, as we are assured, a heart full of magnanimous emotions toward her disarmed and discomfited antagonist; and yet, as if mastered by some mysterious spell, silencing her better impulses, her words and acts are the words and acts of suspicion and distrust.

Would that the spirit of the illustrious dead whom we lament today could speak from the grave to both parties to this deplorable discord in tones which should reach each and every heart throughout this broad territory, "My countrymen, know one another, and you will love one another."

Lamar's delivery was impassioned. At the close, few eyes in the House were dry. He had the North crying for Sumner, the South crying for itself. Although some Republicans condemned Lamar for duplicity, most Yankee statesmen had had enough of the internecine rancor. Lamar's eulogy was an appropriate signal to bury the hatchet, and Lamar was an appropriate symbol for reconciliation.

Lamar became known as the Great Pacificator. Securing valuable financial aid for the South, he secured his own election to the Senate and, with it, an impregnable position as America's favorite token Southerner. Hence, his appointment by Grover Cleveland, first, as Secretary of the Interior and then to the Supreme Court. Wherever he was, he was the South's best friend, reopening the hallowed pork barrel for his constituents and, until his death in 1893, casting his ultraconservative prestige behind his old states' rights position, which he never ceased to propound.

TWILIGHT
OF THE OLD GUARD

Lucius Lamar accomplished a great deal for the South in Washington. Wade Hampton did even more, serving as both the leader and prominent symbol of the old aristocracy. No one could have played the role better. The richest man in the South before the Civil War, Hampton was also one of the most imposing—a giant over six feet tall, and weighing nearly two hundred and fifty pounds, all muscle. Like Lamar, Hampton had a fine education and was trained as a lawyer. Additionally, he was a superb horseman, whose wartime legion of blue-blooded cavalrymen was the elite corps of the South. As one who successfully combined cavalry and chivalry, Hampton can best be described as a cultured General Forrest. Because he survived Forrest by three decades, his noble image was an essential psychological crutch and rallying point for the beleaguered South.

Wade Hampton's ancestors, arriving in Virginia from England in 1620, only one year after the Jamestown landing, became one of America's first families. First in time, though, didn't automatically mean first in wealth. The initial Hampton was a tobacco planter, the second a clergyman. The third, fourth, and fifth generations all were Virginia farmers with varying degrees of success, but never quite equaling that of the Byrds or Randolphs. Like so many second sons of these Old Dominion families, Anthony Hampton of the fifth generation was precluded from any inheritance. He set off in the 1760s for the South Carolina frontier to create his own estate. Unfortunately, he, his wife, and one of his five sons were scalped by Cherokee Indians in their log cabin in 1776.

Surviving them was a son, Wade, who realized all his father's ambitions. The first key to his success was military, for which his frequent early hand-to-hand combat with the Indians had been excellent training. During the Revolution, Hampton, who rose to the rank of colonel of the cavalry, was instrumental in defeating the British in South Carolina. His heroics were further rewarded by his election to the House of Representatives. Having become increasingly sophisticated through his government contacts, not to mention his three high-society marriages, Hampton was encouraged to amass land near his home in the up-country. The price was more than right, as was his timing: he began planting cotton, then a negligible crop, at the same time Eli Whitney invented the cotton gin.

By 1799, the log cabin had become a lordly plantation. Having taught himself to read, Colonel Hampton built an impressive library, along with a stable whose mounts won all the races in Charleston. The old families there were at first shocked by the up-country upstart, but soon welcomed him into their exclusive fold. He was a winner, in every sense, owning over a thousand acres, eighty-six slaves, and an annual cotton crop valued at $90,000. He was rich, Charleston rich, and this was only the beginning.

Wade's son, Wade II, burnished both the family's fortunes and its image. Fighting beside his father (now a general) at the Battle of New Orleans, Wade II was appointed the bearer of the glad tidings of the victory of Andrew Jackson, a family friend. He rode almost nonstop through the wilderness from New Orleans to Columbia, South Carolina, on one horse in only ten days—a remarkable record. His passion for horses led Wade II to expand his father's stables into the very best in the country. Further, he bought an empire of cotton plantations, stretching all the way to Louisiana, and had it tilled by over a thousand slaves. The main Hampton barony, Millwood, near Columbia, dispensed some of the most lavish hospitality in the entire Cotton Kingdom.

Wade II formed a Columbia-Charleston axis by marrying Anne Fitzsimmons, the daughter of a powerful low-country shipbuilder. Their first son, born in 1818, was named, of course, Wade III. This Wade had a privileged youth typical of the class. Raised by his "mauma" (not mammy) named Nelly, he was sent to the finest tutors and to South Carolina College, of which Wades I and II had been trustees. After his classical education, he went on a highly lavish

European tour, where he enjoyed the hospitality of such hosts as the
Duke of Wellington.

Adding further order to Wade III's perfectly ordered life was his
marrige to his beautiful old-line Virginia cousin, Margaret Preston.
Their first child, born in 1840, was Wade IV. When Margaret died in
1851, Wade remarried, this time the equally beautiful Mary McDuffie,
daughter of a late South Carolina Governor and Senator. Wade next
decided to enter state politics, easily winning election to the House in
1852, then to the Senate in 1856.

Yet, for all this ordered splendor, there was more than a touch of
the wilderness mountain man in Wade III. To begin with, he looked
frightening—a huge hulk whose fine Anglo-Saxon features were in
adulthood all but concealed by a huge mustache erupting into enormous mutton-chop whiskers. Women of the period found this tonsorial style immensely appealing. The favorite sport of this bear of a
man was hunting bear, but he was distinguished from other outdoors-
men in that he eschewed firearms. Instead, he went stalking into the
woods with his hounds, armed with only a huge knife. When he found
one of the black bears, he would attack it directly, and stab it to death;
then, hoisting the four-hundred-pound beast onto a waiting horse, he
would ride back to the plantation in triumph. Wade III was said to
have killed eighty bears in this manner, and had the claw marks all over
his body to prove it.

Although Wade III had not been a doctrinaire secessionist, he had
no choice but to cast his lot with his region when the war broke out.
He raised his own crack legion of a thousand men, numbering some of
the most aristocratic scions in the state. The men were as distinguished
sartorially as they were socially, resplendent in uniforms of fitted gray
jackets, gold buttons, plumed hats, and special swords over three feet
long. In addition to the legion, Hampton donated a million dollars'
worth of cotton to the Confederate government. He also sacrificed his
son Preston, who died beside his father from a bullet in the groin
received while leading a charge against the enemy in northern Virginia.
Wade IV was almost fatally wounded on the same day. Wade III
himself supplemented his bear scars with many battle scars.

Like Bedford Forrest, Wade Hampton was an uncompromising

general. He promised General Sherman two executions for every Southern prisoner killed by Northern captors. In one letter of warning to Sherman, Hampton accused him of being more savage than the Indians who had massacred Hampton's great-grandparents; even Indians didn't rape women and children, he stated. Sherman responded by trying to blame Hampton for the burning of Columbia. Sherman claimed that the city went up in smoke because Hampton had ordered all the city's cotton torched rather than have it become Yankee spoils. Nothing could have made Hampton more furious than this accusation, for Columbia was his home. The controversy simmered for years until the crafty Sherman, in his memoirs, finally admitted that he had concocted the charge "to shake the faith of his people in him [Hampton], for he was, in my opinion, boastful and professed to be the special champion of South Carolina."

Although Sherman's rumor-mongering did not hurt Wade Hampton, the war did ruin him financially. With his three thousand slaves liberated and his property plundered, he went from being the South's biggest planter to one of its biggest bankrupts. In one of the South's most ignominious foreclosures, he declared bankruptcy, owing over one million dollars in personal debts. With his plantation in decay, he was forced to move into an overseer's shack. But rich or poor, his old constituents still worshiped him. Despite his efforts to withdraw from politics at the war's end, he still nearly won—by a write-in vote—the first postbellum South Carolina election for governor. Hampton's reason for not running was that the Radical Republicans would have severely flayed South Carolina had the state elected him. When Congress proceeded to flay South Carolina anyway, Hampton changed his mind.

The Old Guard was galled by the decadent Franklin Moses administration and by the sight of a government run by their former slaves. They believed that blacks were fit to raise cotton, not points of order. Accordingly, they resolved to take the government back for themselves. Its former leaders, including Hampton, having finally won full pardons for their wartime activities, the Democratic Party began to rally itself for the 1876 election. And, of course, Wade Hampton III was called upon to be its standard-bearer. Hampton had been faring poorly in trying to eke out a living as a farmer and insurance salesman. When his bankruptcy proceedings required the sale of his priceless antiques and paintings at the Columbia courthouse, the proceeds were $118—there was, sadly, no market for such luxuries. Hampton thus seized on the idea of becoming governor; at worst, it would give him a chance at solvency.

The Democrats faced a seemingly impossible struggle. The Radicals had curbed their excesses after the reign of Moses and in 1874 elected a new Governor, Daniel Chamberlain. A Massachusetts native, Chamberlain was one of the most subdued of the carpetbaggers. His education had been a grand tour of Eastern Ivy—Andover, Amherst, Harvard, Yale. He had come south after the war in hopes of becoming a spoils-rich genteel planter. Although he was far from saintly, compared with Moses, Chamberlain was Thomas Jefferson. His reform administration made him acceptable to much of the white population.

Chamberlain's closest aide was Francis Louis Cardozo, the head of the Union League, and the mulatto ancestor of the future Supreme Court justice, Benjamin N. Cardozo. Cardozo had gone to England as a youth. Graduating cum laude from the University of Glasgow, he returned to New Haven, Connecticut, where he became a prominent clergyman in the Presbyterian Church. Cardozo was tall, fashionably dressed, an excellent accountant, and his skin was nearly white. But nearly wasn't enough for the Hamptonites, now known as Bourbons, after the royal ruling family in France that had been deposed by the French Revolution. To their minds, even the smallest drop of black blood made a person black and, in their minds, incompetent.

The black legislature was still in power during Chamberlain's administration and had elected their deposed savior, Moses, to a sinecure as a circuit judge. Governor Chamberlain ultimately blocked Moses's commission and forced him to flee the state, but the Bourbons did not trust Chamberlain—they wanted complete control, and complete elimination of blacks from power. To accomplish this end, the Bourbons waged a relentless campaign that combined symbolism with fear. The symbolism was provided by the giant Hampton, who was paraded around the state, sometimes in a chariot, like a Roman gladiator, bedecked with laurel leaves. The political rallies were circuses complete with cannons, bands, prayers, and processions. On the dais where

Hampton would speak was a dark sack, containing a hunched-over figure covered with black robes, wrapped in chains, and labeled South Carolina. When Hampton took the rostrum, a miraculous transformation occurred. Out of bondage sprang a beautiful blond girl all dressed in white and all smiles. Other times, there would be a Las Vegas-style revue, in which voluptuous figures of Liberty and Justice would raise a prostrate South Carolina to her feet. A chorus line of the thirty-seven states served as background.

Hampton was the symbol; the Ku Klux Klan was the fear. Although the Klan had theoretically been dissolved by Wizard Forrest, its spirit and violence lingered on in cabals throughout the state. The name was changed from Klan to Democratic Rifle Clubs. The white sheets were discarded in favor of red shirts, "bloody shirts," the symbol of the South's wounds and its new defiance. Women throughout the state began spending all their time making them; this shirt became South Carolina's leading cottage industry.

While the red shirts marched and brandished their guns, Hampton himself did his best to court the black vote. Because blacks were a majority in the state, he could not win without them and could not take the chance that the red shirts could scare enough blacks away from the polls to make the difference. A benevolent slave owner, Hampton still had the loyalty and respect of his former chattels, who became superb campaigners for him among other blacks. The teary testimonials of such old servants as "Mauma Nelly" who raised "Marse Wade" had enormous value in swaying votes.

Despite all Hampton's exhortations to the contrary, violence was the rule. Finally, in October 1876, martial law was declared, and before the election President Grant sent federal troops to quell the disturbances. Nonetheless, the big scare was working. Now nothing could be less politic or more physically dangerous, for blacks or whites, than to speak against the "Straightout" Hampton ticket (whose name meant: get the Radicals straight out). On election day in November fraud and sleight of ballot were rampant. The old Slidell ruse of multiple ballots was particularly popular, with some civic-minded men claiming to have voted twenty times. The final tally was too close to call; both sides claimed it for themselves by scant majorities. Soon two legislatures, one

Democratic, the other Republican, stormed into the state House at the same time, and engaged in a terrible shouting and jostling contest for seats.

The two competing governments went at each other for months. This was also the year of the photo-finish presidential election, Tilden versus Hayes. When Hayes, the Republican, was finally declared victor, after countless recounts, he announced his new policy of withdrawing troops from the South and thereby ending Reconstruction. This was the death knell for Chamberlain and the Radicals. Without military support, they were doomed (as were the prospects for black civil rights). Chamberlain slunk out of the governor's mansion and out of the South. He fared better than his predecessor, Moses, though, becoming a prominent corporate lawyer in New York City. Many of his fellow Radicals, like Cardozo, did worse. Cardozo was sentenced to a two-year prison term by the triumphant Democrats. After being released in 1879 Cardozo went to Washington and became a high school principal. Most of the other carpetbaggers and scalawags also went north, to a variety of careers and crimes. In the next election in 1878, Wade Hampton was reelected governor by 169,550 to 213. There was no competition. The black presence in South Carolina's government was over. It would be nearly a century before it resumed.

Hampton, the hero of the white renaissance, basked in seemingly endless accolades. But his joy was short-lived. Soon after his reelection, he went deer hunting. Having slept late and missed his horse, he took a mule instead. The mule went wild, throwing Hampton and breaking his leg so badly that the bones pierced the skin. His wounds at Gettysburg had been scratches by comparison. The leg was amputated, and Hampton nearly died. Churches throughout the state were packed with his weeping, praying supporters. When he recovered in 1879, the state honored him by sending him to Washington, to the U.S. Senate. He learned to use his wooden leg so well, hunting and fishing like old times, that one could hardly tell the difference.

Regrettably, Hampton's glory road was coming to an end. Despite his political ascendancy and his efforts to appoint fellow aristocrats to high office, Hampton and his class were still very poor financially. Without money and slaves, they could never wield great influence again. That their day was over was signaled by the rise of South Carolina's great mass of poor whites—who were actually now no poorer than the once-noble planters. The poor-white vote had put the Bourbons in power. Now the poor whites decided to dispense with symbols; they wanted the power all for themselves. Their paragon was a one-eyed demagogue farmer named Pitchfork Ben Tillman, so named because of the farm implement with which he threatened his opponents. Tillman despised blacks. Yet he despised "the aristocrats" just as much. This manic agrarian populist vowed to "get" Wade Hampton and hand South Carolina over to the people—poor people, Tillman's people. The success of the Tillman movement was the end of South Carolina's Old Guard.

In 1890, Tillman became governor and one of his men easily routed Wade Hampton from his Senate seat. President Cleveland saved his friend from an ignominious trip to the poorhouse by appointing Hampton U.S. Railroad Commissioner. Spending much of his time in the West, fishing, hunting, and overseeing America's expanding railroad empire, Hampton felt crushed by the Tillman takeover. He returned to South Carolina to die, at age eighty-four, in 1902. Right until the last heart attack, Hampton would ride his horse alone down the shady streets of Columbia, a still-imposing, solitary figure with a flowing white beard. He always waved at the old women who had swooned for him when they all were younger. The women waved back. No one ever forgot him. In many ways, he was the last aristocrat.

VII

The Southern Resurrection: Ward McAllister and Society

Returning to Savannah, we went after quail. One morning, being some fourteen miles from the city, we felt famished, having provided no lunch basket. I asked a friend, who was shooting with us and acting as our guide, if there was a white man's house within a mile or two where we could get a biscuit. . . .

"Oh," he replied, "there is a white man who lives within a mile of us, but he is the meanest creature that lives and will have nothing to give us."

"Who is he?" I exclaimed. He gave me his name. "What," said I, "Mr. Jones, who goes to Newport every summer?" "The same," said he; "do you know him?"

"Know him?" I answered, "why, man, I know no one else. He has for years asked me to visit his plantation. He lives like a prince. I saw him at a great fete at Ochre Point, Newport, several years ago. He turned up his nose at everything there, saying to me, 'Why, my dear fellow, these people don't know how to live. This fete is nothing to what I can do, at my place. . . . Come to my plantation, and I will show you what a fete is. I will show you how to live.'" My friend listened to all this with astonishment.

"Well," said he, "I have nothing to say. That is 'big' talk. Go on to your friend's place and see what you will find." On we moved, four as hungry men as you could well see. We reached the plantation, on which we found a one-story log cabin, with a front piazza, one large center room, and two shed rooms. There was a small yard, inclosed with pine palings to keep out the pigs, who were ranging about and ineffectually trying to gain an entrance. We entered the house, and, seeing an old colored man, my Southern friend opened on the old darkey with: "Where is your master?"

"In Savannah, sir."

"When does he dine?"

"At six o'clock, sir."

"What have you got for his dinner, old man?"

"Pea pie."

"Is that all that he has for his dinner?"

"Yes, sir."

"What is pea pie?" I asked.

"Cow peas and bacon," was the answer.

With this, my Southern friend stepped to the back door of the house, asked the old man to point him out a fat turkey. The old darkey did this, saying, "There's one, sir, but, Lord help me, Massa, don't kill him."

The protest came too late. Up to the shoulder went the gun, and down fell the turkey. Now, turning to the old darkey, he said:

"Old man, pick that turkey and roast him, and tell your Massa four big buckra men are coming to dine with him today, at six o'clock."

Down we sat at his table, and had a dinner of small rice, pea pie, and roast turkey. . . . Our host was a thoroughly local man; one of those men who, when in Paris would say, "I'm going to town," when he proposed returning to Savannah, which, at that time, was to him the metropolis of America. This gentleman then, like others in the South, cultivated the belief that they alone lived well, and that there was no such thing as good society in New York or other Northern cities; that New Yorkers and other people were simply a lot of tradespeople, having no antecedents, springing up like the mushroom, who did not know how to live.

—WARD MCALLISTER
Society as I Have Found It, pp. 94–97.

The above antebellum idyll was chronicled in 1890 by Ward McAllister in his memoir *Society as I Have Found It.* Where society was concerned, Ward McAllister didn't find it; he founded it—at least in New York, which Southerners, like the unprepared host, regarded as only marginally civilized. The toast of Savannah, the snob of snobs, the messiah of manners, Ward McAllister in the postbellum era led New York out of the social wilderness. In the process, he made America socially conscious and preserved, in a new and anomalous forum, the Southern aristocratic mystique. Not only did Ward give New York society a heavy Southern accent, he also studded it with authentic Southerners, Reconstruction refugees for whom Ward was the social gateway. He never forgot his roots.

The post-Civil War period was the era of the robber barons, and

New York had never been richer. During the war itself great fortunes had been amassed by profiteering. Commodore Vanderbilt made millions in equipping the Union forces with ships that wouldn't float. J. P. Morgan scored likewise with guns that shot in the wrong direction. And countless others made enough money, in speculations ranging from gold to tainted food, to spur the birth of a new Northern leisure class. The real problem was how to spend its leisure, and its money. Ward McAllister supplied the answer, in the form of society: worrying about who and what was in and who and what was out, chic and cheap, costume balls, dinner parties, mansions, resorts, *Social Registers,* prep schools, titled marriages, and a host of other expensive pretensions that have continued to obsess the American upper bourgeoisie to the present day. Here, upon these insecure parvenus, was the South's ultimate revenge.

New York desperately needed guidance. Its small Dutch patroon elite had been dispossessed of much of its upstate land holdings years earlier. A few old families were still around, but were hardly a potent social force. The power was with those who had money, especially the Astors and the Vanderbilts, but they weren't sure how to wield it. McAllister led the way, assisted by a fifth column of fellow émigré Southerners, who gave the social order he was forming the gentility it needed. He created the list of lists, the "400," referring to those he determined could fit, physically and socially, into Mrs. Astor's ballroom.

THE CRADLE OF SOCIETY

This field marshal of the social renaissance was hardly a romantic figure. Aside from his wild walrus mustache and scraggly Van Dyke beard, the bald, paunchy, and rumple-suited social lion was completely nondescript. Nor was he dynamic or verbally facile. What did set Ward McAllister apart from the world of nouveaux riches in which he moved was that his riches weren't at all filthy. He was, in the eyes of all the rest, a genuine aristocrat, a Southern aristocrat. As such, all his idiosyncrasies could be overlooked. Ward was born into a prominent family in Savannah in 1827. He always considered himself first and foremost a

Savannahian. This is somewhat unusual, for the mossy metropolis was always much less aristocratic than its neighbor Charleston, a hundred miles up the coast. In fact, Savannah, despite its patina of refinement, was a rather bustling mercantile city, a cotton port, thriving on the trade old-line Southerners scorned when carried on by Yankees.

The principal aristocracy among which the McAllisters moved was a Jewish one. The only creditors in the original debtors' colony had been a community of highborn Sephardic Jews who were fleeing the Portuguese Inquisition. Georgia lay in the same latitude as their holy city of Jerusalem, and it boasted complete religious freedom. Here was the Promised Land of the Western Hemisphere. The leading families were the Sheftalls and the Minises. Indeed, Philip Minis was the first white child born in Georgia.

Because a few English court favorites had taken most of the best land, these early Jews became, not planters, but great merchants, doctors, and attorneys. In time they came to dominate the mercantile society of Savannah. Into their midst in 1784 came a young lawyer, Ward's grandfather Matthew McAllister. The McAllisters were originally Scottish Calvinists who had settled around York, Pennsylvania, in 1732. People of some means, but hardly of royal blood, the McAllisters began as blacksmiths, then bought a large tract of land and farmed it profitably. So profitably, in fact, that Matthew's father, Colonel Richard McAllister, had gone to Princeton and taken on all the trappings of a gentleman farmer, becoming a Revolutionary leader and a member of Pennsylvania's Supreme Executive Council after independence. Despite this political influence, there wasn't enough of it, nor of general opportunity in the crowded Quaker state, to satisfy all of his eleven children. Three of them, including Matthew, went to Georgia to seek their fortune.

With his own Princeton degree and concomitant polish, Matthew McAllister made his mark in the bar as well as in the heart of Savannah's most eligible heiress, Hannah Gibbons. Hannah's father, Joseph Gibbons, was a wealthy Barbadian planter whose special connections at the English court enabled him to secure massive grants of land in Georgia. Hannah and her seven brothers enjoyed a gracious existence at their plantation, Mulberry Hill, where the family grew silkworms.

In 1787, the year of Matthew McAllister's wedding to Hannah, he was appointed Georgia's attorney general. It was no mere coincidence. Hannah's brother Thomas, a three-hundred-pound behemoth, was one of the state's heavyweights in politics as well and was able to give his new brother-in-law Matthew the essential helping hand. Although Thomas had been a loyalist during the Revolution (an offense ordinarily chargeable with high treason), in Thomas's case it was regarded as simply a ploy to preserve the family's property had the Revolutionary plans gone astray. Land was sacred, and Thomas's behavior was accepted simply as a matter of understandable self-preservation. Other members of his family had been notable patriots, and he was more than forgiven. In fact he was elected Savannah's mayor.

While the plantations provided for a seigneurial life-style, titanic Thomas Gibbons preferred the courtroom to the veranda. Busy Savannah impelled men, regardless of their means, to become active in a profession. It was an aberrant phenomenon in a South where the aristocracy, or pretenders thereto, were loath to take on any "career" other than that of plantation lord.

Gibbons was the outstanding lawyer of his day, earning $15,000 annually in legal fees, an astronomical sum at that time. His specialties included such matters as election rigging and the Yazoo Frauds, wherein 64-million acres of the Georgia territorial wilderness were sold off under the most dubious authority to land speculators at the unprincely sum of one and a half cents an acre. His power and prestige helped Gibbons ascend to the position of federal district judge and aided the judicial rise of his brother-in-law Matthew McAllister, whose behavior, in sharp contrast, was irreproachable. Succeeding Gibbons as Savannah's mayor in 1801, McAllister later was appointed a state circuit judge for the Savannah region. On the bench, he waged a futile crusade for a more humane penal code. In one impassioned opinion, he pleaded:

Whipping, pillorying, branding, slitting nostrils, and cutting off ears, instead of having a tendency to reform or deter must have a direct contrary effect. It stimulates to every species of villainy as soon as the punishment is over, whereas this class of offenders would, in all probability, were they confined and compelled to labor, reflect on their past lives, reform and become useful citizens. —THOMAS GAMBLE, "The McAllisters,"
Savannah Morning News, October 5, 1930, p. 4.

Matthew's son, and Ward's father, Matthew Hall, or simply Hall, McAllister, followed his father into public service. Although Hall, born in 1800, inherited an extensive estate from his mother, he preferred the townhouse to the plantation and showed no interest in becoming an idle country gentleman. His disinclination for the rice fields may have been affected by a section of his mother's will which provided for the emancipation of all her slaves. This decision had less to do with Hannah Gibbons McAllister's conscience or magnanimity than her annoyance at Hall's marriage to a half-Yankee wife.

Hannah's will curtly tailored the punishment to suit the crime, dooming Hall to a slaveless urbanity. The sting was tempered by the fact that in commercial Savannah, law had as much, if not more, cachet than planting. Hall prepared for the calling at his family's Princeton and as apprentice to a famous Philadelphia lawyer, Jared Ingersoll. While in the North, Hall in 1822 married a wealthy Boston debutante named Charlotte Louisa Cutler. Charlotte's maternal ancestors were Charlestonians and included General Francis Marion, the "Swamp Fox." Consequently, the nuptials were not considered totally repugnant to increasingly chauvinistic Savannah, despite the discomfiture of Hall's mother. At the same time, Charlotte's Northern connections gave Hall entree to the best of Yankeedom and later enabled their son Ward to keep his own feet gracefully planted in both camps.

Like his father, Hall McAllister soon burnished his legal career, at twenty-seven, with an appointment as U.S. District Attorney and became active in Democratic politics. A staunch supporter of slavery, he opposed equally staunchly the presecessionist policies of Calhoun. (Being a Union man and a slavery man at the same time were, until the eve of the war, not at all incompatible.) Hall served in the Georgia Senate from 1834 to 1837 and turned down his party's nomination for the U.S. Senate because of his distaste for the less than grand life in Washington. Instead, he became Mayor of Savannah, which honored him as much for his famous dinner parties and Madeira fests as for his political sagacity.

Little Ward could not have helped but be impressed by his father's revels. Yet no one impressed him more than the local merchant prince William Gaston, the most hospitable man in the annals of Southern hospitality. Gaston, a bachelor and president of the Planters Bank, gave a huge dinner party every night for visitors to Savannah, whether sailors or sultans. The specialty of these dinners was roast canvasback duck, which became Ward's favorite dish as well. Women guests were always presented with delicate Spanish fans as souvenirs. When Gaston died in 1837, reportedly of overeating, the adoring city fathers erected a huge mausoleum for him that was also to be the resting place for any strangers who died in Savannah, until their relatives claimed their remains.

Deeply moved by the Gaston legend and by his father's high times, young Ward made an early vow to devote himself to similar pleasures. He had passionate debates with his brother Hall over the virtues of a life given over to personal pleasure. His was the planter's mentality, not the ideal of practical, active Savannahians. Ward recalled the conflict:

My second brother, Hall, grew up with the poet Milton always under his arm. He was a great student. At the little village of Springfield, Georgia, where my family had a country house, and where we occasionally passed the summer in the piney woods, I remember as a boy of fifteen years of age, reading the Declaration of Independence on the Fourth of July from the pulpit of the village church to the descendants of the old Salzburghers, who came over soon after Oglethorpe, and it was before an audience of these piney woods farmers, that, with this brother, at a meeting of our Debating Society in this village, I discussed the question, "Which is the stronger passion, Love or Ambition," he advocating Ambition, I Love. I well remember going for him, as follows: "If his motto be that of Hercules the Invincible, I assume for mine that of his opponent Venus the Victorious. With my sling and stone I will enter this unequal combat and thus hope to slay the great Goliath." The twelve good and true men who heard the discussion decided in my favor.   *—Society as I Have Found It*, pp. 8–9.

As Ward mounted his adolescent pursuit of Venus, his father, in 1845, with equal ardor, pursued the governorship of Georgia. But his Unionism and high living did not work in his favor. Attacked as a "kid glove aristocrat," Hall McAllister soon was confronted with a backwoods backlash fomented by his Whig opponent. A typical attack on Hall was carried in the *Athens* (Ga.) *Southern Whig.*

McAllister is the candidate of the aristocratic clique that controls the Democracy. He belongs to the class in Savannah known as the "swelled heads," who think the upcountry people no better than brutes. He never will stand these upcountry "crackers." If you will move the state house to

Savannah and furnish him with wines of the different brands, he may make a jolly governor, but if you put him at Milledgeville [then capital] and give him "bald face" [a popular, if impotable, brand of contraband corn liquor] to drink he cannot stand it. His aristocratic blood will curdle and he will be a dead man in less than six months.

Accordingly, McAllister was slandered with unbased charges that he wanted to disenfranchise the poor whites with a property requirement for voting and that he was an advocate of monopoly. To counter these salvos, McAllister went all-out to appear as a man of the people. He donned a four-cornered slouch hat and brown overalls, then the costume of the piney woods. He campaigned in a rickety carriage. He even got a suntan, which in those days was the stigma of toil rather than the badge of leisure. Still, he lost the election by barely 1,000 votes out of the 70,000 cast. The defeat, his first in politics, was very disheartening.

McAllister's sons found the loss even more disillusioning. For Ward's younger brother Hall, also a lawyer, it loosened the home ties sufficiently to allow him to be ensnared by the romance of the California gold rush. The sybaritic serpent who lured the twenty-three-year-old Hall west was his thirty-four-year-old cousin Sam Ward, of New York, a man who looked almost identical to Ward McAllister and who actually launched Ward on his social mission.

Sam Ward exploded the Southern myth that Yankees were all boorish tradesmen. Sam was an aristocratic playboy, if ever there was one. But the McAllisters took credit for this; after all, they had "civilized" the boy on his frequent Southern visits. Furthermore, his Charleston blood—inherited through his mother, the sister of Ward McAllister's mother—was viewed as the dominant strain. His sister Julia Ward was far less malleable. She totally outraged the Southern branch of the family by marrying a Boston abolitionist named Samuel Gridley Howe, editing his antislavery *Commonwealth,* and later writing "The Battle Hymn of the Republic."

Brother Sam had no causes other than "Venus," the muse he shared with his cousin Ward. His father had been a leading Wall Street banker in the firm of Prime, Ward, and King. Sam was raised as a little prince, prepared at the Round Hill School in Connecticut, educated at Columbia, polished at Heidelberg, and debauched in the fleshpots of Europe.

At twenty-four Sam was said to be New York's best dancer, as well as the most knowledgeable wine connoisseur in the United States. He was also a brilliant mathematician, though he never bothered to add up his expenses. No one in Manhattan could have been more charming or more eligible, and Sam took the conjugal sweepstakes of 1838 in wedding Emily Astor, the granddaughter of John Jacob Astor.

Three years later, Emily died in childbirth, and Sam, unwilling to keep Venus at bay for a protracted mourning period, remarried a voluptuous Creole named Medora Grymes, the daughter of the famed New Orleans lawyer, John Randolph Grymes. The Astors, shocked at Sam's wanton disrespect, kept him from seeing his daugher, Maddie Astor Ward, and excluded him from any of the family's largess. To add to his troubles, Prime, Ward, and King went bankrupt in 1849. Sam, who could not live without lots of money, decided to pull up all roots, leave his wife, and become a forty-niner.

He and Hall McAllister sailed to San Francisco on the good ship *Panama* around the Straits of Magellan. Sam went directly to the gold fields; Hall stopped at the courthouse, or at least the rudiments of one. This was the wild Wild West, and no place could have offered greater opportunity for a young lawyer, once some semblance of civil authority had been established. Hall's motto was "Ten millions or nothing." He was willing to risk anything to be rich. Here his impetuousness paid off. Given his background and shortage of lawyers, he was appointed U.S. District Attorney for the San Francisco area. His salary of $2,000 a year was lavishly supplemented by private cases paid for with bags of gold dust. The possibilities of conflict of interest were legion, but Hall was the soul of integrity. He won his reputation by prosecuting a villainous mob of racketeers known as the Hounds, as well as the terrifying vigilante groups that had sprung up in the law-and-order vacuum. Meanwhile, his private cases were bringing him over $50,000 a year, and there was an apparently insatiable demand for his services.

Hall wrote glowingly of his success to his father and his brother Ward, who was just completing his own legal apprenticeship. Hall begged the two to move west and help him share this legal bonanza. Ward ridiculed his brother's tales as "Arabian Nights stories" until Hall sent home a large sack of gold. That was enough. Sensing the impending confrontation over slavery, still smarting from Hall Sr.'s political setback, and drooling over the fortune that awaited them, the McAllisters pulled up their elegant deep roots and sailed for Mecca-by-the-Bay in 1850.

The bold move was more than justified. Everything Hall promised came true. The McAllister law firm fared extraordinarily well. After several years, the younger Hall was appointed by President Pierce as first Justice of the U.S. Circuit Court for the state of California. The family became not only the preeminent legal dynasty of California but the preeminent social one, too. Among the grasping throngs, the noble Southerners stood out like knights of the realm. Mrs. McAllister was unchallenged as the reigning hostess of San Francisco.

Only young Ward was miserable. After a lifetime of being pampered, he was ill equipped for the rigors of California life (as compared to the South) and he was not the stuff of which great lawyers were made. Venus, not ambition, was all that stirred him. He did, however, find his métier in entertaining his firm's clients. A sample of McAllister's complaint:

Imagine me then, a well-fed man, with always an appreciative appetite, learning, on my arrival in San Francisco, that eggs, without which I could not breakfast, cost $2 apiece, a fowl $8, a turkey $16. One week's mess bill for my breakfast and dinner alone was $225, and one visit to my doctor cost me $50. Gloom settled upon me, until my noble parent requested me to bring back to the office our first retainer (for I was then a member of my father and brother's law firm). It was $4,000 in gold ounces. I put it in a bag and lugged it to the office, and as I laid them by ounce on my father's desk, he danced a pirouette, for he was as jolly an old fellow as ever lived. I went to my work at once in earnest; it struck me that in that country it was "root, pig, or die."

My first purchase was a desk, which combined the qualities of bed and desk. How well I remember the rats playing hide-and-seek over me at night, and over the large barrel of English Brown Stout that I invested in and placed in the entry to console myself with. After six months' hard work, I began to ease up, and feel rich. I built a small house for myself, the front entry 4x4, the back entry the same, one dining-room 12x14, and one bedroom, same dimensions. My furniture, just from Paris, was acajou and white and blue horsehair. My bed-quilt cost me $250; it was a lovely Chinese floss silk shawl. An Indian chief, calling to see me, found me in bed, and was so delighted with the blankets that he seized hold of them and exclaimed, "Quanto pesos?" (How much did they cost?). . . .

A CLASS BY THEMSELVES

As our firm was then making $100,000 a year, our senior partner, my father, asked me to entertain, for the firm, our distinguished European clients, as he had not the time to do so. His injunction to me was, "Be sure, my boy, that you always invite nice people." I had heard that my dear old father had on more than one occasion gotten off a witticism on me as follows: Being told how well his son kept house, he replied, "Yes, he keeps everything but the Ten Commandments," so I assured him if he would honor me with his presence I would have to meet him every respectable woman in the city, and I kept my word. Before we reached the turkey, my guests had so thorough dined that when it appeared, the handsomest woman in the room heaved a deep sigh and exclaimed, "Oh, that I might have some of it for lunch to-morrow?" Such dinners as I then gave, I have never seen surpassed anywhere. It is needless to say that my father was intensely gratified. We had, tempted by exaggerated accounts of the gold fields, French cooks who received $6,000 a year as salary. The turkey, costly as it was at $16, always came on table with its feathered tail intact, and as eggs were so expensive, *omelette soufflé* was always the dish at dessert. Two years was the length of my stay in San Francisco.

—*Society as I Have Found It,* p. 22.

The McAllisters' cousin Sam Ward soon grew less than enraptured with the new frontier. The gold fields didn't pan out, an auction warehouse he established burned down, and a treasure hunt with the Piute Indians brought in no treasure. Although the Piutes made Sam an honorary chief, the chronic *crise de foie* from the Indian cuisine outbalanced any honor. Finally, another prospector bet Sam a sizable sum that he could not learn the Piute dialect in less than three weeks. Sam, who was fluent in French, German, Spanish, and Italian, won the wager easily. It paid his passage back to New York in 1852. Ward McAllister was more than delighted to join him.

Sam set up a very modest brokerage house on Wall Street, but Ward was intent on avoiding work at all costs. The cost was marriage, but of the most convenient sort. The lucky girl was none other than his cousin Sarah Gibbons. In contrast to her gargantuan grandfather Thomas (the brother of Ward's grandmother), Sarah was frail, shy, and homely, anything but Venus. Nevertheless, she was rich, enabling Ward to live in the style to which he had become accustomed. His family had been annoyed at his disinclination toward the law, and had no interest in subsidizing his romantic quests. Self-effacing Sarah was content simply to pay while her husband played. In Ward's mind, she was the perfect wife.

THE MAKING OF THE 400

Ward found Sarah in Elizabeth, New Jersey, on the horse farm her grandfather Thomas Gibbons had used as a summer retreat. He had a mansion there that was a duplicate of the White House in Washington. While in the North in 1817 Gibbons was introduced to the steamboat. The planter-capitalist decided a fortune could be made by operating a ferry across the harbor to New York. He was right, but a legal monopoly on the service had already been granted.

The only monopolies Gibbons believed in were the ones he held himself. Undaunted, he bought a boat and in 1818 hired as his blockade-running captain, for $60 a month, a raw young sailor named Cornelius Vanderbilt. Constantly harassed by the local authorities trying to enforce the monopoly, the slippery Vanderbilt and the price-slashing Gibbons built up a large passenger business. At the same time Gibbons donned his commodious legal hat and began a lawsuit that after six years finally reached the Supreme Court. Chief Justice John Marshall's 1824 decision in *Gibbons* v. *Ogden,* perhaps his most famous, was a great victory for unimpeded interstate commerce. It also made the Gibbonses eternally rich. This in turn enabled Ward McAllister to create a society for the likes of Vanderbilt, whose biggest break in life was his job with Gibbons.

When Thomas Gibbons died in 1826, so fat in his last years that he had to be carried about in a sort of sedan chair, he was worth well over a million dollars and was reputedly the richest man in the South. He had disinherited his son-in-law John Trumball (and all Trumball's offspring) for the crime of failing to testify on Gibbons's behalf in the steamboat litigation. Trumball's loss was Gibbons's granddaughter Sarah's tremendous gain and it was soon to be Ward McAllister's. Sarah inherited the bulk of her grandfather's estate. No sooner had she and Ward said their vows, in 1853, than her new husband deposited her on a large farm in Newport, Rhode Island, and dashed off to Europe to follow in cousin Sam Ward's decadent footsteps. Wherever Ward went, his self-introduction as "an American landed proprietor" won him immediate entree to local society. Sarah may have later joined him; he never mentions her in his writings. (They did live together when he returned to the United States.) The only company Ward was concerned with in Europe was that of his doctor. In France he hired his own traveling physician, whose two-dollar daily retainer Ward supplemented with a daily bottle of 1848 Latour. In his mind, "You owed your existence to [doctors]; they kept you in the world, and not to have a doctor within call was to place yourself in danger of immediate and sudden death."

Hale, hearty, and thoroughly cosmopolitan after his five-year grand tour, Ward returned to conquer America in 1858. He took Manhattan by way of Newport. "The most enjoyable and luxurious little island in America," as Ward called it, had been a Southern summer resort since pre-Revolutionary days, a particular favorite of the Charleston and Tidewater gentry. The rocks, cliffs, crashing surf, and crisp air formed a delightful counterpoint to the flat, stagnant stillness of the Southern swamps. The Southerners' Newport was light-years removed from the circus of ostentation that marked Newport's coming heyday in the gilded age of the 1880s. Discreet hotels, quiet cottages, and a general unobtrusiveness contrasted sharply with plantation grandeur.

Ward McAllister established his Bayside Farm while the Southerners were still in Newport. When the Civil War broke out, he alone of the Southern aristocracy remained to hold court, and hence was viewed by later comers as a gallant symbol of a vanished era. On the issue of the war, the family was divided. The California McAllisters, still nostalgic for the Old South, were leaders of a faction known as the Chivalry Democrats, who had advocated dividing California into a Northern free state and a Southern slave one. The plan miscarried, and the judge and his followers acquiesced in majority rule. Ward's brother Julian, who had graduated second in his class at West Point, was a captain in the Union Army. Ward himself was content to fiddle while Atlanta burned. He spent the war years giving picnics for the noncombatant Northerners, who were beginning to discover that Newport was "the place of all others to take social root in." First came a wave of New England intellectuals: Longfellow, Holmes, Henry James, John Singer

Sargent, Julia Ward Howe. The transplanted Cambridge ambience, Harvard-by-the-sea, was soon shattered by the boisterous, free-spending arrival of the New York nouveaux, led by August Belmont, always in quest of genteel chic.

Ward received them all graciously, and all paid him the appropriate fealty. He preferred calling his picnics *fêtes champêtres,* the English term not conjuring up enough of the élan of these splendors in the grass. Ward had enjoyed such parties on the Georgia sea islands and was eager to transplant the tradition. Because he himself was not a farmer, he would hire entire flocks of Southdown sheep, interspersed with an occasional cow or pig, to give Bayside the appropriate bucolic air. He described a typical affair.

Riding on the Avenue on a lovely summer's day, I would be stopped by a beautiful woman, in gorgeous array, looking so fascinating that if she were to ask you to attempt the impossible, you would at least make the effort. She would open on me as follows: "My dear friend, we are all dying for a picnic. Can't you get one up for us?"

"Why, my dear lady," I would answer, "you have dinners every day, and charming dinners too; what more do you want?"

"Oh, they're not dinners. Any one can give dinners," she would reply; "what we want is one of your picnics. Now, my dear friend, do get one up."

This was enough to fire me, and set me going. So I reply:

"I will do your bidding. Fix on the day at once, and tell me what is the best dish your cook makes."

Out comes my memorandum book, and I write: "Monday, 1 P.M., meet at Narragansett Avenue, bring *filet de boeuf piqué,*" and with a bow am off in my little wagon, and dash on, to waylay the next cottager, stop every carriage known to contain friends, and ask them, one and all, to join our country party, and assign to each of them the providing of a certain dish and a bottle of champagne. . . . My pony is put on its mettle; I keep going the entire day getting recruits; I engage my music and servants, and a carpenter to put down a dancing platform, and the florist to adorn it, and that evening I go over in detail the whole affair, map it out as a general would a battle, omitting nothing, not even a salt spoon. . . .

We would meet at Narragansett Avenue at 1 P.M., and all drive out together. On reaching the picnic grounds, I had an army of skirmishers, in the way of servants, thrown out, to take from each carriage its contribution to the country dinner. The band would strike up, and off the whole party would fly in the waltz, while I was directing the icing of the champagne and arranging the tables; all done with marvelous celerity. Then came my hour of triumph, when, without giving the slightest signal (fearing some one might forestall me, and take off the prize), I would dash in among the dancers, secure our society queen, and lead her the way to the banquet. Now began the fun in good earnest. The clever men of the party would assert their claims to the best dishes, proud of the efforts of their cook, loud in their praise of their own game pie, which most likely was brought out by some third party, too modest to assert and push his claim. Beauty was there to look upon, and wit to enliven the feast . . . and all feeling that they were on a frolic, they threw hauteur, ceremonial and grand company manners aside, and, in place, assumed a spirit of simple enjoyment. Toasts were given and drunk, then a stroll in pairs, for a little interchange of sentiment, and then the whole party made for the dancing platform, and a cotillion of one hour and a half was danced, till sunset. As at a "Meet," the arrivals and departures were a feature of the day. Four-in-hands, tandems, and the swellest of Newport turn-outs rolled by you. At these entertainments you formed lifetime intimacies with the most cultivated and charming men and women of this country.

These little parties were then, and are now, the stepping-stones to our best New York society. People who have been for years in mourning and thus lost sight of, or who having passed their lives abroad and were forgotten, were again seen, admired, and liked, and at once brought into society's fold. Now, do not for a moment imagine that all were indiscriminately asked to these little fetes. On the contrary, if you were not of the inner circle, and were a new-comer, it took the combined efforts of all your friends' backing and pushing to procure an invitation for you. For years, whole families sat on the stool of probation, awaiting trial and acceptance, and many were then rejected, but once received, you were put on an intimate footing with all. To acquire such intimacy in a great city like New York would have taken you a lifetime.

—Society as I Have Found It, pp. 111–119.

By 1870 Ward McAllister and his parties had become legend. In addition to Newport, before the war he had taken whole contingents of revelers for quail-shoots on the Gibbons plantation in Savannah. During the war, he led English fox hunts and other country squire amusements at the Gibbons estate in New Jersey. There was also a townhouse in Manhattan for the opera season and other urban revels. Sarah, the woman who made all this possible, had become an invalid and went into seclusion—though not before giving birth to two sons and a daughter, Louise.

Once she was grown, Louise occasionally served as her father's mistress of ceremonies. But since she totally lacked the requisite sparkle to shine at his endless succession of galas, Ward cast around for a suitable "society queen" to complement his kingship. He found her in Mrs. William Backhouse Astor, Jr.

Mrs. Astor was no more attractive than Mrs. McAllister. She was, however, infinitely more pretentious and outgoing. She was thrilled by the prospect of dancing all night. The most distinguished thing about Mrs. Astor was her Knickerbocker ancestry; she was a Schermerhorn. Otherwise, she was stocky and swarthy, with a baboon face and a clown's bulbous nose. Her beauty lay in the Astor millions, in her gigantic ballroom, and in her Parisian chef. She adored Ward; he called her his Mystic Rose. Their relationship was symbiotic, yet always platonic. Ward didn't believe in mixing pleasure with the business of ruling society.

The Mr. behind Mrs. Astor cared as little for society as the Mrs. behind Mr. McAllister. William Backhouse Astor, Jr., escaped the ballroom to the bottle on his yacht, with its distaff crew. William was the grandson of the fabulous fur trader John Jacob Astor and brother of Emily Astor, the late wife of Sam Ward. Despite the older Astors' continuing antipathy toward Sam, they felt nothing but affection for Sam's ultra-ingratiating cousin Ward McAllister. Sam himself had taken another plunge on Wall Street but had found the perfect niche in Washington as America's "King of the Lobby." Sam's role in politics was analogous to Ward's in society. Styling himself the "gastronomic pacificator," Sam, who snacked on truffles, was credited with saving President Andrew Johnson from conviction. His power-peddling for the railroads kept Sam in champagne, permanently.

With cousin Sam holding down the capital, and his family ruling the West Coast, it was only fitting that the lord of Newport should also take charge of unruly New York. With the Mystic Rose at his side Ward began to give the grandest of Manhattan parties, with an emphasis on costume balls, cotillions, and endless dinners. To exclude the ever-increasing numbers of new rich bloated on war spoils, Ward in 1872 drew up the first of his famous lists, the Patriarchs. The promulgation of this roster of the twenty-five men "who had the right to create and lead society" had only slightly less impact than the Edict of Nantes. New Yorkers evidently needed a strong hand socially, or simply craved authority; Ward certainly provided it. In the same way a Michelin star can make a restaurant, inclusion on a McAllister list could make a socialite. The lucky gentlemen were mostly old Knickerbockers, with a couple of relocated old Southerners and, naturally, the Astors.

These, and only these, were given the sacred right to invite people to Ward's balls. But Southerners were always welcome. Indeed, Ward would receive any new Southern arrival who called on him. He offered sympathy, and better, introductions. Ward became a conduit for tunneling these escaping Southerners into a new high society similar to their own now banished one. Such Southerners became conversation pieces, and their soft drawls and courtly demeanor could hide a multitude of defects. Scorn over slavery? Not a chance. The nouveaux riches, never noted for their conscience, didn't think it was so bad after all, now that they could afford similar servitude.

If Ward McAllister declared Southerners were chic, Southerners were chic. All New York seized the notion. In the period after the war, New York society rapidly developed a plantation image. At the top was Ward, but he had many lieutenants who had swallowed their pride and come north to earn a living or, frequently, to marry one—since the quickest way for the new rich of the North to improve their respectability and status was to marry a "new poor," especially one from the Old South. Dubbed "Autocrat of Drawing Rooms," Ward held the ultimate power, that of assigning seats at dinner parties.

Even less noble Southern types were able to come under Ward's diamond-studded wing. The classic example was an ex-traveling salesman from Loudon, Tennessee, Richard T. Wilson, who made a small fortune in Europe allegedly by selling contraband cotton, blankets, and defective shoes purloined from the Confederate commissary. He then made a bigger fortune as a Wall Street banker, buying up many of the South's bankrupt railways and industries at ridiculously low, unpatriotic prices. Still, Wilson was six foot six, with imperial bearing, a scalawag in planter's dress. Good for the Southern image, if not for the South, Wilson passed as an aristocrat and was embraced by Ward. The attractive, drawling Wilson children thus became prime catches, or catchers, as it were, getting the best dinner table seats and marrying a Goelet, an Astor, a Vanderbilt, and the British ambassador.

Basically Ward McAllister was inordinately fond of himself and all that he represented. That is why he was so enraptured with the South. Richard Wilson's business ethics were no worse than those of his fellow robber barons, with whom Ward was socializing, and his manners were infinitely better. He would never, like John Jacob Astor, wipe his fingers on a woman's ruffled sleeve in lieu of a napkin. Nor would he speak in the dialect of obscenity of Cornelius Vanderbilt, who acted like a stevedore, not a commodore. Southerners were polite if nothing else. Society was big enough to accommodate the Nobs (solid old family) as well as the Swells (chic new money), Ward declared magnanimously.

Ward's open-mindedness was not unusual for the times. The 1870s was truly the era of "anything goes." The administration of Ulysses S. Grant was a giant grab bag, with big salary increases ripped off by Congress. There was more massive graft in the Whiskey Ring scandal inside the Treasury Department, whereby the country was bilked out of a fortune in alcohol tax revenue. The transcontinental railroad, the Union Pacific, linked East and West, but only through enormous fraud and bribery. In Washington "Uncle Sam" Ward, the wizard behind much of this perversion of laissez-faire, was toasting every mile of track. And in New York, cousin Ward McAllister was oblivious to everything except his next ball.

The worlds of politics and society were not mutually exclusive. The debauched Washingtonians loved to come to Manhattan to squander the taxpayers' money they were stealing. When Mrs. Astor's daughter Carrie married Richard Wilson's son Orme, President Grant was the guest of honor. It was a real coup for Ward, who planned the affair. Grant got so drunk that he placed the lightened end of his cigar in his mouth and burned himself badly. He was the only casualty of an affair that netted over a million dollars in gifts for the newlyweds.

Life was a cabaret, or at least a quadrille (an elaborate French square dance). Whether in Mrs. Astor's ballroom or at Delmonico's, on which he seemed to have a perpetual lease, Ward was throwing a party. There was a "Mother Goose" quadrille in which all the men wore pink and sang nursery rhymes, a "Pinafore" quadrille, where everyone dressed as sailors, a "Hunting" quadrille, in which the guests dressed in scarlet hunting coats, and a "Dresden" quadrille, in which the ladies wore white satin, with powdered hair, and the gentlemen white satin knee breeches and powdered wigs, with the Dresden mark, crossed swords, on each of them. . . . The Hostess appeared as a Venetian Princess, with a superb jeweled peacock in her hair. The host was the Duke de Guise for that evening. The host's eldest brother wore a costume of Louis XVI. His wife appeared as "The Electric Light," in white satin, trimmed with diamonds, and her head one blaze of diamonds. The most remarkable costume, and one spoken of to this day, was that of a cat; the dress being of cat's tails and white cat's heads, and a bell with "Puss" on it in large letters. A distinguished beauty, dressed as a Phoenix, adorned with diamonds and rubies, was superb, and the Capuchin Monk, with hood and sandals, inimitable; but to name the most striking would be to name all.

—Society as I Have Found It, p. 354.

For the younger set Ward founded a junior patriarchate, called the Family Circle Dancing Class, and women besieged him with entreaties to get their precious little ones in. "The family always went back to King John, and in some instances, to William the Conqueror," Ward joked. Once "in" the competition and sniping were fierce:

I led the way to the ball-room with the "fairest of the fair," the daughter of one of the most distinguished men in this country (who had not only been Governor of this State, but Secretary of State of the United States). We were surrounded by a noble throng of old New Yorkers, all eager to view the opening quadrille. The ladies were in Colonial costumes, representing Lady Washington and the ladies of her court. As I walked through the crowded rooms, having on my arm one of our brilliant society women, "a flower which was not quite a flower, yet was no more a bud," we met approaching us a lady in indeed gorgeous apparel—so gorgeous, that the lady on my arm at once accosted her with, "Good gracious, my dear Mrs. B—, what have you got on? Let me look at you." Her head was a mass of the most superb ostrich plumes, Prince of Wales feathers, which towered above her, and as she advanced would bend gracefully forward, nodding to you, as it were, to approach and do her honor. Her dress, neck, and shoulders were ablaze with jewels and precious stones, and in her hand she carried an old Spanish fan, such as a queen might envy. The following reply to the query came from this royal dame: "What have I got on? Why, Madame, I had a grandmother!" "Had you, indeed! Then, if that was her garb, she must have been Pocahontas, or the Empress of Morocco!" The war of words beginning to be a little sharp, I pressed on, only to meet another famous lady, whose birthplace was Philadelphia, and who had had no end of grandmothers. She wore a superb dress of scarlet and gold, tight-fitting, such as was worn during the Empire. Another young woman wore her great-grandmother's dress, pink and brown striped brocade, cut like Martha Washington's dress in the Republican Court, in which her great-grandmother figured. The wife of a prominent jurist, a remarkably handsome woman, with a grand presence and a noble carriage, representing Lady Washington, wore, to all eyes, the most attractive costume there.

— *Society as I Have Found It,* pp. 323–24.

Aside from the costumes, the food was the thing. Ward always planned the menus, modeling them after William Gaston's Savannah repasts, with a soupçon of cousin Sam Ward's influence-dinners thrown in. A typical meal would begin with *tortue claire,* followed by *mousse aux jambons,* and terrapin. Next came turkey, bred on Ward's Newport farm and fed on grasshoppers. Then things would begin again. *Paté de foie gras en gelée.* A maraschino sorbet to clear the palate. Canvasback and woodcock to bloat it again. A salad. Camembert. Nesselrode pudding. Washing it all down was champagne, red and white vintage wines, and *après,* Madeira, the Southerner's drink of the gods. It is small wonder that in those days, being thin was not in; it was impossible.

While turning Manhattan into an endless feast in the 1870s, Ward had not forgotten his Newport springboard. With Ward as its grand vizier, once-staid Newport was becoming the world capital of exhibitionism. Beginning with August Belmont's "By the Sea," the cottages of old were replaced by the white elephants, the immense marble palazzos with scores of servants that humbled even the mansions of Natchez. Ward's *fêtes champêtres* were still the chief drawing card, but they, too, had grown far more complex, bearing no resemblance to mere picnics.

Our next great day-time frolic was at Bristol Ferry. There we had a large country hotel which we took possession of. We got the best dinner giver then in Newport to lend us his *chef,* and I took my own colored cook, a native of Baltimore, who had, at the Maryland Ducking Club, gained a reputation for cooking game, ducks, etc. We determined on this occasion, to have a trial of artistic skill between a creole woman cook, the best of her class, and the best *chef* we had in this country. We were to have sixty at dinner; dishes confined to Spanish mackerel, soft-shell crabs, woodcock, and chicken partridges. It is needless to say, the Frenchman came off victorious, though my creole cook contended that the French *chef* would not eat his own cooked dishes, but devoured her soft-shell crabs.

On this occasion we had a grand turnout of drags, postilions *à la demi d'Aumont,* and tandems. I led the cotillion tandems. I led the cotillion myself, dancing in the large drawing-room of the inn; and it all went so charmingly that it was late into the night when we left the place. It was as dark as Erebus. We had eleven miles to drive, and I saw that some of our four-in-hand drivers felt a little squeamish. My old bachelor friend had in his drag a precious cargo. On the box-seat with him sat our nightingale, and I had in my four-seated open wagon our queen of society [Mrs. Astor] and a Baltimore belle. "Is the road straight or crooked?" I was asked, on all sides. Having danced myself nearly to death, and being well fortified with champagne, I found it straight as an arrow, and I was then oblivious to its crooks and turns. Off we all started up the hill at a canter. I remember my friend, the Major, shouting to me, "The devil take the hindmost," and the admonition to him of his old family coachman, who accompanied him that day, "Be careful, sir, the road is not as straight as it might be." Driving along at a spanking pace, the horses fresh,—there was a scream, then another, then a plunge, and a splash of water. Dark as it was, standing up in my wagon, I shouted, "By Jove! He has driven off the bridge."

—Society as I Have Found It, pp. 195–97.

Ward's daily regimen in New York never varied. He would rise at eight, take a light breakfast, and devote nine-thirty to eleven-thirty to "business," which usually consisted of advising, gratis, people who were planning parties. At noon he had lunch with several Patriarchs at the Union Club. In the afternoons, he would enjoy a constitutional, regardless of the weather, paying calls on various Matriarchs and, always, Mystic Rose. Every evening was a party.

THE LAST DANCE

McAllister society was spreading across the country. Other cities began forming their own Patriarchs and having balls. In the 1880s, when the waves of European immigrants began to arrive, xenophobic Americans sought safety in class distinctions. Exclusivity was the watchword; Ward was the last word. The oracle of society was also its apologist.

The mistake made by the world at large is that fashionable people are selfish, frivolous, and indifferent to the welfare of their fellow-creatures; all of which is a popular error, arising simply from a want of knowledge of the true state of things. The elegancies of fashionable life nourish and benefit art and artists; they cause the expenditure of money and its distribution; and they really prevent our people and country from settling down into a humdrum rut and becoming merely a money-making and money-saving people, with nothing to brighten up and enliven life. . . . Fashion soars, it never crawls.   —*Society as I Have Found It,* pp. 160–61.

The leviathan that Ward created and worshiped eventually turned on him. The cozy list of twenty-five Patriarchs was unworkable; every new millionaire wanted in. Ward was pressed mercilessly for a new roster. The result was the 400: those "at ease" in Mrs. Astor's ballroom. He picked the number in 1888; society waited breathlessly for the names for four long years, until 1892. The honor roll was heavy on millionaires and Southerners, short on the arts. When one of Ward's confreres was asked about the cultural void, he snapped, "Remember that Broadway only cuts across Fifth Avenue—it never parallels it."

The list alienated everyone. Those left off were understandably miffed. Those who made it felt it wasn't exclusive enough. Adding to the insult was Ward's book, *Society as I Have Found It,* published in 1890. New York's elite thought it was an outrage that Ward was spilling their secrets to the masses. But the book was more than a primer on how to be socially acceptable. It was a paean to Southern social superiority and a satire of the rich Yankee as parvenu tradesman. To self-conscious Northerners, it was hardly a laughing matter.

The book and the 1892 list finally provoked an uprising of the swells, highlighted by a campaign to ridicule Ward as society's lackey, not its king. Stuyvesant Fish, a leader of the palace revolt, announced, with icy triumph: "McAllister is a discharged servant. That is all." The party line was that Ward was no longer unique. He had brought in too many Southerners and taught his party-giving lessons too well. Society didn't need or want an autocrat any more.

The unkindest cut of all came when Ward's Mystic Rose deserted him. Nervous about her own social security, Mrs. Astor sundered the alliance. This was a major upheaval, big news in an era when society was a front page topic. Every journal sought out Ward for commentary. Not quite comprehending his fall from grace, Ward was delighted to talk. Seeing himself in print deluded him into thinking he was still the voice. Alas, it was simply a matter of being hoist by his own petard of pomposity, as in his "advice" to Chicago on its hog-butcher attempt at society:

We in New York are familiar with the sharp character of Chicago magnates and many of us have learned to our cost that the Almighty Dollar is the trail they are following. I do think these Chicagoans should pretend to rival the East and Old World in matters of refinement. Their growth has been too rapid to allow them to acquire both wealth and culture. Their leaders of society are the successful Stock Yards magnates, cottolene manufacturers, soupmakers, Chicago gas trust speculators and dry good princes.
                                                              —*The McAllisters*, p. 46.

Having deserted his family for his jealous mistress, society, the jilted suitor now found himself in a most unaccustomed position—alone. At first he tried to rationalize his involuntary exile. "I wish society would drop me," he told the *New York Herald* in 1892. "Then I'd have a little time to myself. I really don't care for society, don't you know, don't you understand. It's more of a bore than a pleasure to me. I merely perform my functions, you understand." A bore perhaps, but without those functions, he had nothing to live for. Sam Ward had died in 1885 of a heart attack while gourmandizing in Italy. Brother Hall McAllister, who had risen to Chief Justice of the California Supreme Court, had died in the same year. Ward's closest friend now was his brother, the Reverend Francis Marion McAllister, an Episcopal minister and still society's link with the hereafter. In February 1895, Ward developed the grippe and died after dining—alone—at the Union Club. He was sixty-eight.

The funeral was Ward's last bash. Although the Mystic Rose did not show up, the other Astors and Vanderbilts did, as did nearly every nob and rising swell in New York. Grace Church on Broadway, *the* place to worship, was packed far tighter than Mrs. Astor's ballroom. The fifteen pallbearers were drawn largely from the original Patriarchate. Five clergymen presided, including the Episcopal Bishop of Mississippi. The dirges were played by none other than the ballroom orchestra of John Lander, precursor of Meyer Davis. There was a thirty-voice choir. The church was a jungle of flowers, so alluring that the police had to quell a near-riot of female mourners attempting to steal some of

RICHARD T. WILSON and his wife MELISSA JOHNSTON WILSON. Parents of the "marrying Wilsons," the most successfully conjugal of all Southern families that had gone to New York after the War. The Wilson children married an Astor, a Vanderbilt, and a Goelet.

Richard reputedly made a killing selling contraband cotton as well as a boatload of blankets and defective shoes purloined from the Confederate commissary. Being a robber baron, however, wasn't enough. After all the public discussion about its wealth, the Wilson family wanted respectability.
(Courtesy Wilson Randolph Gathings)

GRACE WILSON.
Daughter of the Wilsons
and wife of Cornelius Vanderbilt III.
A financial panic in the 1880s had reduced the Wilson fortune to barely more than a million dollars. Given the hard times, Grace had to snare a big fish.
(Courtesy Wilson Randolph Gathings)

ALVA SMITH VANDERBILT BELMONT *(1854–1933)*. Mobile beauty who went north
to two brilliant marriages. Her daughter, Consuelo Vanderbilt,
married the Duke of Marlborough in 1895.
*After Perry Belmont died in 1908, Alva tuned out of society and became transformed into a
militant suffragette. Her favorite cause was women's rights in the South. She felt that the
belles of Dixie were the most oppressed women of all, prisoners of hoop skirts and mint juleps.*
(Courtesy Wilson Randolph Gathings)

ALICE HEINE *(1858–1925)*. New Orleans girl who became the first
American Princess of Monaco.
More divisive was Alice's fascination with her suppressed Jewish heritage. This upset her father
and ultimately spelled doom for her marriage.
(New York Public Library)

AMALIE RIVES *(1863–1945)*. Celebrated Charlottesville author and wife
of an Astor and a Russian prince.
Amalie grew up to be a rangy, purple-eyed, golden-curled beauty, and a fearless iconoclast.
She loved to write—on paper, on the walls, even on her petticoats. When she was twenty-five, she
wrote her first novel, The Quick or the Dead. *It was a heavy-breathing best seller.*
(Courtesy Wilson Randolph Gathings)

CHISWELL DABNEY LANGHORNE *(1843–1918)*
with daughter Phyllis. Father of Charlottesville's
Langhorne sisters, America's most famous belles.
When Dana Gibson climbed the steps of Mirador
to ask for Chillie's blessing, the irascible father told
Gibson to take the next train back to New York;
as he said, he didn't want any "damn Yankee
sign painter coming down here to interfere
with my daughter's life."
(Alice Winn)

IRENE LANGHORNE GIBSON *(1874–1956)*.
Wife of society artist Charles Dana Gibson
and model for the Gibson Girl, the ideal of
American beauty for decades.
Irene was delicate, yet voluptuous and had an
angelic singing voice. She received more than
sixty serious marriage proposals and
made a dramatic sweep across the party circuit
from New Orleans to Bar Harbor.
(Alice Winn)

LADY NANCY LANGHORNE ASTOR *(1879–1964)*. Wife of Viscount Waldorf Astor, one of the world's richest men, and the first woman to sit in the House of Commons. *Nancy told Winston Churchill, "If I were your wife, I'd give you poison in your coffee." Churchill smiled and quietly replied, "If you were my wife, I'd drink it."* *(Alice Winn)*

ASA GRIGGS CANDLER *(1851–1929)*. Atlanta druggist's assistant
who founded Coca-Cola.
*Asa's only problems came from Southern religious groups who objected to the beverage. There
were rumors that "the pause that refreshes" did so because the drink contained cocaine. If Asa,
a religious man who had no bad habits anyone was aware of, couldn't silence the opposition,
his brother, a Methodist bishop, could.*
(Courtesy of the Archives: The Coca-Cola Co.)

HENRY FAIRCHILD DE BARDELEBEN *(1841–1910).*
The iron king of Alabama.
Never afraid to take risks, he tried one iron venture
after another, most of which worked. He gambled
heavily, won big, and coined the phrase,
"life is a glorified crap game."
(Birmingham News)

"PITCHFORK" BEN TILLMAN *(1847–1918).* Populist
Senator from South Carolina who fought an
unending battle against blacks and "aristocrats."
He was the greatest rabble-rouser of his time. His
favorite targets were the Reconstruction scalawags and
carpetbaggers, whom he called "blood-sucking
vampires"; Wade Hampton, whom he derided as the
"grand mogul"; and blacks, whom he labeled
"barbarians." He constantly harped on the theme of black
sexual assaults on white women.
(New York Public Library)

DR. CLARIBEL CONE *(1864–1929)* *(left)* and MISS ETTA CONE (1870–1949) *(right)*.
Greensboro, North Carolina, art collectors and heiresses to the Cone corduroy fortune.
*After Alice B. Toklas, Claribel and Etta were two of Gertrude Stein's closest friends. The four
women, who spent endless hours together, made an imposing impression on the Paris
boulevards. The sisters were intimates of Picasso and Matisse and became two of the most
influential art patrons on the Continent.*
(New York Public Library)

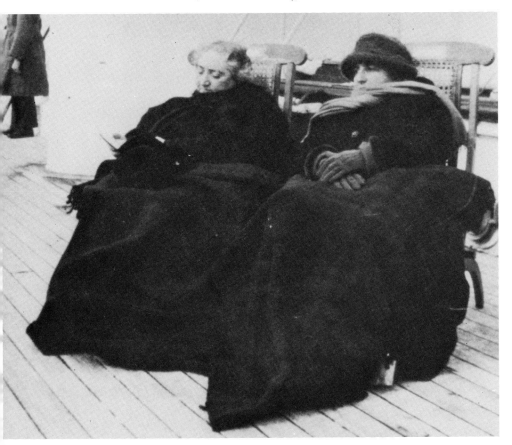

Brodie Leonidas Duke *(1848–1919)*,
Benjamin Newton Duke *(1855–1929)*, and
James Buchanan (Buck) Duke *(1856–
1925)*. Sons of Washington Duke of Durham,
and lords of a great tobacco empire. Brodie
and Buck were involved in a number of
monumental divorces.

*Adding insult to injury, Lillian further claimed
that Buck kicked her out of bed, shook her, choked
her, beat her with a crutch, and had his
housekeeper in his New Jersey estate deprive her of
both vegetables and flowers. That was no way for a
Southern gentleman to treat a lady.*
(Duke University)

DORIS DUKE (daughter of Buck Duke). Shown with Latin Playboy
PORFIRIO RUBIROSA at El Morocco, New York.
(Jerome Zerbe)

ZACHARY SMITH REYNOLDS *(1912–1932)* and LIBBY HOLMAN REYNOLDS *(1906–1973)*. The heir to the Camel cigarette fortune and his wife, the Broadway torch singer, who was charged with his murder.

Libby Holman may at first have been amused at the adolescent crush of the chubby, rich teenager, who thought he was an amalgam of Lindbergh and Valentino. But Smith's dogged, worldwide persistence began to pay off. No one, not even the sexiest woman in America, could simply ignore a Reynolds.

(Z. Smith Reynolds Foundation)
(Louis Botto, Playbill)

RICHARD JOSHUA REYNOLDS, JR. *(1906–1964).* Older brother of Z. Smith Reynolds
and oft-wed international sybarite.
When Dick's yellow Rolls-Royce was found overturned in Long Island Sound, at the end of an
abandoned pier, the worst was feared. A worldwide dragnet went out. But a few days later,
Dick was discovered, not in Dakar or Timbuktu, but in a chop suey parlor in St. Louis,
accompanied by a beautiful blonde.
(Z. Smith Reynolds Foundation)

ELMS COURT. The Surgets's Natchez mansion, from which Jane Surget Merrill was evicted due to her affair with her cousin, Duncan Minor.
Elms Court reigned supreme as the social center of Natchez.
(Courtesy Wilson Randolph Gathings)

GLENWOOD, also known as Goat Castle. The end of the Natchez tradition.
(Courtesy Wilson Randolph Gathings)

Master bedroom of Goat Castle.

Filth rivaled only by the Augean stables. Goats, pigs, cats, chickens, and ducks had replaced the belles and beaux who used to pass through the Doric pilasters.

(Courtesy Wilson Randolph Gathings)

Octavia Dockery *(1864–1948)* and Dick Dana *(1870–1947)*. The owners of
Goat Castle and survivors of the Southern aristocracy. They were prime
suspects in the murder of Jane Surget Merrill.
Octavia was a destitute ex-debutante who was forced to support herself by raising chickens and
goats. Dick was a gifted pianist who became the "wild man of Natchez," spending much of
the three decades preceding the murder gamboling in the woods,
sporting only a gunnysack and a three-foot beard.
(New Orleans Times-Picayune)

the wreaths. Conspicuous in her absence, but true to form, was Ward's wife.

Ward's estate was a mere $10,000, barely enough for a quadrille. Sarah Gibbons McAllister had held the millions, but, true Southern lady that she was, she had been too gracious ever to apply fiscal sanctions to her absentee husband. Sarah died quietly at age eighty, in 1909. Her daughter Louise, despite her preeminent eligibility, stayed in the shadows with her mother. Years later, when she was in her eighties, Louise finally married an elderly Maryland horse breeder, but she died six months after the wedding.

Ward, Jr., cleared out of the Eastern party circuit as soon as he finished Princeton and Harvard Law School. He went to San Francisco, where he enjoyed great status in the McAllister-dominated bar. Eventually he found even Nob Hill too claustrophobic. He escaped to the wilds of Alaska, where he served as federal judge for the territory.

Only Heyward Hall McAllister was a man after his father's heart. Nominally a broker but actually a playboy, he divided his time between the Gibbons New Jersey estate, the Waldorf-Astoria, and the Hotel Balmoral in Menton, on the French Riviera. His first marriage, to a daughter of one of the 400, was a failure; his second marriage was a shock. Heyward had told his family he was going away on a hunting trip. He returned with the catch of a young, unpedigreed, French girl who spoke no English and was said to be a chambermaid. Heyward was summarily dropped from the *Social Register,* and he spent the rest of his life in France. None of the McAllisters had any children.

Perhaps the best commentary on what happened to society after Ward McAllister is the man who took his place. Harry Lehr was a shrillish Baltimore homosexual with distinct transvestite proclivities. He had two special talents. One was being able to wiggle his nose from side to side. The other was the bitchy insult. When at a Newport ball, *the* Mrs. Astor, laden with diamonds, clanged by him, Harry pulled some roses from a bowl and hissed, "Here, you look like a walking chandelier. Put these on. You need color."

She loved it, as did her queenly successors, Mrs. Stuyvesant Fish and Mrs. Oliver Hazard Perry Belmont, a Mobile belle who kept the South's social hegemony alive. They made Harry their pet, let him give their parties, found him a Main Line wife whom he never touched, and lauded him as Ward's successor. "Wardie was the voice crying in the wilderness who prepared the way for me," Lehr trilled. Poor Ward must have been turning over in his grave. It was a sorry end for the swellest nob of them all.

VIII

Wedding Belles: Marital Reconstruction

Ward McAllister's equation that Southern equals Social was of inestimable benefit to a large number of calculating families seeking their way out of the morass that was the South after the Civil War. A calculating Southerner? Wasn't that out of character? Definitely not. After the Civil War, every family for itself was the rule rather than exception. Interestingly, the families that were resourceful enough to do so by hieing themselves north and trading on their Southern charms were, by and large, not the old aristocrats like Ward McAllister. Rather, they were the middle class or lower, a cut above white trash, but many notches below the plantation gentry that had once dominated the Old South.

Whatever their origins, these ambitious Southern families were discovering that the greatest asset of all was neither land nor slaves, nor even lineage. They could gloss over all that in the haze of the romantic past. No, Dixie's hidden asset, its secret weapon, was simply the Southern woman—the *belle.* This remarkable damsel seemed to always get her man, be it a Yankee plutocrat or a foreign aristocrat. In the process, a new group of great Southern families was launched. Through the belle, the South finally conquered the North, by love rather than war.

THE MARRYING WILSONS

Without a doubt, the most successfully conjugal of all Southern families were the "marrying Wilsons." Starting from the humblest of backwoods beginnings on the Georgia and Tennessee frontiers, Mr. and Mrs. Richard Thornton Wilson married their daughters and son to the very best of New York and British families.

A rough farm girl, Mrs. Wilson came to be regarded as the leading lady of Manhattan society. How did the Wilsons do it? To begin with, they were Southern. They sounded great. And they were big–husband and wife over six feet tall–so that they looked even more imposing than the Jefferson Davises. (In fact, R. T. Wilson was said to have been Margaret Mitchell's inspiration for Rhett Butler in *Gone With the Wind.*) But, most important, the Wilsons were incredibly cunning. Rich when the South was starving, they were accused by Southerners of being the worst of scalawag turncoats, feasting on the spoils of the Confederacy. New York, however, wasn't tuned in to Southern nuances. The Wilson act was the best in town.

The Wilsons referred to themselves as an "old Southern family." Yet, unlike other such families, their pre-1865 genealogy always seemed to have been lost in the postwar shuffle. Industrious social chroniclers, however, were able to dig back further, to the Wilsons's undoubted chagrin. Richard T. Wilson was born in Gainesville, Georgia, in 1829, the son of a Scottish tanner. He went on the road at an early age, selling trinkets or trading them for cotton. Most of his customers didn't have cash, but cotton was literally as good as gold. One of his customers was as intrigued by the lanky Wilson as she was by his knickknacks. This was Melissa Johnston, a proverbial farmer's daughter in Loudon, a hamlet in western Tennessee. They were soon married. Wanting his new son-in-law off the road, Melissa's father helped the couple set up a little general store. At the outbreak of the Civil War, Wilson's trading experience won him the rank of major in the Confederate commissary department.

At the close of the war, the Wilsons suddenly and miraculously became extremely rich. The family's story was that Richard Wilson had made a fortune by speculating in the Confederate bonds being sold in Europe. But no one made a fortune on that ill-fated issue, except John Slidell's in-laws, the d'Erlangers, who had devised the bond scheme. The Wilsons did go to Europe in those final days of the Confederacy, riding a flatcar camouflaged with branches to Wilmington, North Carolina, where they ran the blockade. Arriving in England, Richard reputedly made a killing selling various supplies that belonged to the Confederate commissary. He may have posed as a Southern agent, though his only principal was himself; not a cent of his sales ever saw its way into Dixie's empty coffers. Once his fiscal deals were made, Wilson made another, dashing to the American embassy and taking the oath of allegiance.

Persona non grata in the South, Wilson went from England directly to New York, one of the first of the Southern émigrés. With his ill-gotten gains, Wilson bought a Fifth Avenue mansion and opened a Wall Street investment house. Now the scalawag, entrenched in the North, became a carpetbagger. He began buying up Southern railroads and industries devastated by the war. One of his shrewdest acquisitions was a bankrupt Virginia bleach plant that he developed into the mammoth Olin-Mathieson chemical company. More fortunes were made in street railways from Brooklyn to Detroit, transactions that were heavily tinged with questionable financial wizardry. But this was the age of the robber baron. Anything went.

Being a robber baron, however, wasn't enough. After all the public discussion about its wealth, the Wilson family wanted respectability. They got it in 1877 when their daughter, May, married Ogden Goelet, a member of an old Knickerbocker real estate dynasty. That May towered over her dwarfish, bumbling husband didn't bother her parents at all. But when the Wilsons encouraged her romance with Ogden, they were betting on a dark horse. Ogden was only one of many nephews of the bachelor Peter Goelet, who was worth over $25 million. Other eligible girls did not expect Ogden to be the lucky heir, and they paid no attention to him. But the Wilsons seemed to have had an inside tip.

Soon after the wedding, Peter died, leaving Ogden everything. It was said that old Peter felt that Ogden was so pathetic that he needed the money more than any of the other Goelets.

The bequest made Odgen significantly less pathetic and, combined with the superrespectability of the Goelet name, made the Wilsons socially invincible. May and Ogden set off for Europe on their new yacht, taking May's sister, Belle, along for the cruise. Belle lived up to her name; her soft voice, honey-blond hair, and delicate hands, were legend on two continents. Belle entranced the Prince of Wales, who had a weakness for American women, especially tall ones with Southern drawls. She was the first young woman from the United States to be presented to Queen Victoria. Belle's introduction to *Burke's Peerage* climaxed at Wilton House, a famous stately home where she met Michael "Mungo" Herbert, brother of the Earl of Pembroke, and one of the brightest lights of the British diplomatic corps. Like so many British aristocrats, Herbert was land rich, but money poor. What lured him as much as Belle's charms was her dowry. For the Wilsons, Herbert's name and background were sufficient quid pro quo.

Four years before the Herbert-Wilson wedding in 1888, Belle's stunningly handsome brother, Orme, hit another jackpot by marrying Carrie Astor, daughter of Ward McAllister's Mystic Rose—*the* Mrs. Astor, queen of New York society. Carrie didn't come cheap. Richard T. Wilson had to put up half a million dollars for Orme to match Carrie's own half-million-dollar wedding gift before the Mystic Rose would consent to the match.

The final jewel in the Wilson conjugal crown was mounted in 1896 when their youngest and most attractive daughter, Grace, wed Cornelius Vanderbilt III. A financial panic in the 1880s had reduced the Wilson fortune to barely more than a million dollars. Given the hard times, Grace had to snare a big fish. She had been spurned by Cecil Baring, an Englishman whose family owned the great banking house of London, because of her family's relative penury. Now Grace was twenty-six and desperate. Her parents wouldn't settle for anything less than a Croesus, and for this young Vanderbilt was ideal. The only catch was his father, Cornelius II. Alone in New York, Vanderbilt, Sr., saw the Wilsons as irreparably tainted by their war-profiteering though why he should object to profiteering was anyone's guess, since his father, the commodore, was involved in enough ruthless schemes to make Richard Wilson seem the saint of Wall Street.

Despite the formidable opposition, Cornelius III was in love and would not be deterred. The family rancor gave his father a stroke, and Cornelius took advantage of this unfortunate diversion to marry Grace. Cornelius II recovered enough to see that his son was totally cut out of his $100-million fortune. Yet Cornelius III had over ten million of his own, enough to keep the Wilsons afloat. Once married, Grace Wilson Vanderbilt became the most conspicuous consumer of all American dowagers, eventually taking Mrs. Astor's place in the early twentieth century as the queen of Fifth Avenue and of Newport. In one generation, then, the Wilsons had made themselves the American equivalent of a royal family. When Richard T. Wilson died in 1908, the New York papers paid him great homage as both a financial wizard and a social patriarch. The Southern papers maintained a scornful silence.

ALVA SMITH
VANDERBILT BELMONT

Another Southern belle who won in the Yankee marital sweepstakes was Alva Smith of Mobile, who married in succession both William K. Vanderbilt, son of the commodore, and Oliver Hazard Perry Belmont, son of August. Although they weren't pariahs in the South, like the Wilsons, the Smiths were certainly not the social success in Dixie they wanted to be. Their failure was not from lack of ambition, for Alva's mother, Phoebe Ann Desha Smith, the descendant of a long line of Kentucky colonels, was as ambitious as a Southern mother could be. During the cotton boom she had relocated to Mobile with her Virginian husband, Murray Smith, a prosperous commission merchant, and she did everything she could to live well beyond their means and thereby attract the appropriate plantation suitors for her four daughters. In Mobile, she failed dismally.

First, she tried to establish the Mobile equivalent of a salon. Regrettably, Mobile was a bit short on the literati and artists Mrs. Smith needed. But even if she had them, Old Mobile would have ignored her anyway. Mobile had its own Creole elite, which was highly xenophobic, especially toward pushy new arrivals like the Smiths. Spurned by Mobile and impoverished by the war, Mrs. Smith somehow managed to scrape together enough funds to take her daughters to Paris in the late 1860s. When that became too expensive, she moved to New York, where she slaved away at a boardinghouse to support her girls' Worth gowns and fancy schooling.

Mrs. Smith's sacrifices paid off handsomely. Southern ties in Manhattan were quite strong, almost clubby. Through Dixie matchmaking, one of the Smith girls married Fernando Yznaga, the son of a rich Creole-Cuban sugar planter who divided his time between Natchez and Havana. Because of the Cuban interests, the family was still wealthy and lived elegantly in New York. Alva became best friends with Fernando's sister, Consuelo, who had been quite an iconoclast in Natchez, doing such outrageous things as smoking cigarettes, playing a guitar, dancing the flamenco, and singing black spirituals at debutante balls. In New York, Consuelo Yznaga took Alva under her wing and helped her break into society.

The Yznagas frequently traveled to Europe in high style and in an exalted circle. One of their friends was the Duchess of Manchester, whose son, George V. D. Montague, would soon inherit the title as the eighth Duke of Manchester. George was planning a tour of the United States, and his mother entrusted him to the Yznagas. Title-hunting Yankee adventuresses were a prominent feature of American society, and the duchess counted on the Yznagas to protect the heir from any predatory American women. The Yznagas shielded their guest from everyone—except Consuelo. She and the young lord wed in New York in one of the most celebrated nuptials of 1876.

Consuelo's social stock was booming, and Alva's went up, too, for Consuelo had introduced her to Willie K. Vanderbilt, yachtsman and son of the commodore. For all their New York Central millions, the Vanderbilts were still considered parvenus and felt that any friend of the regal Consuelo was a friend of theirs. In 1875 there was no opposition when Willie wed Alva as there was two years later when Cornelius III wed Grace Wilson. Alva's mother may have been a social climber, but at least her father was no scalawag. Furthermore, after his first wife died, the old Commodore Vanderbilt himself had married a Mobile girl named Frank Crawford. So the Vanderbilts had a built-in partiality for Alabama, which favored Alva, whose dark, busty chubbiness was considered the height of feminine allure in those times.

Alva and Willie K. named their daugher Consuelo, in honor of their matchmaker. Of course, Alva wanted her Consuelo to have a title, too. But as a young woman the swanlike Consuelo, famed for the supposed grace of her endless neck, had none of her mother's aggressive Southern belleishness. Shy and retiring, she was perfectly content, at nineteen, simply to wed one of her fellow Fifth Avenuers. Not so her mother, who trekked to England in 1894 to sign up the foppish Charles Richard John Spencer-Churchill, ninth Duke of Marlborough. His dubious masculinity notwithstanding, Alva made him an offer he couldn't refuse, in a prewedding gift of millions of dollars' worth of blue-chip New York Central bonds. She also gave a ball in his honor at her renowned $2-million Marble House in Newport. This five hundred guest extravaganza was perhaps the most lavish in Newport history, featuring a Chinese teahouse, an African rain forest, a Hungarian gypsy camp—and Southern renaissance. Leading off the dancing with Alva was none other than Richard T. Wilson.

The young duke was dazzled. Consuelo was less pliable. The swan quickly became an ostrich, burying her head against her mother's urgent entreaties. She hated Spencer-Churchill and threw a tantrum that seemed to have no end. As an antidote, Alva locked Consuelo in her room, then hired a team of physicians to warn the girl that she was suffering from a rare disease that could be fatal if she didn't calm down. Better wed than dead, Consuelo must have thought, and eventually went through with the ceremony in 1895. This gave Alva an excuse for another of her famous parties, this one featuring a sixty-piece symphony and the transformation of New York's St. Thomas Episcopal Church into a botanical garden. Money couldn't buy love, though. The marriage was a royal flop.

While Alva Vanderbilt was masterminding her daughter's marriage, she was also working on another of her own. A frequent guest on yacht trips on the *Alva* from Cannes to Calcutta was Oliver H. P.

Belmont, the playboy son of the superbanker August Belmont. Perry Belmont, five years younger than Alva, was smitten by the still-sexy, early-fortyish woman of the world. During the torrid affair between Alva and Perry, Willie K. had one of his own with a Nevada girl named Nellie Neustetter, who had become a courtesan in Paris. Willie K.'s indiscretions, so far beneath his station, shocked society more than the high-level one of Alva and Perry. A divorce was quickly arranged in 1895, and Alva soon became a Belmont. It was sweet revenge for Alva, whose mother had been snubbed in Paris by Belmont's relatives, the Slidells. The South may have turned the Smiths down cold, but Alva more than settled the score in New York.

One of Alva's sisters, Mimi, met and married another English nobleman through her Yznaga connections. However, the fourth, Armide, was so repelled by the whole marriage-go-round that she became both a defiant spinster and an activist in the women's rights movement, a disciple of the Grimké sisters. And, amazingly enough, after Perry Belmont died in 1908, Alva herself tuned out of society and became transformed into a militant suffragette. The catalyst for her conversion was her travels; the plight of the Italian peasant women was especially effective in shocking her out of her Fifth Avenue insulation. That society would gossip self-righteously about her divorce from Willie K. Vanderbilt also annoyed and emboldened her. "I was one of the first women to get a divorce from an influential man," she fondly boasted.

Whatever the cause, Alva went to the barricades with a special zeal. She now used her funds for feminist rallies, not 400 parties. She founded the Political Equality League, brought the English dynamo, Christabel Pankhurst, to America for a lecture tour, and joined with Elsa Maxwell to produce a suffragette operetta. Later, she branched out into the trade union movement and even helped fund a socialist journal. But her favorite cause was women's rights in the South. Alva felt that the belles of Dixie were the most oppressed women of all, prisoners of hoop skirts, mint juleps, and expectations of perpetual passivity and coquetry, if not chastity. Though she still enjoyed her own mint julep up to the time of death in 1933 at eighty in her Paris palais, no one could have ever accused her of being passive.

THE FIRST JEWISH PRINCESS

The two Consuelos weren't the only Southern girls to marry foreign royalty. Another was Alice Heine, who married the Duc de Richelieu and then the Prince of Monaco. Alice's father, a New Orleans business-man, was a member of a Hamburg banking family who had come to New Orleans in its antebellum cotton boom years to open an American office. There he married Marie Miltenberger, one of the most eligible Jewish girls of the French Quarter, where her family had been mer-chants since the earliest Creole days.

Like all the Creoles, the Heines were ruined by the war. And like so many other Southerners, they looked to their svelte, blue-eyed, blond-haired teen angel to salvage their future. Sent to Europe by her father, Alice came through splendidly. Her European relations were promi-nent in French banking circles and were delighted to introduce their American cousin. Her family had her converted to Catholicism, to prevent any bars to marriage.

Alice was so gorgeous, it is unlikely that religion would have mat-tered. At seventeen, in 1875, she wed the twenty-six-year-old Duc de Richelieu and moved to his ancestral Château de Haut-Buisson. She never forgot her family. Shortly after the marriage, the Heines left New Orleans for good and became, with Alice's royal contacts, one of the leading bankers in France. The duke died five years after the marriage, and Alice, then twenty-two, moved to the Portuguese island of Madeira. Her mourning period was brief.

With an inheritance of nearly $15 million, Alice was one of the most sought-after widows in Europe. Any title could have been hers, yet she seemed inexorably drawn back to her roots. In succession, she fell in love with two Jewish doctors. Each time, however, her father swept onto the scene and broke up the affairs. Wanting another title in the family, he finally got it in Prince Albert of Monaco. A renowned oceanographer doing deep-sea diving off Madeira, the prince was hooked on Alice at first sight. In 1889, she became his princess.

The marriage began brilliantly, with Alice turning Monte Carlo into something more than a gambling den. She brought the famous impresario, Raoul Gunsbourg, to direct the opera house, and he, in turn, brought the Diaghilev ballet there. However, after a decade of marriage, the prince and princess began to draw apart. For one thing, Alice got seasick at the mere thought of water and refused to set foot on either of the prince's two yachts, which he had named *Alice I* and *Alice II.*

More divisive was Alice's fascination with her suppressed Jewish heritage. This upset her father and ultimately spelled doom for her marriage. While Prince Albert stood fast with her in her highly publicized support of Captain Dreyfus, there was nothing he could do when Alice became the amorous *patronne* of a handsome young British composer named Isidore Cohen, who changed his last name to de Lara. De Lara wrote popular songs as well as opera, and sang his compositions to a wide audience of admiring women. His "Garden of Sleep" was the Victorian equivalent of a gold record; it made him the Mick Jagger of his time. Alice gave a huge production in Monaco for anything he wrote. In fact, she was spending on the opera more than the profits from the casino.

Not surprisingly, by the time Alice was forty-four, the prince could take no more. The couple separated in 1902, but Alice kept her title as well as de Lara. Notables continued to flock to her salons, which were a veritable movable feast, ranging from her Haut-Buisson château, to her Paris townhouse, to her London flat. Some of her most welcome guests were Southern belles on their own title search. Alice was always delighted to give them advice.

THE CHARLOTTESVILLE SIRENS

One of Alice Heine's friends was another Southern American princess who needed no lessons in love, marriage, or, for that matter, anything. This was Amalie Rives of Charlottesville, Virginia, something of a breeding ground for beautiful girls who made beautiful marriages.

Beatrice Ashley and the Langhorne sisters were the prime examples. But Amalie was first. She was from one of Virginia's oldest and finest families and grew up in one of the Old Dominion's most imposing ancestral homes, Castle Hill, down the road from Jefferson's Monticello, Monroe's Ash Law, and James Madison's homestead. In fact, Charlottesville, with Jefferson's elegant university, situated amid the rolling splendors of the Blue Ridge, was Virginia's Valley of the Kings. The Rives clan was vital to the local aristocracy.

Amalie's grandfather, William Cabell Rives, had been a law student of Jefferson's, a Senator, and the American Minister to France. His son, Alfred Landon Rives, could boast General Lafayette as his godfather. Queen Amalie of France was godmother to the Riveses' daughter and the namesake of Amalie to come. Alfred L. Rives, Amalie's father, was chief of engineers of the Confederacy. After the war, he was reduced to taking odd jobs in railway construction around the South. Still, the Rives had their gracious Castle Hill, where Amalie was surrounded by old-time nannies and tutors who were too loyal to the family to seek positions elsewhere.

Amalie grew up to a rangy, purple-eyed, golden-curled beauty, and a fearless iconoclast. She loved to write—on paper, on the walls, even on her petticoats. In 1888, when whe was twenty-five, she wrote her first novel, *The Quick or the Dead.* It was a heavy-breathing best seller about a woman who was torn between her passions for her dead husband and those for her new lover. While *The Quick or the Dead* was becoming the talk of the nation, selling a phenomenal 300,000 copies, Amalie opted for the quick. She married the hell-raising John Armstrong Chanler of New York, a rakish big-game hunter whom she had met at her first season at Newport and who was the model for the live protagonist of her book.

One of the famous Astor orphans, Chanler himself had a great deal of blue Southern blood. His mother, Maddie Astor Ward, was the granddaughter of William Backhouse Astor and the daughter of the ubiquitous bon vivant Sam Ward, perhaps the North's greatest Dixophile. Chanler's father, John Winthrop Chanler, was well-rooted in aristocratic Charleston. Chanler's Astor-Ward mother died of a fever she caught at her Astor grandfather's funeral, and his father died of a fever he caught at a croquet match shortly thereafter, leaving Chanler and his siblings the richest orphans in the world.

John Armstrong Chanler was strange. Although he had graduated from Columbia and was a qualified attorney, he preferred the other side of the law. He was charged with at least one murder, ate wild duck and ice cream for breakfast, lounged about in leather pajamas, and spent a fair amount of time at New York's Bloomingdale Asylum for the well-to-do-insane. He also believed that he could change the color of his eyes and the shape of his head at will and sincerely thought that he was the reincarnation of Napoleon Bonaparte. Those in the know called him "the General."

Because the South treasures its eccentrics, Chanler became a cult figure. Charlottesville loved him. His wife Amalie was less enthused. After six turbulent years of a marriage which shuttled between Virginia and Europe, Amalie got a divorce on grounds of incompatibility. Now she decided it would be much more fun to be a princess than an Astor. Through her decadent friend, Oscar Wilde, Amalie met and married the émigré Russian artist Prince Pierre Troubetzkoy. Wilde had been drawn to Amalie by a fascination with her old black mammy, whom she brought to England with her. He felt that Amalie and Pierre were the two most beautiful people in London and were destined for each other. Amalie, also an esthete who believed it sinful for beautiful women to be wasted on ugly men, found Pierre irresistible. So did Chanler. He bought an estate in Charlottesville and settled into a loose friendship with the prince and princess, who lived in the Riveses' ancestral Castle Hill. Chanler's home was called, appropriately enough, Merrie Mills.

The Troubetzkoys turned Castle Hill into a domiciliary melting pot, mixing early American antiques with Byzantine chests and Italian baptismal fonts. The servants learned to serve borscht and risotto with the fried chicken to the international parade of celebrities who came to visit. While Pierre painted his portraits, Amalie continued to be a prolific writer. She also became a morphine addict, and described her painful withdrawal from the drug in her next acclaimed book, *Shadows of Flames,* a pioneering American work about the taboo subject of narcotics. She also wrote poems and Broadway plays, always working at

Castle Hill. There she rode horses and reveled in her role as "the
Virginia Princess" nearly until her death at eighty-two in 1945.

Another Charlottesville girl who married a Chanler and hit the big
time was Beatrice Ashley, the daughter of a local lawyer. The Ashleys
weren't an FFV family, like the Rives, but Beatrice always aspired to be
like Amalie, the idol of all the local girls. Rather than daydreaming, the
determined Beatrice really followed through. She went to New York
and became a chorus girl, where her long legs and classical features were
noted by producers and socialites alike. Her first hit came in the play,
The Greek Slave, belting out a number called "I'm a Naughty Girl." She
followed this with a Chinoiserie called *San Toy,* in which she stopped
the show with the song, "Rhoda, Rhoda Ran a Pagoda."

Beatrice's theatrical success brought half the 400 to her stage door,
including Morgans and Vanderbilts. But Beatrice wanted to follow
Amalie and, accordingly, in 1903, when she was seventeen years old, she
married William Astor Chanler, John's brother. William Astor Chanler was also a glamorous playboy, but without his brother's kinks. After
her marriage, Beatrice bowed out of the theater, turning her talents to
sculpture, writing, and philanthropy. Unlike Amalie, she spent her
time in Manhattan and Paris, and never returned to Charlottesville,
possibly because she didn't have a Castle Hill to return to.

BEAUTY AND ITS REWARDS

The biggest Charlottesville success story of all, though, was not the
unconventional Amalie or the ambitious Beatrice. Rather it was the
effortlessly beautiful Langhorne sisters. In this land of Randolph and
Rives, the one family that became synonymous with Charlottesville
didn't even arrive until 1892. When they came, however, they did so
with a splash. The waves never subsided.

The Langhorne hegemony was founded not on politics, not on
tobacco, not on bloodlines, but on good looks. The family was a living
refutation of the old adage that "beauty isn't everything." The five
Langhorne sisters were America's reigning belles of the gilded age, at
the turn of the century. They received more marriage proposals than

any other women in American history. With the marriage of Irene Langhorne to Charles Dana Gibson, the country's most influential social chronicler, and that of Nancy Langhorne to Lord Waldorf Astor, the world's richest man, the Langhornes hit the conjugal jackpot. The rest of the family enjoyed the social spoils, as did Charlottesville itself.

The town became a marital El Dorado, with the most eligible suitors from home and abroad paying anxious calls at the Langhornes's estate, Mirador. In the course of these courtships, the swains also discovered the pastoral delights of the Blue Ridge. Even when these gilded youth left without a Langhorne girl, they consoled themselves with lush memories of horses, hounds, and the beauty of the mountains, not to mention the bevy of local belles who served as consolation prizes. Their glowing tall tales, combined with those of the English nobility whom Nancy Langhorne, as Lady Astor, later brought to Mirador, gave Charlottesville a high society mystique and put the Langhornes in the ranks of Dixie royalty.

For a family that had been virtually destitute at the close of the Civil War, this social renaissance was no mean feat. The unlikely patriarch of this house of pulchritude was the girls' father, Chiswell Dabney Langhorne, a rotund, stocky man, distinguished by his walrus mustache and his deadly aim with the juices from his chewing tobacco. Along with the spit was a modicum of polish. The Langhornes were actually one of the First Families of Virginia, descendants of a Welsh anti-Cromwell Royalist, who had come to Virginia in 1672 and served in the colony's House of Burgesses. Although they did not amass the wealth of the Byrds or the Carters, the Langhornes settled in Lynchburg, acquired land and slaves, and operated one of the larger flour mills in the state. The entire family fortune was destroyed during the Civil War, forcing young Chillie, as he was known, to start from scratch. While Lee was surrendering his sword at Appomattox in 1865, Chillie, who served as a private in the Virginia infantry, surrendered his bachelorhood at twenty-two to a seventeen-year-old girl he met when stationed in Danville. Nancy Witcher Keene was descended from Irish immigrants; her family had been minor local politicians. However, she was ravishing, with the deep blue eyes, high cheekbones, blond hair, and overall patrician bearing that would make her daughters the most wanted women in the entire country.

Chillie once cataloged his postbellum assets as "nothing but a wife, a ragged seat to my pants, and a barrel of whiskey." In later years he could have added to that list his family of five girls and three boys. To support his expanding brood, Chillie took a long succession of odd jobs. First, he was a night clerk in a hotel, where he was dismissed for ringing the fire alarm to alleviate his boredom. Then he rented a mule and buggy and became a traveling piano salesman. His inability to play more than one chord (due to an alleged sprained wrist) kept him from becoming another Steinway, and his only sale occured when he threw in the mule and buggy to close the deal. From music, Chillie ventured into art, hawking a variety of masterpieces, from Romeo and Juliet to Stonewall Jackson, for the price of seven dollars (Robert E. Lee cost nine). Next came tobacco auctioning, and greater success. Chillie is given credit for having invented the gobbledygook auction cant that still echoes incomprehensibly throughout warehouses in the Southeast.

By 1885, the mumbo jumbo had made Chillie solvent, if not rich. He moved his large family from Danville to a small house in the metropolis of Richmond. But here his silver tongue began to lose its luster. The tobacco business declined so steeply that Chillie was planning to appeal to the mercies of a cousin near Charlottesville, when his former Civil War commander, now an executive with the Chesapeake and Ohio Railroad, offered him a job managing the semi-chain gangs that laid the rails. A benevolent despot where blacks were concerned, Chillie proved quite adept at his new task. His managerial skills, combined with a good-old-boy conviviality that brought the C & O much business, eventually made him a millionaire.

At last the Langhornes could begin to live in the style to which their ancestors had been accustomed. They started to spend their summers at the mountain spa of White Sulphur Springs, West Virginia, the Saratoga of the South—although their life-style was by no means Astorian. They had a small cottage on Virginia Row, not a suite in the grand Old White Hotel, where the wealthy outlanders stayed. Instead of a phaeton and a team of proud horses, they brought a goat and a cart for the children to play with. Nevertheless, Chillie's personality, his jokes, his songs, and his infinite drinking capacity carried the day. He became the toast of the Springs, the center of attention—until his sixteen-year-old daughter Irene was "discovered" in 1889 by a roving

Ward McAllister. Savannahian McAllister knew a Southern belle when he saw one. With McAllister's support, Irene became *the* belle of the nation. McAllister invited her to come to New York and lead his Patriarchs Ball at Delmonico's, the crowning event of the Manhattan social season. Chillie couldn't say no and allowed Irene to enter the tightly chaperoned world of the 400. Irene was delicate, yet voluptuous, and had an angelic singing voice. She received more than sixty serious marriage proposals and made a dramatic sweep across the party circuit from New Orleans to Bar Harbor.

While Irene's beauty was making her father famous, his railroad business was continuing to make him rich. Because Irene was entertaining so many prominent suitors, Chillie decided that he needed a great estate to receive them in the proper Southern manner. When Virginians decide to live seigneurially, Charlottesville is the place they go. To that end, in 1892, Chillie purchased the elegant, Georgian-style Mirador, seventeen miles outside the city. Instead of coming to Charlottesville as a poor relation seeking a handout, Chillie now arrived as Colonel Langhorne, a tycoon eager to dispense the largess of his hospitality.

The house overflowed with eligible men, fierce rivals who were frequently piqued by having to share rooms with each other. The melee for Irene's hand ended with the arrival of Charles Dana Gibson, the dashing society artist who had met Irene at Delmonico's in 1894. (Dana Gibson had many distinguished Dana relatives; he was also the cousin of the "wild man of Natchez," Dick Dana of Goat Castle.) When Dana Gibson climbed the steps of Mirador to ask for Chillie's blessing, the irascible father told Gibson to take the next train back to New York; as he said, he didn't want any "damn Yankee sign painter coming down here to interfere with my daughter's life." Chille was only teasing, however, as was his wont. He rolled out the red carpet, poured a pitcher of mint juleps, and welcomed Gibson into the fold. The couple were married in Richmond the following year, with an epicurean reception held at the Jefferson Hotel, whose grand staircase was used in the movie, *Gone With the Wind*.

Dana Gibson's new bride became the inspiration for the Gibson Girl, the wholesome embodiment of American femininity until the advent of the flapper. In Gibson's sketches, the Gibson Girl was the ultimate decorative object. She didn't have a career; she didn't need one. Beautiful, elegant, wise, and loved by all men, she was the standard of perfection that American women of the era strived for. She also made Dana Gibson the richest artist of his time, with a $100,000 contract from *Colliers,* among other lucrative assignments. He and Irene led a most glamorous existence in New York, interspersed with frequent jaunts to Europe, where Gibson lampooned the foibles of nouveaux riches Americans abroad in comic-strip-style tableaux. His favorite targets were calculating American dowagers intent on marrying off their bejeweled daughters to nouveaux pauvres European noblemen. Although Gibson made fun of social climbing, the climbers themselves were his most avid devotees.

While Dana Gibson was satirizing strategic matrimony, his wife, Irene, was unabashedly aiding it. She talked Chillie into sending two of her younger sisters, Nancy and Phyllis, to finishing school in New York, where she could introduce them to all the "right" people. Both girls were superb horsewomen, though it has been said that Nancy's intrepid jumps caused her mother to die of a heart attack at the Lynchburg Horse Show in 1903. The two girls did deliver premature shocks to their mother by embarking upon unhappy marriages with two polo-playing Harvard Yankees. Nancy wed Bobby Shaw, a Boston Brahmin, in 1897; Phyllis married Reggie Brooks, a New York Knickerbocker, in 1901. In both cases, the husbands quickly began to miss the thrill of the chase, despite the heralded good looks of their wives, and the marriages failed.

In an attempt to assuage the twin shocks of divorce and the death of Mrs. Langhorne, Chillie sent Nancy to England to ride her blues away. Her depression was quickly dispelled when, on the ship's journey across, Waldorf Astor fell madly in love with her. (Such precipitous infatuations were standard for the Langhorne sisters.) The $100-million-plus Astor fortune was founded on Oregon furs and Gotham real estate and had done wonders for the Wilsons, Rives, and Ashleys. The Astors clearly had a weakness for Southerners. Now it was the Langhornes' turn to reap the benefits of Astor passion. Waldorf's father, William Waldorf Astor, had run for political office in New York and lost. Scorning the rebuff of the electorate as representing the ignorance of the masses, Astor, Sr., decided, in 1890, to move to England and live the cloistered life of a landed aristocrat. He acquired a title, a stately home, Cliveden, on the Thames, and sent his sons to Eton and Oxford. The transition from American robber baron to regal English baron couldn't have been easier.

Astor, Sr., was displeased with his son Waldorf's selection of a wife. Instead of the princess he envisioned for Waldorf, he was getting a Virginia divorcee, the daughter, not of a lord, but of a former auctioneer and figurative slave driver. He conveniently developed a case of gout and vowed to miss the 1906 wedding. Chillie, who would be upstaged by no one, got an even worse case of gout and said he would stay home as well. Happily, by wedding day, both men made miraculous recoveries and were present at the ceremony. Chillie gave his daughter away, while Waldorf's father gave the couple Cliveden, as a wedding gift. There Nancy would play hostess to the likes of George Bernard Shaw, Lawrence of Arabia, Mahatma Gandhi, and an endless parade of world notables. The Langhorne-Astor union turned out to be an extremely happy one, with five children.

Nancy's talents extended beyond those of a good hostess and mother. When her husband, Waldorf, ascended to his father's seat in the House of Lords, Nancy ran for his vacated seat in the House of Commons and won, becoming the first woman to sit in the House. In all her years in the Commons, Nancy did her best to look like a commoner, usually dressing in a plain black coat and skirt, white blouse, and the black tricorn hat that became her trademark. Her apparel was designed to be the equivalent of the dark suits of the male members of Parliament.

Ironically, the chief crusade of this woman from the land of the bottomless highball was one of temperance, against the British liquor interests. But Lady Nancy Astor was actually far more distinguished for her bon mots than for her legislative record. One of her rare enemies was Winston Churchill, who resented the millionairess's presence in Parliament and would have liked to banish her and her Southern drawl back to the Blue Ridge forever. Their repartee is famous. Chauvinist Churchill once said to Nancy, "When you took your seat, I felt as if a woman had come into my bathroom and I had only a sponge with which to defend myself." Nancy snapped back, "Winston, you're not handsome enough for that sort of trouble." On another occasion, Nancy told Churchill, "If I were your wife, I'd give you poison in your coffee." Churchill smiled and quietly replied, "If you were my wife, I'd drink it."

Nancy's feud with Sir Winston was mere fun and games, however, compared to the controversy that arose during the pre-World War II era over her alleged pro-Nazi sympathies. The world press made an endless succession of snide innuendos and outright accusations about what was called the Cliveden Set, Nancy's charmed circle of aristocrats and intellectuals. As the leader of a pack that, it was said, would rather switch than fight, Nancy was pilloried for her Southern background. Because she had freely admitted, only half in jest, that she felt Virginians were a "master race," because Virginians had been slave owners, and because she had grown up in a very nativist, racist America that was closing its gates to non-Aryan immigrants by vicious quotas, Nancy was regarded as a prime candidate for the Nazi movement and for Hitler's propaganda. Once the war came, though, Nancy disproved all her critics by the fiercest patriotism and by limitless contributions to the war effort. Her courage and spirit helped keep British upper lips stiff; even Churchill had to admire her for it.

Just as Irene had assisted Nancy and Phyllis with their first weddings, Nancy, once ensconced in the peerage, also took up the role of marriage broker. Her youngest sister, Nora, had as many suitors as Irene, but was terribly indecisive. Chillie, wanting Mirador to himself for once, begged Nancy to help put Nora in wedlock, once and for all. The lucky man was Paul Phipps, a young architect educated at Eton and Oxford, whose American-born mother was vice-chairman of the London City Council. Phipps was considered something of a Southerner, which delighted the Langhornes, because his mother's ancestors were Natchez cotton planters. His American grandparents were the William Butler Duncans, of One Fifth Avenue, New York's most redoubtable address.

Despite Phipps's blue-chip background, however, Nora was somewhat less than thrilled with him, even after the nuptials. During the alliance, she twice eloped with Maurice "Lefty" Flynn, an All-American football hero from Yale, who became a silent movie star in a number of Westerns. On the first elopement, to the Midwest, Dana Gibson led a successful rescue party. On the second, to the Côte d'Azur, Nora proved, for once, decisive. She divorced Phipps, wed Flynn, and left Europe for Greenwich, Connecticut.

After her separation from Reggie Brooks in 1912, her sister Phyllis moved back to Mirador while Chillie moved across the road to a new estate, which he christened Misfit. He had retired in 1903 at age sixty, because, as he put it, only "Yankees and Negroes" worked past that age. He thereafter assumed the role of full-time Virginia gentleman, shuttling between England and Charlottesville until his death in 1918. Phyllis herself left Mirador in 1917 to marry still another gentleman of Nancy's selection, an English patrician by the name of Robert Brand, later Lord Brand. Brand was the managing director of Lazard Brothers, the international merchant bankers, as well as a director of Lloyd's Bank and the London *Times,* and a prominent economist.

The least celebrated of the five Langhorne belles was no less beautiful; she was simply older (twenty years Nora's senior) and less flashily married. Elizabeth Langhorne was the wife of Thomas Moncure Perkins, a Richmond pork broker, and also a social power broker because of his FFV lineage. Perkins and his wife died young, in 1914, within weeks of each other. Their two little daughters, Nancy and Alice, were raised by various Langhornes and by Charlotte Noland, Mr. Perkins's cousin. "Miss Charlotte" was the legendary headmistress of the Foxcroft School in Middleburg, Virginia, renowned for infusing Southern charm into the Northern rich who filled its rosters. After Foxcroft, Nancy and Alice went to England, where their Aunt Nancy continued her matchmaking, setting the girls up with most eligible husbands.

With all the distaff fireworks, it is easy to overlook the three Langhorne brothers, handsome specimens all. The first two, Keene and Harry, were both charming social drinkers, whose drinking, unfortunately, ruined their health. Both men died very young, without children. The youngest son, Buck, was more conventional and restrained. He lived on a farm near Mirador, married a plain, nonsociety girl, and showed little inclination for the pageantry of the Cliveden Set.

He did win election to the Virginia legislature, though, with one of the most laconic campaigns ever conducted in the South. Buck used only two phrases: "To Hell with Prohibition," and "That's a question every man must decide for himself." That was real diplomacy.

Like Amalie Rives, Nancy Astor never forgot her Virginia roots. She went back to Charlottesville nearly every year, taking huge entourages of the English peerage with her. Nancy was at her best in taking the starch out of her guests' ultrastiff collars, as when she served them local treats like hog jowls and turnip greens in place of their habitual *haute cuisine*. They invariably loved it. Nancy was Virginia's biggest booster. During World War II, she always sought out Virginia soldiers and entertained them at Cliveden. "When you behave yourself here," she told them, "say that you are from Virginia. When you get drunk and disorderly, tell people that you are from New York." Nancy's favorite motto was "Once a Virginian, always a Virginian." When she died in 1964, at eighty-five, she was buried with a Confederate flag in her hands.

IX

The Day of the Farmer: The "New South" Millionaires

THE SOLID GOLD PITCHFORK

We reorganized the Democratic party with one plank, and only one plank, that "this is a white man's country and white men must govern it." . . . They [the blacks] said—"The President is our friend. The North is with us. We intend to kill all the white men, take the land, marry the white women, and then these white children will wait on us." . . . Clashes came. . . . It was a fight between barbarism and civilization, between the African and the Caucasian, for mastery.

It was then that "we shot them [the blacks]"; it was then that "we killed them"; it was then that "we stuffed ballot boxes." . . . We had decided to take the government away from men so debased as were the Negroes—I will not say baboons; I have never called them baboons; I believe they are men, but some of them are so near akin to the monkey that scientists are yet looking for the missing link. We saw the evil of giving the ballot to creatures of this kind. . . .

I would lead a mob to lynch any man, black or white, who had ravished a woman, black or white. . . .

I have three daughters, but, so help me God, I had rather find either one of them killed by a tiger or a bear and gather up her bones and bury them, conscious that she had died in the purity of her maidenhood, than have her crawl to me and tell me the horrid story that she had been robbed of the jewel of her womanhood by a black fiend. The wild beast would only obey the instinct of nature, and we would hunt him down and kill him just as soon as possible. . . .

Civilization peels off us, any and all of us who are men, and we revert to the original and savage type whose impulses under any and all such circumstances has always been to "kill! kill! kill!" —*Congressional Record*, January 21, 1907, pp. 1440-1441.

Thus spoke Benjamin Ryan Tillman, not at a Ku Klux Klan rally or before a lynch mob, but on the hallowed floor of the United States Senate. "Pitchfork Ben" Tillman earned his nickname from his threat to stab President Grover Cleveland in the ribs with his farmer's helper. By waging a vicious political campaign, he easily displaced the regal Wade Hampton as the political overlord of South Carolina. The one-eyed Tillman, who served several terms as governor and Senator, was a violently angry man whose hatred was directed at two prime targets— blacks and "aristocrats." Both groups, in his mind, had ruined his fair state. Tillman's constituency was comprised of small farmers, a huge group encompassing moderately prosperous homesteaders as well as shiftless poor white trash. Until the Civil War, the people of the middle-to-lower classes had been a silent majority. Now they found a voice in Pitchfork Ben Tillman. And because of the power vacuum created by the slow death of the Old Guard, Ben became the prototype of the region's New Guard. In the wide-open New South, Pitchfork Ben Tillman became what he hated most—an aristocrat.

Actually, the antebellum Tillmans, despite all Ben's protests to the contrary, were not that far from South Carolina's inner sanctum of old, rich families. The Tillmans came to Virginia from England in 1638, before the Byrds and the Randolphs. Although they were among the very first of the First Families of Virginia, Ben never mentioned this. The dispersion of the FFVs saw the Tillman clan scattered throughout the South. Though none became as rich as members of the Hampton family, most of them were fairly prosperous. The South Carolina branch settled in Edgefield, a farming district in the up-country (as the area inland from the coastal marshes was called). Edgefield was not as fashionable as Charleston, although its cotton fields did support its own plantations, slaves, and other Southern graciousnesses. Ben Tillman's parents had their own mansion—Chester—ninety slaves and over three thousand acres. For their seven sons and three daughters, there were fine clothes and private tutors. One of the boys was even sent to Harvard.

For all its wealth, however, there was something about the up-country that prevented it from assuming aristocratic airs. Perhaps it was the atmosphere of frontier violence that seemed to pervade the place. Edgefield liked to boast that it was the home of Preston Brooks, the man who nearly caned Charles Sumner to death in the Senate, and William B. Travis, defender of the Alamo. Ben Tillman's father and his Harvard-trained lawyer brother, George Dionysius, both had committed murders. George, who had previously wounded another man and beaten up Preston Brooks, too, fled to Nicaragua after his most serious crime and became a mercenary insurrectionist. But he soon became homesick, returned to Edgefield, and served a two-year prison sentence. When he was released in 1860, he was treated like a hero by Edgefield residents, who admired his feistiness. Two other brothers were murdered in rows over alleged insults to family honor. The Mexican War claimed the life of a third brother, while a fourth was killed in the Civil War. A fifth died of typhoid fever.

Ben, born in 1847, was the youngest Tillman son, and in keeping with the fates of his brothers, he did not go through life unscathed. He enjoyed an idyllic plantation childhood playing marbles, swimming, hunting, and eating "possum and 'taters" with his slave playmates. He read extensively and enjoyed the best of local private academies. He, too, might have gone to Harvard, but because of the war, he stayed on the plantation to help his mother. In 1864, when he reached conscription age, an unfortunate event prevented him from enlisting in Confederate military service, that ultimate badge of courage for Southern youth. After an afternoon swim in the family millpond, Ben developed an eye abscess; two months later, his eyeball had to be removed. The empty socket, especially when coupled with his sneering mouth, swarthy skin, and bearish physique, made him a terrifying sight to behold. His life from then on seemed an effort, both to compensate for his lack of war credentials, and to live up to his fierce image.

When the war was over, Ben Tillman married Sallie Starke, an eighteen-year-old girl who was the daughter of a farmer. His mother, whose estate had been much less ravaged than others in the state, gave the couple a wedding gift of four hundred acres, on which Ben built a three-room cabin. Now he became a farmer himself, which was no mean calling in the postbellum period. The war had been a great equalizer—the old planters had gone from riches to rags, while the small farmers, having stayed in rags, were physically no worse off than before and psychologically much better off. Unlike the planters, they had not enjoyed the luxury of slaves. They knew how to work, and hard work was the only way out of the slough of Reconstruction. Virtually every success story in the South after the Civil War involved these "little people" who labored their way to the top. Although relatively speaking, Ben Tillman had begun his career with a silver spoon (or perhaps one should say a silver pitchfork), he was willing to toil as if he had had nothing.

For over a decade Tillman worked endless farmer's hours with no thoughts of politics. Like other farmers, he deferred to the Hampton-Charleston elite that had always dominated the state; the government belonged to the aristocracy, Ben assumed. His first involvement in public affairs of any sort came in 1876, when the Radical Republicans were driven out of the state by the Hamptonites. Ben participated in various riots in which blacks were killed and otherwise frightened away from the polls, events that he found thrilling. When Ben's felon brother, George Dionysius, was elected to the state legislature and to Congress in 1878, Ben was inspired to follow in his footsteps.

Beginning with a lowly position in the Sweetwater Sabre Club (a Klanlike, black-baiting politico-military group that aided the Democrats in winning back the state government), Ben worked his way up the political ladder over the next fourteen years. First, he organized a group known as the Farmers' Association, whose overt purpose was lobbying, although its covert aim, which proved successful, was to instill class consciousness among the farmers. Ben Tillman became known throughout the state as the "Agricultural Moses" (biblical, not Franklin J.).

From the Farmers' Association, Ben moved on to bigger stakes—the Democratic Party. With his colorful speeches, he was the greatest rabble-rouser of his time. His favorite targets were the Reconstruction

scalawags and carpetbaggers, whom he called "blood-sucking vampires"; Wade Hampton, whom he derided as the "grand mogul"; and
blacks, whom he labeled "barbarians." While successfully appealing to
the white masses' vanity by stressing their superiority to blacks, Ben
also fanned their frustrations by blaming the once-rich plantation
whites for monopolizing all political power. And he underscored their
worst fear by constantly harping on the theme of black sexual assaults
on white women. If his speeches didn't win him converts, his bar-
becues—at which he served his listeners unlimited helpings of baby pig
roasted over hickory logs—did. His rallies were like circuses—whole
towns came out to see him. In 1890, Ben was elected governor by a
near-landslide and four years later South Carolina proudly sent him to
the Senate, where he put on a continuous show for the next three
decades.

No sooner had Ben entered office than he began to implement his
number one campaign promise: the disenfranchisement of blacks,
which he considered essential to his own continued hegemony. There
were 100,000 white voters in South Carolina, 60,000 of whom were
Tillmanites; the remainder were Hampton conservatives. But there
were also a possible 120,000 black voters, who could control the state if
they stayed together. Tillman's crusade was to keep them not only
disorganized, but completely excluded. To accomplish this, he devised
an incredibly crafty voter regulation law. Any male South Carolinian
could vote if: he lived in the state for two years, the county for one year,
the voting precinct for four months; if he paid his poll tax six months
before the election; if he could read and write a section of the Constitution or had $300 worth of property; and if he had not been found guilty
of a long list of crimes, including wife beating, adultery, thievery,
housebreaking, arson, and attempted rape.

These crimes were considered "black" ones; "white" crimes, such as
murder and fighting, were not on the list. The residence requirements
were most effective against blacks, who tended to be migratory. Furthermore, so little money was appropriated for black education that few
could expect to pass the literacy test, which was administered by whites
in the most arbitrary manner. Without having to resort to blatantly
unconstitutional ruses like "grandfather" clauses, under which suffrage

was granted to descendants of Confederate Army veterans, Ben Tillman effectively eliminated the black vote. In 1900, fewer than 4,000 of the 120,000 potential black voters went to the polls. Ben's promise that "this is a white man's country and white men must govern it" had been kept, to the letter.

Ben's other enemy, the "aristocrats," were nearly as submissive as the blacks. Most of them were too busy trying to scrape together a living to become involved in politics. Even Wade Hampton bowed out gracefully once he knew the numbers were against him. The only remaining spokesman for the Old Guard was Narciso G. Gonzales, a Columbia newspaperman whose sister had married Wade Hampton's nephew. Gonzales was the son of Ambrosio José Gonzales, the descendant of Spanish grandees and himself a rich Cuban sugar planter who had led the fight for Cuba's independence from Spain. Apparently, A. J. Gonzales liked to fight, since he also served as a Confederate officer in the Civil War. His son, Narciso, abandoned the cry of *"Cuba libre"* for that of "Down with Tillman." Gonzales was outraged at everything about Tillman—his profanity, his bluster, and especially his advocacy of lynching and mob violence. While the old families silently expressed their contempt by excluding the Tillmans from all social events, Gonzales actively voiced his in one scathing article after another on Tillman demagoguery.

Ben Tillman liked to say that Gonzales should be "sued for libel or flayed with a stick." His nephew, Jim Tillman, supported Ben's sentiments toward Gonzales and also had a personal ax to grind with Narciso. A tall man, with long, flowing black hair and a satanic glare, Jim was a man after his uncle's heart, heavily involved in drinking, gambling, cockfighting, and beating blacks. Through Ben's control of the state, he got himself elected lieutenant governor. His major political position was his support of closing down the black schools altogether.

Jim Tillman's long feud with Gonzales had begun when Gonzales branded him "unfit for association with gentlemen" and thereby blackballed him from a social club Jim wanted to join. When Jim ran for the governorship in 1902, Gonzales conducted an all-out campaign against him. Comparing Jim to Franklin J. Moses, Gonzales called him a "proven liar, defaulter, gambler and drunkard." The result was that Jim lost the governorship and Gonzales lost his life. Shortly after the election, in 1903, Gonzales was strolling, unarmed and triumphant, down a shady Columbia street when Jim walked up to him and shot him. Uncle Ben pulled out all the stops to save the nephew who had silenced his most powerful critic. He had Jim's trial transferred to a small backwoods town where the Tillmans were treated as gods. With Ben on prominent display at the defendant's table, a loaded jury accepted Jim's remarkable plea of self-defense, and acquitted him. This was Southern justice at its worst.

The aristocrats, however, finally got their revenge. This occurred in the same year that Gonzales was shot, when Ben's oldest son, Ben, Jr., married Lucy Frances Dugas. Lucy was descended from the Pickenses, Edgefield's oldest and finest family. Lucy's great-great-grandfather was General Andrew Pickens, a major Revolutionary War celebrity in South Carolina; her great-grandfather was Governor Andrew Pickens; and her grandfather was still another governor, Francis Wilkinson Pickens. But her most famous ancestor of all was her mother, the fabled Douschka Olga Nova Franceska Eugenie Dorothea Pickens Dugas. The name came from Russia, where Douschka's father was serving as James Buchanan's Minister. Born in 1858, in the imperial palace in St. Petersburg with the czarina as her godmother, Douschka (Russian for "little darling") was given a christening as regal as her name, attended by representatives from many foreign countries and the entire Russian court.

Douschka was blond, blue-eyed, and altogether perfect. She was the image of her mother, Lucy Holcomb, of Nacogdoches, Texas, supposedly the most beautiful woman in the South. Lucy Holcomb's picture appeared on the Confederate hundred-dollar bill. When Pickens left Russia to serve as South Carolina's governor during the Civil War, the imperial family was broken-hearted, and every subsequent year on her birthday, sent Douschka a package of jewels and other treasures. South Carolina loved the little girl just as much as her Russian friends did. At age three, she was taken to Charleston's Battery, where General Beauregard held her in his arms, placed a match in her hands, and let Douschka light the cannon that fired the first shot on

Fort Sumter. The South Carolina legislature formally invested Douschka with the title "The Child of South Carolina." When Governor Pickens died at the close of the war, none of his slaves wanted to accept their emancipation. They stayed on the Edgefield plantation, loyally taking care of Mrs. Pickens and Douschka.

Other former slaves in the area were far less docile. Things became so tense in the early 1870s that the local blacks, spurred on by scalawags and carpetbaggers, began looting homes and threatened to burn the town. A teenaged Douschka came to the rescue. Donning the then-scarlet robes of the Ku Klux Klan, the blond beauty rode on a white horse at the head of an endless procession of 1,500 Klansmen. During the night the Klan marched in silent anger throughout Edgefield in what was to blacks a spectacle so terrifying that it caused them to flee and to hide in the woods for days. There were never any further expressions of discontent in the area.

As Douschka grew up, she proved immensely able. She took over the Pickenses' cotton plantation, Edgewood, and made it most profitable by putting her ex-slaves on an incentive system. They received not only a salary but also a percentage of Edgewood's earnings. Other local farmers followed Douschka's lead in treating the freed blacks as employees rather than as slaves. Soon the entire state was benefiting from the results. In her leisure time, Douschka became South Carolina's premier horsewoman and fox hunter. She married one of the most eligible men in Georgia, banker-physician Dr. George Dugas, whose father founded the Medical College of Georgia. The couple produced a pretty daughter, Lucy, who was her maternal grandmother's namesake.

Ben Tillman was not at all pleased to learn that the aristocratic Lucy Frances Dugas was to become his daughter-in-law. He was appalled that his constituents would see him as consorting with the enemy. Actually, the Pickenses were just as reluctant to see the two families united as Ben was, though they were more discreet in their opposition.

Venus triumphed over politics, however. Ben, Jr., and Lucy were madly in love and wed in spite of all warnings. But Ben, Sr., never stopped sowing the seeds of discontent, and eventually he got his son to see the light. By 1908, Ben and Lucy separated, and the two families went head to head in a stupendous custody fight over the couple's two young girls, little Douschka and Sarah.

First, the Tillmans spirited the girls away, then the Pickenses took them back. Finally, Pitchfork Ben stepped in. South Carolina had an archaic statute giving a father complete and arbitrary control of his children. One of the Tillman-appointed judges ordered the girls turned over to Ben, Sr., to whom Ben, Jr., had deeded the babies under the law. With Ben, Jr., standing by and gloating, his father became the figurehead custodian. This move, however, was universally unpopular. Mothers around the state were up in arms, Ben, Sr., was condemned as a kidnapper, and endless petitions were circulated to repeal the father-asking law. Ben, Sr., was even hanged in effigy. Eventually, the Pickenses appealed to the state's highest court, which declared the law unconstitutional and returned Lucy's babies to her. Two days after the decision came down, Ben, Sr., had a stroke, which nearly killed him.

Ben recuperated by following various homespun remedies. His favorite lifesaver was an onion diet, consisting of raw onions and tomatoes for breakfast; buttermilk, bread, and eight boiled onions for lunch; and cheese, tomatoes, and more raw onions for dinner. Before long, he was back in the Senate, a little wobbly, but nastier than ever. In Washington, he locked horns with Presidents Roosevelt and Wilson, fighting over issues that tended to involve the power of the Eastern establishment. When Ben wasn't flailing blacks, denouncing women's suffrage as "heresy and leprosy," and pork-barreling jobs for his friends and relatives, he was a true populist. He was a spokesman for the farmer, the laborer, and the common man. Had he spoken just a bit more softly instead of waving his pitchfork, he might have been a force to reckon with on the national political scene. As it was, his most memorable act in the Senate may have been a bloody fist-fight with his fellow Senator from South Carolina. Shades of his countryman, Preston Brooks! Nonetheless, when Tillman died in 1918, he had become the prototype for the New Southern politician—heavy on sound and fury, short on substance, and immensely popular with voters hungry for a good show.

FROM THE PINEY WOODS

While the Tillmans were joining the Pinckneys and the Rutledges on the roster of great South Carolina families, other dynasties were also emerging throughout the South. The roots of these families were embedded in the middle and lower classes. Some of the clans, such as the Bankheads from the piney woods of Jasper, Alabama, elevated themselves through politics, thus following the Tillman pattern. John Hollis Bankhead was the son of a poor South Carolina farmer and Indian fighter who moved the family west toward the more fertile fields of the black belt. After minor heroics in the Civil War, Bankhead methodically worked his way up the political ladder. He began by a tour of duty in the Ku Klux Klan, terrifying blacks from the voting booths. He did so well with the blacks that he advanced to the wardenship of the state penitentiary, and then finally the U.S. Senate, where he sponsored road bills that preceded the interstate highway system. Most of his senatorial work, though, was completely parochial and consisted of securing federal funds for Alabama public works. The state showed its appreciation by sending Bankhead's son, John Hollis II, to his father's Senate seat and by electing his other son, William Brockman Bankhead, to the House, where he eventually became Speaker, though the latter Bankhead was better known for his actress daughter, Tallulah, than for his high office. Only an extremely indulgent father could have allowed this most iconoclastic of all Southern belles to develop her unique personality. Tallulah observed no conventions. She exposed herself in public, held interviews in the toilet, carried on with blacks up in Harlem, took cocaine, and generally lived a life of total decadence. Nonetheless, she was a great performer. And because she limited her debauches to New York and London, and always acted demure—well, almost demure—in Alabama, the folks in Dixie never stopped loving her.

Although politics may have been one way to found a dynasty in the postbellum era, the best way was money. And the best way to make money was by industry, an almost alien Yankee concept in the South prior to the Civil War. Now, with the absence of slave labor, manufacturing took the place of farming as the most profitable occupation. Thus, the greatest families of the New South constituted not an agrarian aristocracy as in the past, but rather an industrial plutocracy. There weren't any white-columned plantations and endless acres for these people, just gloomy factories. The mansions, planters' whites, and other trappings came later, after the money had been made.

Perhaps no family in this plutocracy was more successful than the Candlers of Georgia, who gave the South—and the world—America's most enduring symbol, Coca-Cola. The Candlers came from old Southern stock, similar to the Tillmans—prosperous farm people, a notch below the refined planter class. The family patriarch, Zachariah Candler, had come to North Carolina in 1736. A Cromwellian officer, he had left England because his Irish wife's religion had caused him to be legally disqualified from public office (the intolerant English viewed any relationship with Catholics as guilt by association), and to be ostracized by his anti-Catholic family. In America, Zachariah's son, William, married a girl named Elizabeth Anthony, whose Italian father was a merchant seaman who had been captured by Barbary Coast pirates and sold into slavery in Algiers. Anthony subsequently killed his owner and fled to Virginia, where he became a substantial farmer.

In search of frontier acreage, William and Elizabeth Candler moved to Georgia, where they produced eleven children over the next many years. Daniel, the founder of the most accomplished family line, was on the verge of a fine career in politics when he killed a man in a duel. Unable to cope with his guilty conscience, he exiled himself to his room and fasted to death. Daniel's son, Samuel, moved away to another small town, called Villa Rica, the site of a supposed gold rush which never materialized. The hamlet originally had borne the name Hick Town but such full disclosure discomfited the residents, who sought to elevate things a bit with an Italianate touch. Villa Hicka, the first effort, was still too close to home, and the name Villa Rica was ultimately chosen. Quickly rising to prominence as the town's leading farmer and merchant, and as its representative to the Georgia legislature, Samuel Candler held court in his general store, the center of Villa Rica society. He took a fourteen-year-old bride, who bore him eleven children.

Although the war prevented the Candlers from giving their off-spring an inheritance, they gave them something just as valuable—discipline. While the sons of the great planters languished, the unspoiled Samuel Candler clan went out of Villa Rica to conquer Georgia. Milton Candler became a leading lawyer and was elected to Congress. Another lawyer, John Slaughter Candler, became a judge on the state Supreme Court. A third brother, Warren Akin Candler, became a bishop of the Methodist Church and president of Emory College. A cousin, Allen Candler, served both in Congress and as Georgia's governor. A Tillmanesque character, Allen Candler had lost an eye during the Civil War and played it up for all it was worth. A stunning stump speaker, billed as "the one-eyed plowboy from Pigeon Roost" (his birthplace), Allen charmed the crowds by saying that he had returned from the war with "one wife, one baby, one dollar, and one eye." The pitch worked beautifully.

But it was Asa Griggs Candler who made the family internationally famous. Asa had always dreamed about becoming a physician, but such dreams rarely came true in the postbellum era, when there was barely money for food, much less for higher education. Consequently, Asa settled on becoming a pharmacist. With $1.75 in his pocket, Asa went to Atlanta in 1873 to find an apprenticeship.

At the end of his first long, dusty day in the town which would later become a great metropolis, Asa found a job in a place called Howard's Drugstore. He was provided with living quarters in the upstairs attic, and was assigned the responsibility of being available to fill emergency prescriptions during the night. After a few years, Candler married Lucy Howard, the druggist's daughter, and soon took over the business.

One of the local pharmacists who had rejected Asa as a job applicant was Dr. John Styth Pemberton, who was always looking, in vain, for new patent remedies that would make him rich. One of his elixirs emphasized the kola nut, which had gotten a reputation as an aphrodisiac among blacks. By mixing this nut with coca leaves, which supposedly possessed highly invigorating cocainelike properties, Dr. Pemberton felt that he had come up with the ideal pick-me-up. With a bit of poetic license, he arrived at the name Coca-Cola and test-marketed this syrup at a nearby soda fountain, where it was mixed with carbonated water and served on ice. Despite lavish claims that the drink would cure everything from a hangover to hysteria, business was slow. Dr. Pemberton was said to have sold only fifty dollars' worth of Coca-Cola in its first year, 1886. In 1888, Asa Candler bought out the frustrated doctor, who himself died soon afterward of a digestive disorder later thought to be stomach cancer.

Asa was a born entrepreneur. As a child, he had killed minks in the woods and sold their pelts for a dollar each; now he began playing for higher stakes. His big product was to have been an item called BBB, Botanic Blood Balm; however, once he acquired Coca-Cola, he put all his efforts behind it. Within a decade, Coca-Cola was one of the happiest success stories in the history of American business.

Asa's only real problems came from Southern religious groups who objected to the beverage. Coke was fun; besides, there were many rumors that "the pause that refreshes" did so because the drink contained cocaine. The Bible belt got no kick from cocaine, nor from anything else that smacked of decadence. If Asa, a religious man who had no bad habits anyone was aware of, couldn't silence any opposition by his upright presence, his brother, Bishop Warren Candler, could. Having risen to the top of the Methodist Church by his fire-and-brimstone revival preaching, Warren spoke out against his chosen symbols of depravity. Aside from the regulation vices, Warren hated plays, movies, dancing—and baseball! But not Coca-Cola, to which he gave his influential blessing. Coke, thereupon, became unassailable. In return, Asa donated over $8 million to his brother's Emory College, moved it to Atlanta, and transformed it into one of the South's leading schools.

If Asa was good to Emory, he was even better to Atlanta. The city had been little more than a railroad terminus at the time General Sherman marched through and implemented his own version of urban renewal. From the ashes, Atlanta grew at a phenomenal rate, both because of its central location and because of Coca-Cola. Atlanta's most famous industry was also its most altruistic. When a 1907 real estate panic struck the city, Asa bought a million dollars' worth of homes to stabilize prices. And in a 1914 cotton panic, he built a forty-acre warehouse to store a fortune in bales until prices went back up. Atlanta showed its gratitude by electing him mayor in 1916. Asa's generosity was at its best when it extended to members of his own family, whom he rewarded with profitable Coca-Cola stock and executive positions in the company.

Meek, mild-mannered, and bespectacled, even when he became Atlanta's Croesus, Asa never showed off, never became a conspicuous consumer. To look at him, no one could have guessed that he was anything more than a corner pharmacist. His complete lack of flair was the one salient characteristic that he shared with most of the New South millionaires. One exception to this rule of bland anonymity was Henry Fairchild de Bardeleben, the iron king of Alabama. The dark, mustachioed de Bardeleben looked like a riverboat gambler and, in his financial deals, acted like one as well. He made and lost several fortunes and in the process, he put Birmingham on the map by building its great blast furnaces.

De Bardeleben was the great-grandson of a Hessian mercenary who had come to South Carolina during the Revolution to fight for King George III. Finding the wild woods to his liking, the soldier stayed on in America and settled in the forest. Eventually, his grandchildren moved out of the wilderness to the relative urbanity of Montgomery, Alabama. Henry, born in 1841, began working in a grocery store at the age of ten, when his father died. It was young Henry's good fortune that his mother was a New Yorker. Normally, in the South, this would have been a liability but, because they were so few, Yankess tended to stick together. One of Mrs. de Bardeleben's best friends was Massachusetts-born Daniel Pratt, the wealthiest man in Alabama, who had made his fortune as a cotton gin manufacturer after having come to Savannah, penniless, as a journeyman carpenter. His gin works in Prattville were the largest in the world. As a favor to Mrs. de Bardeleben, Pratt took Henry to live with him, and just as Asa Candler married his employer's daughter, Henry de Bardeleben in 1860 married Ellen Pratt and became superintendent of his father-in-law's ginnery.

With Pratt capital, Henry became involved in coal mining, which brought out all the backwoodsman in his genes. He once said, "I'd rather be out in the woods on the back of a fox-trotting mule with a good seam of coal at my feet than be President of the United States. There's nothing like taking a piece of land, all rock and woods—ground not fit to feed a goat on—and turning it into a settlement of men and women; making pay rolls; bringing the railroad in; starting things going. . . . Nothing like boring a hillside through and turning over a mountain! That's what money's for!" Henry turned his pioneer vision into numerous realities. Never afraid to take risks, he tried one iron venture after another, most of which worked. He gambled heavily, won big, and coined the phrase "life is a glorified crap game." When de Bardeleben died in 1910, Alabama enshrined him as a hero symbolizing financial success.

Less flamboyant, but even more successful than de Bardeleben, were the Cones of Greensboro, North Carolina, the world's largest denim manufacturers. Herman Cone (né Kahn) was born in Bavaria in 1828 and had come to America as an itinerant peddler in the South. He sold enough wares to trade his pushcart in for a country grocery store in Jonesboro, Tennessee, where he married another German Jew, Helen Guggenheimer, whose father was also a merchant. The couple had thirteen children. After the Civil War, the Cones moved to Baltimore and entered the wholesale cigar and grocery business. Many of their customers were the company stores of Southern cotton mill villages. Because of the shortage of cash, the Cones accepted cotton goods from the mills to settle the accounts. Gradually as they realized how disorganized the small mills were and how ineptly they were managed, they became involved in the cotton business themselves, built their own mills in the water-power belt of the Carolina Piedmont, and became multimillionaires.

While the Cone sons worked diligently at the business, two of the daughters more than compensated for the family's colorlessness. Claribel Cone, to her family's dismay, was not the marrying kind; she wanted to be a doctor. Fortunately for her ambitions, she graduated first in her class from Baltimore's Women's Medical College and did advanced studies at Johns Hopkins. When Gertrude Stein, one of Claribel's fellow students and best friends, went to Paris at the turn of the century, Claribel followed, and Claribel's devoted sister Etta in turn followed her. After Alice B. Toklas, Claribel and Etta were two of

Gertrude's closest friends. The four women, who spent endless hours together, made an imposing impression on the boulevards. The Cones were both stately and portly. They dressed in exotic Moroccan djellabas, Indian shawls, and black Victorian dresses adorned with Renaissance jewelry. The foursome eventually broke up (Gertrude wanted Alice more than anyone else) but they all remained friends. Etta loyally typed Gertrude's most famous manuscript, *Three Lives,* and Gertrude in turn introduced the sisters to modern art. They were intimates of Picasso and Matisse, and became two of the most influential art patrons on the Continent. Claribel loved art so much that she abandoned her promising medical career in favor of full-time art collecting. The sisters' adjoining apartments in Baltimore, which served as home between trips, constituted one of America's greatest private collections, the very best of the modern French masters. Claribel died of pneumonia in 1929 at Lausanne, but Etta kept right on traveling and collecting for another twenty years until her death at the Cone mountain estate in Blowing Rock, North Carolina.

THE DUKES OF DURHAM

Though the Cones may be North Carolina's leading Jewish family, many other Jewish Carolinians are also products of the Southern Industrial Revolution. The turn of the century saw a large influx of East European Jews to all parts of the eastern seaboard. To North Carolina came numerous Polish and Russian cigarette rollers to work for the Dukes of Durham, a family that, more than any other, was responsible for the phenomenal growth of the South's most progressive state. Always referred to as "the valley of humility between two mountains of conceit" (Virginia and South Carolina), North Carolina had historically been a state of small farmers, not great planters. But the day of the small farmer had finally come and no one seized the moment better than the Dukes.

The Dukes had been a part of that mass of slaveless farmers of English ancestry who had been in America since the late 1600s. They were the unlucky ones, unable to amass land. Their hard work had only gotten them more hard work, and no one worked harder than Washington Duke (1820–1905) on his small farm outside the tiny town of Durham, North Carolina. He didn't go to school, he never traveled, he didn't philander, he didn't sow wild oats—he just tilled his fields. Washington's only recreation was his local Methodist congregation, whose praise-the-Lord sermons and church suppers added spice to an otherwise monotonous existence. When the secession controversy broke out, Wash Duke was all for the Union. Not owning slaves themselves, he and his fellow subsistence farmers had nothing in common with the lords of Natchez, except for a Southern drawl. Nonetheless, swept up by the patriotic call to arms, Wash Duke fought for his region.

In 1865, Wash, then forty-five, was captured by Union troops and imprisoned until Lee's surrender. When he was released, he traded his Confederate money for a fifty cent coin, found an abandoned wagon and two discarded blind mules, and trudged back to Durham to make his fortune. There he was aided by his three young sons—Brodie Leonidas, Benjamin Newton, and James Buchanan—whose mother had died when they were young. The boys knew nothing but long hours and backbreaking chores. Loading up their tobacco—the only crop they had left—on the wagon, the family traveled about the rolling hills and pine barrens. To make the tobacco more salable, they prepared it for smoking and packed it in burlap bags with the label, "Pro Bono Publico."

Soon, "Pro Bono Meo" appeared to be a more suitable appellation. A good smoke was one of the few luxuries the South had left, and the Dukes' tobacco business took off. By the 1870s, they had a large factory in Durham and more money than they knew what to do with. With no idea about how to consume their proceeds, the frugal Dukes plowed the cash back into the business. Their one major competitor was Bull Durham, the world's largest smoking tobacco manufacturer. From its factory foghorn, specially designed to sound like a bull's bellow, to its trademark—the fierce Durham Bull, which appeared on posters throughout the world, including the pyramids at Giza—the Bull, as their competitor was known, was intimidating.

The Dukes knew they couldn't beat the Bull in the pipe tobacco market, so they shifted their energies to cigarettes. In the 1880s, the cigarette was an effete European item used only in America by globe-trotting cosmopolites. The Dukes set out to change all that, using advertising as their tool. Their first great discovery was that sex sells. A beautiful French actress named Madame Rhea, who was stopping shows in an Atlanta music hall, was signed up to appear in an ad in the *Atlanta Constitution.* The lithograph showed her holding a pack of Duke cigarettes and was captioned "Atlanta's Favorite." In terms of sales results, the charm of Madame Rhea turned out to be more effective than the alarm of the Durham Bull. The Dukes followed this up by inserting picture cards of chorines and other belles in cigarette packages, which promptly became collectors' items. Further, a smashing redhead was hired as the firm's first female traveling salesperson. Within a few short years, the whole nation had caught cigarette fever. The hand rollers were replaced by a machine that made upward of a quarter-million cigarettes a day. Bull Durham had been critically gored.

The Dukes relished the rewards of monetary success. Their cigarettes were sold all over the world, and they became the fulcrum of the great "tobacco trust" that monopolized the smoking industry until the government broke it up in 1911. Washington Duke retired from the firm and quietly enjoyed his old age, traveling about Europe, signing in at grand hotels as Washington, Duke of Durham. The misplaced comma went a long way—he was treated like royalty, despite his home-spun ways. Wash's son Ben took after his father. True to the colorless prototype of the Southern millionaire, Ben spent all his time at work, at church, with his family, and in philanthropy, culminating in the creation of Duke University. Ben married the daughter of the mayor of Durham, built a big Victorian house in Durham, and led a settled life. Not so his brothers, Brodie Duke and James B. (Buck) Duke. Just as sex had been their blessing in business, after hours it was their curse.

Brodie had begun his manhood auspiciously enough, wedding the daughter of a local Presbyterian minister. When she died in 1888, Brodie quickly remarried, this time an Alabama girl. The couple separated after the new Mrs. Duke felt the family fortune could be more profitably consumed in the oasis of Southern California than in Durham, where Brodie was king. The 1904 divorce drove the ruggedly bearded Brodie both to drink and into the consoling arms of a host of rapacious women. He feebly sought to excuse the alcohol as a health aid, claiming that the combination of liquor and milk was good for his ailing stomach. As for the women, Brodie made no excuses at all.

Of all the distressing damsels who came to Brodie's side, the craftiest of the lot was Alice Webb, whom Brodie, then fifty-eight, married in New York. Brodie and Alice staggered to the altar in December 1904, following a two-week debauch which included one of Alice's friends named Agnes Des Plaines, as well as a doctor, a nurse, and a masseur. The orgy of drink and drugs took place at a hotel in uptown Manhattan on the edge of Harlem. When word of Brodie's activities reached the folks in straitlaced Durham, they promptly proceeded to lace the offender up in a straitjacket and have him declared insane.

The entire affair grew even more embarrassing after the background of Brodie's bride became known. Alice, whose age was variously estimated from thirty-two to fifty, and whose most prominent features were her expensive clothes and "determined jaw," described herself as a businesswoman. Others did, too, but not in the kind of business discussed in polite society. Although Alice claimed to be a relative of the Vanderbilts, it turned out that she had been involved in numerous "marriages" around the country in which she claimed to be related to a first family in the particular city in question. The *New York Times* quoted law enforcement authorities as saying:

There are in this city cliques of women who are making it a business to set pitfalls for wealthy men susceptible of the kind of allurements they know to place in their way; that these women maintain furnished flats in different parts of the city to receive their victims when these have fallen into their meshes. Drugs or intoxicants are stated to be employed until, by predatory methods, all the money obtainable has been acquired. —*New York Times,* January 10, 1905.

Alice fit the mold. She had a respectable veneer and presented herself as the president and secretary-treasurer of the Texas-Cuba Tobacco Company of Nacogdoches, Texas. Apparently, she made Brodie an offer on unseen tobacco lands that he just couldn't refuse, as long as Alice was part of the bargain. When he was carted away, Alice was found to have nearly $20,000 he had given her. Brodie had another

$40,000 in cash in his pockets. Despite these revelations, however, Brodie was still madly in love. He mooned away for Alice first in the psychopathic ward of Bellevue Hospital and then in a private sanitarium in Queens, from which his lawyers finally had him released by a writ of habeas corpus.

Upon his release, Brodie was sobered up by the news that arrest warrants had just come in from Nacogdoches for Alice, where she had become notorious as the "Tobacco Queen" and was being charged with large-scale swindling. Brodie fell out of love as quickly as he had fallen in. Now he went along with his family's plans to have the marriage annulled. He realized that Alice and her friends had embarked upon their orgy to lure a stoned-drunk innocent to the altar. Further damaging evidence came from one of Alice's former "husbands," George Hopkinson, with whom Alice had vainly tried to prove a marriage contract. Hopkinson knew Alice but hotly denied any relations with her other than those that transpired when they met, as he claimed, in a New York bordello. The last outrage, as far as the Dukes were concerned, were numerous affidavits attesting to Alice's involvement with "Polo Jim," an unsavory black racetrack character.

Stripped of Brodie's support, Alice was arrested on the Texas charges and imprisoned in the Manhattan Tombs for nearly three weeks. Meanwhile, a new judgment came in from Arkansas, holding Alice liable for $10,000 of overdue notes. Desperately in need of alimony, she sued Brodie for separation on grounds of abandonment. But poor Alice was no match for the phalanx of Duke Wall Street lawyers. Brodie conveyed all his property to trustees and was placed on an allowance of a hundred dollars a month. The divorce was granted with little trouble. Alice was crushed in her alimony suit and left New York empty-handed. The last that was heard of her was a year later in Chicago, where she was again being held in jail, without bail, for defrauding a hotel with seventy-five dollars' worth of bad checks, drawn on a bank in Nacogdoches.

Brodie, on the other hand, did not disappear. In 1910, at sixty-two, he again went to the altar, knowingly and willingly, with a twenty-eight-year-old Durham beauty named Wylanta Rochelle. The couple eloped to Washington, D.C., where the first pastor they approached refused to perform the ceremony. They moved onward to Camden, New Jersey, where they found a more tractable preacher and took the vows that lasted until Brodie's death in 1919. Neither of his brothers attended his funeral, having never forgiven him for being such an unashamed bon vivant.

Actually, brother Buck, for all his attempts at discretion, had no right to be so judgmental of Brodie. His own divorce made as many headlines as Brodie's, though, in contrast to his brother, he was sober through it all. Buck was indeed a rather stolid character. A brawny farm boy, he had few of Brodie's vices. When he went to New York in 1884 to establish the Duke office, which evolved into the enormous American Tobacco Company, he stayed far away from the brothels and the bright lights of the Bowery, then the entertainment district. His own recreation after a twelve-hour working day was to stroll through the streets at night, counting discarded cigarette packs and exulting that most of them were Duke products. And his only real extravagances were buying horses and custom-made shoes to fit his pigeon-toed feet.

Despite Buck's unromantic bent, his immense financial power gave him enormous appeal. (The family was said to be worth well over $100 million.) In 1893, he fell under the spell of another designing woman, though a more subtle one than Alice Webb. This was a voluptuous blonde named Mrs. Lillian Fletcher McCredy. Lillian had grown up in Camden, New Jersey, and had aspired to become a concert singer in New York. Instead, she became a socialite-equestrienne and married a rich coffee broker, who later divorced her on grounds of adultery. Lillian's checkered past didn't faze Buck. She became his mistress, lavishly kept in a townhouse off Central Park, while Buck pretended to live in a hotel. The charade lasted a decade, until Buck's upright father and his brother Ben gave him some strong hints about marriage. Always the dutiful son, Duke followed family policy and married Lillian in late 1904.

What Buck didn't know was that Lillian had been much less than honorable herself. She had been conducting a second affair with "Major" Frank Huntoon, a sixty-six-year-old bachelor who was in the mineral water business. This old soldier was still quite agile, climbing in and out of the windows of the Duke townhouse while Buck was away. She and Huntoon had even spent her wedding's eve together, neither willing to give the other up, and during the honeymoon, they exchanged cryptic love notes, telegrams, and personals placed in the *Paris Herald Tribune,* such as this item from the major:

Oh, memories that bless and burn! This separation is killing. Please don't wear low necked dresses. Shall enjoy your house until octopus returns, when that pleasure shall cease.   —*New York Times,* March 22, 1906.

Buck didn't like being called "octopus," nor did he like being cuckolded. Suspicious from the outset, he hired a staff of detectives to trail his wife, and they did so on trolleys, in cabs, and even on bicycles. Lillian and Huntoon were particularly fond of romantic drives to Coney Island, as well as cozy champagne evenings in Buck's bedroom while he was away. To spice up their rendezvous, Huntoon would often arrive with a half-dozen nightgowns for Lillian to model for him. According to Buck's spying maid, Lillian vowed that Buck himself would never be given the pleasure of seeing her in these outfits. To lay a further trap for Lillian, Buck took another trip, alone, to England. The moment after Lillian waved bon voyage, she dashed to a hotel near the docks for an afternoon tryst with the major.

All this came out in Buck's divorce action in 1906 barely a year after the nuptials. Given the aggravation caused by the romantic escapades of Brodie and Buck, poor Washington Duke had passed away in 1905 at the age of eighty-four. Intent on making Wash proud of him, even if posthumously, Buck Duke put his entire legal armada into the divorce case. Lillian, now forty to Buck's forty-nine, tried to counter with accusations about a wretched honeymoon on which, she alleged, Buck "in a most inhuman fashion, insisted and compelled [her] to take and continue long journeys in an open vehicle, exposed to rain, hail and snow, and cold, over a large part of Italy and France, travelling every day, depriving [her] of sleep, exposing her to hunger, and that [he] caused her to lose twenty pounds in weight, affected her with pain and sleeplessness, and wrecked her nerves and physical health." Adding insult to injury, Lillian further claimed that Buck kicked her out of bed, shook her, choked her, beat her with a crutch, and had his housekeeper in his New Jersey estate deprive her of both vegetables and flowers. That was no way for a Southern gentleman to treat a lady.

The court was unmoved and Buck got his divorce. Lillian got no alimony, and she lost Major Huntoon to boot. Furthermore, an unscrupulous Wall Street wizard named "Colonel" Lindsey stripped her of the small fortune in cash and jewels Buck had given her during their marriage. She became a music teacher and died a pauper. Where Buck was concerned, the family didn't want to take any more chances. They hustled up a romance with a thirty-five-year-old Atlanta beauty named Nanaline Holt Inman. The widow of a cotton merchant, Nanaline's lean, delicate, aristocratic good looks were somewhat belied by the fact that her mother was a seamstress in Macon, Georgia. Nonetheless, she looked and acted refined, which was enough for Benjamin Duke, who had met Nanaline at a North Carolina mountain resort and who seemed to act as a parent for both Brodie and Buck. Buck and Nanaline wed in 1906. As a love nest, he built her a grand $2-million mansion on Fifth Avenue (now the site of New York University's Institute of Fine Arts).

With Buck taken care of, it was now Ben's turn to sing the altar blues. Buck had urged Ben to build his own Fifth Avenue palazzo. Durham, Buck felt, was beneath the dignity of a tobacco titan. Reluctantly, Ben followed suit and awkwardly released his children, Angier and Mary, into the fast life of Northern society. But the pace was too fast, and the Dukes were soon devoured, in a string of romantic alliances, by a branch of the Philadelphia Biddle family. Although the Biddles were not wealthy, they did have a good deal of polish, and the Bible school they ran was appealing to the pious Ben.

In 1915, Angier Duke, thirty-one, wed Cordelia Biddle, sixteen, while Mary Duke, twenty-eight, wed Anthony J. Drexel Biddle, nineteen, who had just graduated from prep school at St. Paul's. Eventually, both marriages ended in divorce. Angier Duke, who at one time had left tobacco for the delicatessen business, seemed to succumb to the habits of his Uncle Brodie. Giving up the delicatessens, he settled into a Gatsby-like existence. He was involved in a number of auto wrecks in his Rolls-Royces, along with other sporting mishaps, including the loss of his hand in a gun accident. In 1923, Angier drowned at a Greenwich yacht club, following one of his many evenings of roaring twenties frivolity.

New York having proved a morass of bad publicity, Ben and Buck Duke concentrated the efforts of their later years on North Carolina. The state had been nothing but good to them, and the Dukes felt it only right to show their appreciation. After all, North Carolina had stood for centuries in the shadow of the Southern aristocracy. Now the Dukes, for all their foibles, were one of the South's first families. The Old South's great dynasties had given the nation brilliant leadership, and gracious living; the New South Dukes were merely providing titillating scandal, along with a product whose effects on health were already being questioned.

Wanting to leave the South something more than a cloud of cigarette smoke, the Dukes lavished their fortune on their home state. They built a great electric power system; they built churches; they built hospitals; they built schools for black and white. In all, their $40-million Duke endowment helped make North Carolina the most progressive state in the South. Their greatest philanthropy, of course, was the university that bore their name. Just as in the case of the Candlers and Emory, and the Vanderbilts and Vanderbilt, the Dukes took a small Methodist college, Trinity, in Durham, North Carolina, and transformed it into a great national university. On their trips to England, the Dukes had been impressed with the colleges of Oxford and Cambridge, and decided to build their university in the Oxbridge image. The result was a splendid Gothic-Tudor assemblage of quadrangles, spires, and luxuriant gardens that many consider America's most beautiful school. Moreover, they used their money wisely to lure a high-quality faculty that matched the setting. Although a hostile press lampooned the Dukes for trying to create overnight the equivalent of a stage set for a grand university, the ends justified the means, and Duke University quickly became an important educational center.

Buck himself had little schooling, but that hardly impeded his success. Although he wasn't quite sure what purpose his university would serve, he rationalized its utility thus: "I don't believe that a college education does a man much good in business, except for the personal satisfaction it gives him. But when you have a great community growing like the Carolinas, you've got to have five kinds of leaders whose minds are trained. The first is preachers, the second is teachers, the third is lawyers, the fourth is chemists and engineers, and the fifth is doctors." Duke University admirably filled Buck's prescription.

Buck Duke died in 1925, shortly after being sued for support a final time by his bitter former wife, Lillian (who herself died of a cerebral hemorrhage two weeks after Buck passed away); Ben died in 1929. Both were interred in lifelike marble sarcophagi in the Canterbury-like Duke University cathedral, in the same fashion as the archbishops of the cathedral's English counterpart. Yet, outside the cathedral is a uniquely North Carolina touch—a huge bronze statue of Buck Duke, heartily brandishing a cane in one hand, and a cigar in the other. This grand old man was indeed the Duke of Durham—a fact he didn't want future generations to forget.

X

Dynasts and Decadents

They were having a "pig pickin'." Fastidious outlanders might call such
an affair a barbecue, but this was no mere matter of sirloin and charcoal.
Whole pigs were roasted on spits over hickory wood. Then the meat
and the crackling skin were finely chopped and mixed with vinegar and
spices. The resulting concoction, known simply as "barbecue," is to
North Carolina gastronomy what foie gras is to that of Perigord. The
barbecue was served to a ravenous crowd, along with such comple-
ments as collard greens cooked in pork fat. The greasy residue of vegeta-
ble juices was known as "pot liquor" and here considered ambrosial.
Then there were deep-fried sticks of corn meal, or "hush puppies,"
supposedly so scrumptious that they kept the hounds at bay. Other
parts of the pig were devoured as well, most notably the small intes-
tines, or chitterlings. When fried, these "chitlins" were considered the
greatest of delicacies. Finally, with their fingers, the guests would pick
the carcass clean, hence the name of the feast.

This particular extravaganza was not occasioned by a Baptist
Church supper or a 4-H Club harvest celebration. Tonight, July 5,
1932, the barbecue wasn't being washed down by iced tea, but by an
array of alcohol ranging from corn liquor to champagne. And the pig

was being picked, not in some fellowship hall, but at Reynolda, one of the great Southern estates of one of the greatest Southern families, the Reynoldses of Winston-Salem, North Carolina.

By any standards, the estate was grandiose. The sprawling white million-dollar mansion, two stories high and with endless wings, sat on six hundred rolling landscaped acres. In addition to a private landing strip, golf course, extensive stables, and twenty-acre artificial lake, Reynolda had its own post office, general store, and Presbyterian Church. No convenience, including God, had been overlooked. The temporal lord of this realm and host of the evening was the twenty-year-old Zachary Smith Reynolds, international bon vivant, globe-circling aviator, and one of two male heirs to the Camel cigarette fortune, worth well over $100 million.

The young tycoon tried his best to look the part, but he came across more as a caricature of Fitzgerald's gilded youths. Awkward, overgrown (well over six feet and two hundred pounds), and with a hush-puppy drawl, Smith Reynolds put too much pomade on his dark hair and seemed to be bursting out of his custom-tailored suits. Still, along with his older brother, Dick, he had won the nation's attention as the most prodigal of Southern sons, two of the most spoiled children in American history.

Holding court with Smith was his recent and second wife, Elspeth Holman, twenty-six, who was not the typical rich, sweet Southern belle one would expect to be married to a tobacco heir. Smith's first wife, Anne Cannon, heiress to the vast towel empire, had met those criteria. She and Smith had married as teenagers. It was a storybook love affair, but it didn't work. Libby Holman, on the other hand, was the ideal fantasy mate for the boy who had everything. She was sexy, sultry, smart, and pure show business, the queen of Broadway torch singers. During her musical career in New York, she had popularized such numbers as "Body and Soul" and "Moanin' Low," and had come to epitomize their unvarnished sensuality.

Like all Smith Reynolds's parties, the pig pickin' was a smash. The dozens of guests, mostly landed Southern youth, were blissfully devoid of Depression concerns. They swam in the lake, cavorted in the woods, gourmandized on the barbecue, and drank themselves into oblivion.

Herself a New Yorker by way of Cincinnati, Libby Holman Reynolds tried her best to adapt her palate and drinking capacity to the expansive Southern style. After taking the laurels in several corn-liquor drinking contests, the besotted young woman excused herself to return to the great house. Somewhat later a shot rang out; the host also had left the party—forever. Z. Smith Reynolds, a young man with everything to live for, was found on his sunporch with a bullet in his head. Speculation as to suicide quickly yielded to assertions of premeditation, and the South's virulent xenophobia was unleashed upon the exotic outlander, Libby. A month after the shooting, Libby was indicted for her husband's murder. Her alleged accomplice was Albert Walker, Smith Reynolds's inseparable boyhood friend. The motive? Greed.

Smith's brother Dick, twenty-six, who himself had just been released from a prison term for manslaughter, was cruising off Africa on his yacht. He didn't make it home for the funeral, but he did arrive for the ensuing fireworks over who killed Smith Reynolds and who would inherit his vast estate. The august Reynoldses wanted it. So did the august Cannons. And so did Libby Holman. The resulting free-for-all was a great family feud, a high-class Hatfields versus McCoys. Gone were Southern gentility and dynastic reverence—a fortune was involved.

Families of the industrial New South would fight over fortunes the way families of the Old South fought over honor. Agrarian antebellum Dixie possessed enough frontier wealth to satisfy all ambitious comers. Theirs was an aristocracy of leisure, with an abundance of time for chivalric concerns. Now the ruthless competition of capitalism was the order of the day, and the highest honor was that of having the largest net worth. Money was everything, an end justifying all means. And the means had grown much more complex. In a modern age where great riches came from manufacturing rather than agriculture, the duel had evolved into the lawsuit.

The Reynolds debacle was the first of two great Southern murder-scandals that would jolt the region in the long, hot summer of 1932. The one in Natchez a month later involved Jane Surget Merrill, a princess of the Old South. This one in Winston-Salem spotlighted a prince of the New South. The fact that one was an affair of recluses and goats, and the other of celebrities and money, was emblematic of the relative positions of the two societies.

With the old order in decay, the post-Reconstruction New South came to be dominated, socially and economically, by an order composed of families that had previously been strictly middle class—shopkeepers, independent farmers, small-time lawyers, and the like. These people, accustomed to hard work, were quick to fill the power vacuum created by the dispossessed, traumatized planter class unaccustomed and averse to toil.

No family better exemplifies this nobility sprung from the bourgeoisie than the Reynoldses. This family, however, was much less opportunistic than merely plodding. The land grabs that had created so many of the first First Families were no longer possible; consequently, those who became the second set of leading families usually achieved their status through toil rather than artifice. As such, the Reynolds success story is rather undramatic, much less striking than the up-from-nothing saga of their fellow tobacco titans, the Dukes. Still, the background of the Reynolds fortune is typical of the New South plutocracy. The drama is provided by the heirs.

EMPIRE BUILDING

The Reynoldses sprang from a place called No Business Mountain, in Patrick County, Virginia, the picturesque hill country along the North Carolina border. The family had originally come to the area from Pennsylvania, around the time of the American Revolution, as part of a great wave of Pennsylvania emigrants, of the hearty stock known as Scotch-Irish. These people were accustomed to an uprooted life. Their name derives from the Lowland Scots, Presbyterians who settled in Northern Ireland in the early 1600s at the behest of the intolerant James I, son of Mary Queen of Scots. James hoped that they would help to "civilize" the untamed Irish, and the repercussions of that experiment are still being felt in Ireland today.

The transplanted Scots thrived for a century until the British Parliament gave them a double-edged coup de grace. The 1699 Woolens Act limited the export of Irish wool to England and Wales alone. In addition to this financial blow, the 1704 Test Act was a gross abridgment of the Presbyterians' civil and religious rights. After the great famine of 1727, all roads seemed to lead to America, and to the unfettered freedoms of Pennsylvania in particular. As the Quaker state grew oversaturated and overpriced, thousands of Scots found their way down the Great Wagon Road through the Blue Ridge Mountains to the back country of Virginia and North Carolina. Accustomed to the rough frontier life of Pennsylvania, they thrived in their new Southern setting.

Like their fellow clansmen, the Reynoldses did not become great planters, but were small farmers who cultivated their soil themselves. Slavery didn't fit the Scottish ethos of self-reliance. Besides which the semimountainous terrain was a far cry from the black belt and did not support planting on a grand scale. Nevertheless, by the time of the outbreak of the Civil War, the Reynoldses had built a modestly prosperous tobacco business.

Hardin Reynolds (1810–1882), father of the family's first tycoon, Richard Joshua Reynolds, had been so chagrined at the low prices paid for raw tobacco and by the early realization that the manufacturer, not the grower, was making all the money, that, around 1830, he talked his own father into the joys of vertical integration. Consequently, the Reynoldses bought some licorice, some equipment, and even a few slaves, and began making their own chewing tobacco. The armchair luxury of chewing and spitting was one of the great Southern pastimes, and the Reynoldses enjoyed a wide market for their product.

Hardin and his brother David would make long wagon trips to Georgia, South Carolina, and Alabama, receiving cash for their tobacco or exchanging it for sugar, cotton, rice, bacon, even Madeira, which they sold in a makeshift little store near the Patrick County courthouse. His brother's death in 1836, followed by that of his father a year later, left Hardin the sole heir to the growing business. Finding that he desperately needed assistance, Hardin in 1843 took a bride from neighboring Stokes County, North Carolina. His new wife, a farmer's daughter named Nancy Jane Cox, provided him with all the help he could ever need—sixteen children, including two sets of twins, over the period from 1844 to 1870.

This formidable matriarch, who lived to be seventy-nine, had probably inherited her gusto from her grandfather, Joshua Cox, who had come to America as an English captain in the French and Indian War. Cox was captured by the Indians, who were so impressed by his bearing and six-foot-six-inch frame that they decided to make him an honorary member of the tribe. Soon escaping by swimming many miles down the Susquehanna River, the massive soldier settled in North Carolina. Captain Cox won further acclaim for his heroics during the American Revolution against his former fellow Tories. So robust was the captain that he was said to have lived into the ripest old age without ever losing a tooth, which was not easy in those prefluoride times.

As Hardin Reynolds's family was growing, so was his slave force, which rose from nine in 1840 to fifty-nine in 1860, Scottish self-reliance notwithstanding. Possessing several thousand acres, albeit many rocky ones, Hardin, at the beginning of the Civil War, stood near the threshold of the planter class. His home, which began as a two-room brick cabin, had grown to a respectable six chambers, plus an outside kitchen. It had even been modernized in the fashionable Greek Revival style, with both Doric and Ionic columns framing the front entry. It had also acquired the more respectable name Rock Spring Plantation. Nor was the interior any more that of a pioneer dwelling. The furnishings included an Empire rosewood piano from Baltimore—which Hardin reputedly acquired for Nancy in exchange for selling a treasured but rambunctious slave, who was part of her dowry—and a large Empire mahogany bed, where all sixteen of the children were delivered.

The Civil War proved only a minor setback to the enterprising Captain Reynolds. (He acquired the title by dint of his financial assistance in equipping the county militia during the hostilities.) After Emancipation, Reynolds converted nearly all of his freed slaves, and many of those of his neighbors, into his tenant farmers. In return for one-half the tobacco crop, Reynolds furnished lodging, tools, mules, and food. He was a strict accountant, and his carefully overseen profits gradually multiplied from the increasing sales of manufactured chewing tobacco and from his general store, whose lines of credit undoubtedly kept his tenants continually beholden to him and thus hard at work.

All of Hardin's children, and later their spouses, assisted in some way with the business, a prime example of the virtues of family unity. Yet none of them burnished the family name as well as did Richard Joshua, or R.J., who was born in 1850. R.J., who enjoyed conveying the misimpression that he had risen to international prominence from the darkest heart of the piney woods, always boasted that he began toiling as a tobacco processor at the tender age of seven. That his major factory contact at that time consisted of smuggling a bit of licorice for his own use is more likely the case, but it is true that in his teens his father put him on the road peddling chewing tobacco. A most resourceful trader, R.J. outhustled his competitors by traveling on foot to the most desolate areas that other salesmen would never bother with. He also would accept virtually anything as a medium of exchange, from rare antiques to groundhog hides. His loads of goods usually exceeded in value what he would have normally gotten in cash, if any of his backwoods customers had had cash to give.

R.J.'s bartering was interrupted at eighteen by an education, which his father bestowed on all of his children, both male and female. R.J. was sent to nearby Emory and Henry College, where he excelled at arithmetic but did wretchedly in everything else (possibly because of a visual disability). He fared better at Bryant and Stratton Business College in Baltimore, where he could calculate away to his heart's content, unfettered by courses in literature and the other liberal arts. In later life, R.J. was lampooned as a functional illiterate. He laughed right along, for this only enhanced his cracker mystique.

While in Baltimore, R.J. continued to work for his father, drumming up orders in his spare time and learning that the cities as well as the backwoods were full of chewers and spitters. He also became increasingly aware that the market for tobacco products was unlimited. Consequently, he returned to the Rock Spring Plantation in 1876 and talked his father into staking him to a new operation sixty miles south in Winston-Salem, North Carolina. The town had been founded by the Scotch-Irish and the equally industrious Moravians, who had also come from Pennsylvania. A burgeoning metropolis, it was more central to power and transportation, and closer to a better grade of tobacco than that grown at home in Virginia. R.J.'s first factory, in a small wooden building, could produce a modest 150,000 pounds of chewing tobacco a year, which he sold largely to his Baltimore contacts.

The business grew so quickly that by 1880 R.J. called upon his brother William Neal Reynolds to move down to Winston-Salem to assist him. After their father died in 1882, the rest of the family refocused their efforts on R.J.'s prospering venture. Of course, he welcomed them all with fraternal zeal; family came first. One of R.J.'s brothers, Harbour, who was a likable lush, moved to Winston and started manufacturing, with R.J.'s help, a brand called Red Elephant, after Harbour's favorite whiskey. Red Elephant was advertised as having one thousand "spits to the chew," which made it the undisputed top of the Reynolds line. By 1887, the Reynoldses had eighty-six different brands, something for every spitter, which were being sold throughout the nation.

The momentum never ceased. A new six-story factory was built, mass advertising was begun, incentives were provided for new rail links to Winston-Salem, scientific flavoring methods made each spit sweeter, and a new smoking line, Prince Albert, became a monumental success. By 1900 R. J. Reynolds Tobacco Company was selling nearly six million pounds of tobacco a year, and the Reynolds family was one of the richest in the South.

R.J. was a bear of a man, well over six feet tall and seemingly as broad. His full head of hair, and even fuller mustache and luxuriant goatee, gave him a mountain-man appearance that definitely signaled an empathy with his backwoods clientele. Aside from a passion for thoroughbreds, tobacco and family were his entire life. When he finally took time out to marry at the late age of fifty-four, he kept the match in the family as well, wedding in 1905 his twenty-five-year-old cousin, Mary Katherine Smith, whose grandmother and R.J.'s mother were sisters.

R.J. seems to have been fixated on Mary Katherine from her early childhood. Having boasted that he would marry her when she grew up, R.J., quite characteristically, fulfilled his intentions. Always pragmatic, even in romance, the fatherly R.J. courted his cousin, not with hearts and flowers, but by having fresh milk delivered to her daily. Whether Mary Katherine's heart was won by R.J.'s milk, or by his millions, is a matter of speculation. In any event, the consanguinity that was a curse to Duncan Minor and Jennie Merrill was never an obstacle here.

Never one to tarry, R.J. fathered four children, two boys, two girls, in the six years following his wedding. His dynastic obligations satisfied, he returned his fullest attention to the business, leaving his wife the task of overseeing the development of the monumental Reynolda estate. His presence at the plant was sorely needed, for the Reynolds Tobacco Company had entered into an uneasy monopoly with the archrival American Tobacco Company. This latter worldwide institution was owned by the Dukes of Durham, who actually had risen from the backwoods poverty that R.J. loved to feign.

Buck Duke and R.J. were each too big and too independent to fit into the same organization, and had the government trustbusters not sundered the two in 1911, there would have been an enormous amount of internecine bloodshed. Instead, there was a war of the marketplace. Association with the Dukes had convinced R.J. that the future of the golden weed lay in cigarettes. Accordingly, in 1913 Reynolds introduced Camels, which Americans were apparently delighted to walk miles for. Within a year, Camels were the number-one brand in the country. Their market share soon rose to an enormous 40 percent. At R.J.'s death in 1918, at sixty-eight, his company was selling over 100 million pounds of tobacco products annually for nearly $100 million.

Everybody associated with R.J., whether a relative or not, seemed to be getting rich, through the company's democratic stock-purchase and profit-sharing plans. Another multimillionaire spawned by the Reynolds nepotocracy was R.J.'s nephew, Richard S. Reynolds. Richard, who began work in 1903, at age twenty-two, as a $50 a month clerk, rose to vice-president of sales. While on the job, he invented a new tin tobacco container to replace the cheesecloth bags that had previously been used. Inspired by his own resourcefulness, he left the company in 1912 to found what was to become the behemoth Reynolds Metals Company, headquartered in Richmond, as well as Wall Street's Reynolds Securities Company. Aluminum king Reynolds was known as the poet-industrialist, composing odes to home building and other joys of capitalism.

Where capitalism was concerned, Richard Reynolds's muse must have been his uncle R.J., whose estate at his death was estimated at $150 million. His widow, Mary Katherine Smith Reynolds, had a brief mourning period, then remarried a Baltimore schoolteacher-turned financier. R.J.'s estate went directly to his children. With only a trust allowance from R.J., the former Mrs. Reynolds moved north to a much less grandiose existence than that at Reynolda, and died a few years later, in 1924. Her young children came under the guardianship of their horse-racing uncle William Neal Reynolds, and his wife, though the actual care was provided by governesses, tutors, and private schools. R.J.'s will stipulated that each child would receive a fourth of his estate at age twenty-eight; until then the orphans could live lavishly on the interest income from their trust.

The daughters were fairly typical heiresses. They spent most of their adolescence living in Manhattan, grand touring in Europe, and attending exclusive Rosemary Hall, a finishing school in Greenwich, Connecticut. Nancy Susan Reynolds, at nineteen, married Henry Walker Bagley, an Atlantan who worked in the advertising department of Condé Nast Publications. Her sister Mary Katherine, at twenty-one, married Charles Henry Babcock, a rising New York executive. Both girls had families and led Fifth Avenue lives that were, for millionaires, rather conventional. The sons, Z. Smith and R.J., Jr., were anything but conventional.

Z. SMITH REYNOLDS

In the crisp fall early morning of November 7, 1929, a black limousine sped through the dark North Carolina pinehills toward the South Carolina state line and the hamlet of York. The town's main street was deserted, except for a lone patrolman. The chauffeur stopped on arrival and asked the trooper where he might find a justice of the peace. There was a wedding to perform. The big black car looked important; the trooper agreed to wake up the probate judge. Such impromptu nuptials were almost the sole function of York and other border communities, since South Carolina, as opposed to its more formal sister to the north, had no waiting period for anxious lovers, young or old.

The limousine did not belie the stature of its passengers. Inside were Joseph F. Cannon, heir to the towel empire of Cannon Mills, his nineteen-year-old daughter Anne, and her eighteen-year-old husband-to-be Z. Smith Reynolds. The patrolman roused the York probate judge and city clerk, and the secret ceremony was performed. There was the same absence of fanfare at the birth of Anne Cannon Reynolds, the couple's child and one of the South's greatest heiresses. Normally such an event would have been the highlight of the Southern society calendar, but the dream marriage had already failed.

The problem was that the couple had almost nothing in common, other than their roots. The bride's grandfather James Cannon (1852–1921) was, like Smith's grandfather Hardin Reynolds, a Scotch-Irish Presbyterian, large family loyalist, who plodded his way to prosperity. His father in turn was a Concord, North Carolina, farmer who, after the Civil War, sent young James to work in a nearby Charlotte general store for four dollars a month. After this subsistence apprenticeship, James returned to Concord and a job in his brother's general store, which expanded via cotton trading and banking activities with its always-indebted clientele. Observing the ways of business, James Cannon concluded that a fortune could be made if the cotton grown in the South could be manufactured into cloth there as well, rather than shipping it to the distant and labor-expensive New England mills. Assisted by capital from the North, Cannon built his first mill in 1887, and vindicated his hypothesis by building many more, both in North Carolina and in neighboring states.

One bright idea begat another. In 1898 James Cannon determined that the march of civilization dictated an improvement upon the rough, nasty flour sacks then used by most people to dry their dishes and faces. If the rich could have linen towels, the rest should have soft cotton ones. This brainstorm made him a multimillionaire. The South's first towel factory, outside Concord, grew into one of the world's largest and most altruistically organized mill towns, named Kannapolis in honor of its founder. It had churches, schools, parks, the

South's biggest YMCA, and a contented work force that produced, in 1914, over 300,000 towels daily.

Anne Cannon's father, Joseph, along with his five brothers, stepped into this empire, first as clerks but soon as directors. Anne grew up as an idolized Southern princess, sent to boarding school at Holton Arms with the Washington, D.C., political elite, and then on to join her fellow debutantes at Salem College in Winston-Salem. There the delicate, fair Anne met Smith Reynolds. Smith had just dropped out of the ultragenteel Woodberry Forest School in Orange, Virginia, where Anne's brother was also enrolled. While his classmates were pondering whether the fraternities and social life of Charlottesville were better than those of Chapel Hill, Smith envisioned a far faster life than that of a Greek-letter cavalier. He wanted to be an international playboy, an ambition not unrealistic in view of his resources.

Following the example of his sybaritic older brother Dick, Smith reasoned that any playboy of the roaring twenties should know how to fly. He began piloting his own plane at sixteen, and soon hired French flying ace Jean Assolant to accompany him on trips to Europe and the Orient. His increasing involvement with aviation matched his high-flying life-style, which centered in Manhattan. All of this proved incompatible with Anne, who was made for the country club rather than the speakeasy. Though the Cannon family thought the match was ideal, as seen in the rush across the state line to consummate the affair, Smith and Anne quickly found it to be a disaster. Smith's disenchantment was underscored in April 1930, when he first saw the sensuous Libby Holman appearing on stage in Baltimore.

If the demure Anne Cannon was the embodiment of purity, Libby Holman represented sin itself. And Smith Reynolds wanted sin. Libby's appearance—tall, raven-haired, with olive skin and a voluptuous figure—was in direct contrast to the slender, fair Anne. Furthermore, Libby sang even more seductively than she looked. And she was bright and cultured. She was a girl with everything, and Smith thought she fit perfectly the image he desired for himself.

The daughter of a Cincinnati attorney, Libby had been a prelaw student at the University of Cincinnati. After graduation she went to New York to attend Columbia Law School. However, her real ambition was to be a singer. Soon her dream came true. She was sidetracked from Wall Street to Broadway by a throat operation that resulted in a most distinctive, husky voice. It wasn't lost on the New York producers, who gave her her first role in a 1924 off-Broadway play entitled *The Fool*. Libby was cast as a prostitute. She advanced to the Great White Way the next year as a chorine in *Greenwich Village Follies,* catching many influential eyes and ears. By 1929, she was a full-fledged star, a smash in the *Little Show* and *Three's a Crowd,* and a headliner at the Roxy Music Hall. Her Harlem-inspired blues made her one of the hottest of talents. She began performing around the country and throughout Europe. A smitten Smith became her biggest fan.

Smith and Anne were separated within months of their marriage. Smith was constantly flying about the world and chasing Libby Holman; Anne returned to her family in Concord. Anne's life was not completely uneventful. She rejoined the party circuit shortly after her baby was born, in August 1930, though her pristine façade began to show signs of cracking. One of her new beaux was Tom Gay Coltrane, the twenty-seven-year-old scion of one of the area's wealthiest families. Tom Gay worked at the Concord Bank and Trust Company, which had been founded by his grandfather and of which his father was director. The courtship ended tragically with Tom Gay's mysterious death on December 4, 1930, in the yard of a friend's house after a party.

Given the almost pathological aversion of prominent Southerners to even the possibility of scandal, Coltrane was buried without discussion, and rumors of foul play were never investigated. His demise was attributed to "a fall and exposure," though an autopsy had indicated that there was no skull fracture and that his external bruises were not enough to have caused death. Shortly thereafter Anne began seeing her childhood sweetheart, Frank Brandon Smith, who worked in his father's hardware store in Charlotte.

Smith Reynolds was oblivious to his wife's adventures. Libby Holman may at first have been amused at the adolescent crush of the chubby, rich teenager, who thought he was an amalgam of Lindbergh and Valentino. But Smith's dogged, worldwide persistence began to pay off. After all, no one, not even the sexiest woman in America, could simply ignore a Reynolds. He followed her, first to Florida, then to

Paris. And when Libby rented a summer home in Port Washington, Long Island, in 1931, Smith took the house next door. No suitor was ever more determined. Smith proposed to Libby time and again. But now instead of laughing, she actually began to go out with him.

Meanwhile, Smith flew Anne to Reno in his private plane for an amicable divorce in October 1931. Anne stayed at Cornelius Vanderbilt's Lazy Me ranch until the divorce, based on "incompatibility," could be granted. Smith told reporters that the reason for their separation was that "she liked big parties and I liked little parties." Anne readily accepted Smith's settlement, which she hardly needed, of $500,000 for their daughter and $500,000 for herself. Anne's mother was given custody of the baby, and the two young people went off to their respective parties. Anne Cannon soon married Frank Brandon Smith. Smith Reynolds now prepared an all-out marital assault on Libby Holman.

In October 1931, shortly before Smith's divorce, Libby had accepted an invitation to Reynolda, which evidently gave her a new, eye-opening perspective on Smith and his proposals. The day after his divorce, Smith called Libby and threatened to kill himself unless she married him. She gave in five days later, when Smith pursued her to Pittsburgh. They agreed to keep their marriage a secret for several months, for the sake of postdivorce decorum. Because Smith was still a minor, another border wedding was in order, this time in Monroe, Michigan, where parental consent was not required. They spent their honeymoon across the state line in a Toledo, Ohio, hotel, after which Smith left for a round-the-world flying trip. Libby met him in Hong Kong in April 1932 and they enjoyed another honeymoon, both in the Orient and for two weeks at the Ambassador Hotel in New York, where the marriage was finally announced. Smith and Libby, between plays, then headed South to Reynolda for the summer and for Smith's final fete of July 5.

The pig pickin' was part of the July Fourth bacchanal, which seemed as if it would continue all summer. It was a typical Reynolds extravaganza, in which mass inebriation was de rigueur. Consequently, when Libby, who was with Smith when he was shot, claimed she remembered absolutely nothing, except Smith's calling her name, followed by a "brief flash," no one, at the outset, questioned her veracity.

At first, suicide seemed a plausible explanation for Smith's death. When called before the coroner's jury on July 14, Libby was joined in her endorsement of the suicide motive by Albert (Ab) Walker, the twenty-year-old son of a local real estate broker, who was Smith's oldest friend and personal secretary, and who had vainly driven Smith to the hospital following the accident. The bombshell at the courtroom was Libby's hysterical revelation that Smith was impotent. (His child by Anne Cannon must have been a fluke, or Anne was less inhibiting than the formidable Libby.) Libby reported that Smith was always pulling out his revolver and threatening to shoot himself because of his sexual inadequacies. To have relentlessly wooed and finally won an international sex symbol and then be unable to rise to the challenge must have been the height of frustration. The racy testimony was a true eyebrow-raiser for the high propriety North Carolinians.

On the Sunday before the party, Ab reported, he and a despondent Smith had spent the night getting drunk at Winston-Salem's ritzy Robert E. Lee Hotel. There, Smith had confessed that Libby found him sexually repulsive. Libby, of course, had professed her undying love and assured Smith that his misperceptions were totally unfounded. A confused Smith, it was said, had promised "to get his head examined." Even during the evening of the party, Walker stated, Smith had brooded that Libby might be off in the woods with some virile stranger. He had vowed "to end it all."

Other lovelorn suicide threats were introduced, one a will from Smith's Woodberry Forest days which read "My Girl has turned me down. Goodbye forever . . . goodbye cruel world," and made such bequests as his car to Ab and his "good looks" to his sister Mary, "who needs them." And one other suicide motive, adduced by the coroner himself, was that Smith had just learned that Libby Holman, née Holtzman, was originally Jewish, though she now was a disciple of Christian Science. The disclosure of Libby's Semitic roots was likely to have a greater impact upon intolerant Bible belters than it may have had on the worldly Smith. When combined with all the shocking discussions of sex, it did little to better the actress's tarnished image among the locals.

In addition to being a Jew, Libby was also a Yankee, and a Broadway Yankee at that. Nice Southern girls didn't sing black-rooted blues songs. Libby thus began to appear to the Winston-Salem community as a modern Salome, a designing woman, the epitome of female treachery. Moreover, aspersions were now being cast upon her relationship with the lanky, boyish Ab Walker. Apparently, on the night of the party, Ab and Libby had been seen, clad in scanty bathing suits, going for a midnight swim in the Reynolda lake. The public imagination was inflamed by reports that they had been kissing, though such indiscriminate displays of affection were commonplace at Smith's parties. Further scorn was heaped upon Libby due to the presence of other show business figures at Reynolda at the time of the slaying: Blanche Yurka, the distinguished actress and director who was Libby's friend and drama coach, and Walter Batchelor, Libby's stage manager. Together with Ab Walker, an unlikely thespian, they had been reveling in champagne, rehearsing lines from a new play that Libby was considering. There was gossip that a Broadway conspiracy might have been at work.

Ballistics tests and a reconstruction of the shooting supported the suspicions of foul play. Smith was left-handed, but he had been shot through the right temple. The trajectory of the bullet indicated that someone other than Smith had fired the shot. Furthermore, despite a supposedly thorough search, the weapon itself was not discovered until four hours after the slaying, when it fortuitously appeared in plain view by the bed. Aside from the testimony about Smith's instability, the suicide theory did not fit the evidence. The conclusion of the coroner's jury that Smith's death came at someone else's hand was echoed by county officials, who pressed on in their investigation of the mystery. On August 4, a month after the tragedy, a county grand jury indicted Libby Holman and Ab Walker for the murder of Smith Reynolds.

Ab Walker was arrested immediately and held without bail at the Winston-Salem jail, where he was treated to the Southern comfort of fried chicken dinners prepared by the noted cooks of the Robert E. Lee Hotel. Meanwhile, Libby had gone home to Cincinnati, refusing to appear in North Carolina until her father retained an aggressive Winston-Salem attorney named Benet Polikoff to handle her case.

Libby's return to North Carolina on August 8 to submit to arrest was a sideshow worthy of Times Square. Dressed completely in black, with a veil, the actress arrived in a long motorcade, along a route thronged with thousands of spectators. The circus atmosphere had

been charged with the earlier arrival from New York of Samuel Leibo-
witz, famous as counselor to the underworld, who had been asked by
unspecified "Broadway friends" to look into the Reynolds case. He was
en route to the federal penitentiary in Atlanta to visit another prominent client, Al Capone.

The most exciting disclosure of all was unleashed by lawyer Polikoff inside the mobbed courtroom, where he was seeking to have Libby
released on $25,000 bond, as Ab Walker had just been. Libby was
pregnant! The news convinced the judge to accede to Polikoff's bail
request. It also set off fireworks within the Reynolds family, which was
beyond distress at the publicity.

If Smith's suicide was predicated upon his impotence, as Libby had
sobbed, her pregnancy would be at odds with her defense. Unless the
child's father was someone other than Smith, that is. The Reynoldses
didn't even want to contemplate *that* possibility. Smith's brother Dick,
twenty-six, who had already served a prison term in England for manslaughter and was a frequent headliner for his reckless epicureanism,
was more than enough embarrassment. The family determined that it
was better to let Smith rest in peace, his end unrequited, and to accept
Libby's child as one of them, than to subject Smith to further posthumous humiliation.

On October 10, William Neal Reynolds, family spokesman and
Smith's guardian, wrote a letter to the judge and county prosecutor
stating that the family would be "quite happy" if the case against Libby
and Ab were dropped. Though the elder Reynolds asserted that Smith's
"attitude toward life was such that he would never have intentionally
killed himself," the evidence marshaled thus far failed to prove "con-
clusively" that Smith had been murdered. Thus spake Reynolds, and
thus ended the case. Or so the family thought.

The Reynoldses' alacrity to close the books may have stemmed
from Smith's will. Under the will, Smith's entire share of his father's
estate, valued conservatively at $30 million, was to be divided equally
among his brother and sisters, except for a relatively paltry $50,000 each
to Anne Cannon and daughter Anne Cannon Reynolds. No sooner was
Libby Holman freed, than she announced, through attorney Polikoff,
her intention to contest the will.

Libby's case was enhanced by the birth of a son on January 10, 1933, a month premature. Christopher Smith Reynolds was a sickly baby of a mere two pounds, eleven ounces, but at least he bore the Reynolds name. The removal of the specter of the murder charge, combined with the lure of a vast inheritance, left Libby with no possible incentive for disputing the child's paternity. She didn't, and the Reynoldses were delighted to start discussions of a settlement. They were anything but delighted when the Cannon family entered the picture that April.

Theoretically, the $1-million divorce settlement upon Anne and daughter Anne, now two years old, was to have satisfied all their claims to Smith's fortune. But with a dazzling $30-million estate up for contest, nobody was satisfied, not even millionaires like the Cannons. Anne's family retained counsel and announced their contention that the divorce settlement was invalid, on the grounds that Anne was ill at the time and agreed to the divorce only because of Smith's duress.

Meanwhile, the Cabarrus Bank and Trust Company of Concord, guardian of little Anne, also filed suit to declare the Nevada renunciation agreement null and void. Their additional grounds were that a minor's (little Anne's) rights could not be waived. The entire legacy was claimed by the bank, not for big Anne, but for the little girl. Anne Cannon was incensed that the bank, of which her uncle Charles Cannon was president, had dared to speak for her side of the family, especially if they were going to leave her out altogether. Charles Cannon and his brother Joseph (Anne's father) had had a terrible falling out over the settlement of their father's immense estate. They had not only not spoken for five years but, as Anne described it, were in a state of "armed neutrality." Anne accused the bank of getting involved only to collect a huge fee for handling the matter.

The Reynoldses, too, were incensed, that their fellow Southern aristocrats had the gall to file suit over money that was clearly superfluous. If the Cannons wanted to challenge them, the Reynoldses were not about to refuse to pick up the gauntlet. A family war was on. Smith's brother and sisters threatened that they, the Reynoldses, would demand the entire fortune for themselves. Libby Holman, who was living with her son in the quiet luxury of a Park Avenue hotel, stayed discreetly on the sidelines. Her legal wizard Benet Polikoff was keeping his eagle eye on every move in the increasingly bitter game.

Poor Frank Brandon Smith was also incensed. Anne Cannon had divorced Frank in 1933 when she began to assert her claim to the Reynolds inheritance. Feeling like the bartered bridegroom, Frank blamed Anne's family for coercing her into a divorce. The jury was more than sympathetic. They responded to Frank's alienation-of-affections suit against Joseph Cannon by awarding Frank a verdict of $125,000, the largest civil damages in North Carolina history up until that time.

After three years of courtroom proposals, backroom counterproposals, and the most vicious innuendos regarding Smith Reynolds's virility, Libby's veracity, and Christopher's legitimacy, the war of the Tar Heels ended in a draw. Of the $30-million estate, little Anne received approximately $8.5 million, while little Christopher was awarded $7 million. Libby Holman graciously accepted $750,000 and the guardianship of Christopher. The remaining millions went to Smith's three siblings who, spurred by their father's philanthropic traditions and by the tax laws, agreed to donate it all to charity. They formed the Zachary Smith Reynolds Foundation, whose first major endeavor was a giant program to combat North Carolina's alarming incidence of venereal disease. Smith might have been amused.

Despite her inheritance, Libby Holman's torch never again glowed with the same intensity. In 1935 she returned to Broadway in a musical comedy entitled *Revenge with Music.* She was, however, more interested in serious drama than in singing. Determined to forge a new image, she even gave up "Body and Soul" and other trademark numbers for folk music. Although she performed in numerous summer-stock productions and some Broadway shows, her new career never regained the pre-Smith high. In 1939, Libby remarried, at thirty-three, a twenty-two-year-old actor named Ralph Holmes. This alliance also ended tragically with Holmes's death six years later from an overdose of barbiturates.

Throughout her travails, Libby used Christopher's Southern inheritance to raise him as the most privileged of Yankees. Feeling that they had had enough publicity to last a lifetime, Libby sheltered Christopher in a half-million-dollar Connecticut manor, complete with seven bodyguards and three Great Danes. The wraithlike, slim, refined, and intellectual Christopher was as unlike the Reynoldses as Putney, his progressive Vermont prep school, was different from his late father's stuffy Woodberry Forest.

But like his father, Christopher's life ended tragically. He thrived at Putney, where he headed the student council and was one of the top students in his class. As a graduation adventure, the well-rounded eighteen-year-old decided to join his classmate Stephen Wasserman in scaling Mount Whitney in California. They chose the most challenging approach, a sheer face that had been conquered only once before. They never returned. Libby Holman went on to a notorious drug-filled affair with the predominantly homosexual actor Montgomery Clift. In 1962 Libby remarried once more, this time Lou Shanker, an artist, but she was unsuccessful in her efforts to resume her career. She never again sang her torch songs of blues, loss, and despair. They hit too close to home. She committed suicide in 1973.

As for Anne Cannon, the protracted legal battles left her with a jaundiced view of wealth. She moved away from her Concord towel fiefdom, became a social worker in Philadelphia, and settled into a happy and unsung marriage with a gray-flanneled, sedate Main Liner. Little Anne, who was raised by her grandmother in Concord and in the lush North Carolina mountain resort of Blowing Rock, likewise refused to become a prisoner of wealth. On November 29, 1948, as an eighteen-year-old freshman at Duke University, she eloped with her childhood sweetheart, Lloyd Patrick "Junebug" Tate, the twenty-two-year-old son of her riding instructor. Tate, just discharged from the Navy, worked in his father's stables in Blowing Rock and in the equally exclusive holiday and golfing center of Pinehurst. There the couple spent the 1948 Thanksgiving holidays fox hunting, and from there they ran off—like Anne's parents—to a South Carolina wedding ceremony. But her marriage was somewhat more durable. It lasted long enough to produce four children, after which Anne divorced Junebug and remarried, this time a local physician.

Finally, for Frank Brandon Smith, all ended less than well. Before he had a chance to begin savoring his record 1935 lawsuit award, a judge overturned the jury's $125,000 verdict as excessive. Frank was eventually left with only $12,500 and a restraining order prohibiting him from maintaining any further actions against Anne's allegedly beleaguered father. Frank returned to his father's Charlotte store and the mundanities of hammers and nails. He learned, the hard way, that joining a great Southern family was by no means a passport to financial bliss.

RICHARD JOSHUA REYNOLDS, JR.

If Frank Brandon Smith was tantalized and tormented by proximity to wealth, R.J. (Dick) Reynolds, Jr., the incarnation of wealth itself, suffered even more by possessing it. Money, sex, and drink had been the ruin of Smith Reynolds. Dick, who was five years older than his brother, had started this tradition of dissipation and spent almost an entire lifetime observing it religiously. With his blue-chip hell-raising providing front page news for decades, Dick Reynolds was the paradigm of the high class good-old-boy.

Dick, born in 1906, preceded Smith at Woodberry Forest. Neither seems to have been imbued with much of the gentlemanly reserve that school was noted for. Both of them husky six footers, with slick brown hair, and overdressed in expensive clothes, the two heirs were fat Gatsbys, with deep Southern drawls which they never lost despite long absences from Dixie. Dick's first departure was at age seventeen, when he ran away from Woodberry Forest and apprenticed himself on a German freighter under the pseudonym Kid Carolina. Dick enjoyed the lusty seaman's view of the world, but he decided that first class, instead of steerage, would be even more fun. Accordingly, he purchased a giant freighter, and fitted out lavish yachtlike accommodations for himself. The remainder of the ship was used to transport tobacco and other cargo across the ocean. In addition to Dick's desire to indulge his personal fancies, there was an economic incentive for the vessel's configuration: R.J., Sr.'s will contained a provision that for every dollar his sons earned, the estate would pay them two. This was over and above their annual allowance of more than $100,000. Although Smith never bothered to avail himself of the opportunity, Dick, truer to the family's Scotch-Irish heritage, was more industrious. He actually made a great deal of money on his cruises, creating a harmonious union between business and pleasure.

Smith's passion for flying was derived from his brother, who even kept a plane on his ship, to solo whenever the spirit moved him. Inspired by his cargo successes, Dick determined, in 1926, to exploit his father's will provision in the air as well as at sea. He bought a fleet of fourteen Fokkers and Curtiss Field on Long Island and organized Reynolds Airways. This proved to be yet another prosperous venture for Dick as he demonstrated once again his father's aptitude for financial success.

Had Dick confined his considerable energies to business, the expansion of the Reynolds empire might have been unlimited. But with one of the world's great fortunes at his command and without parents to restrain him, Dick went the hedonistic route. His first capitulation was to Broadway, which proved to be a fatal influence upon his brother Smith. Though Dick lacked the Midas touch as a producer, he was successful with the female side of the theater, and was often seen squiring around the most stunning showgirls in New York, often several at a time.

In 1927, one of Dick's productions, *Half a Widow,* won national attention—not for its reviews, which were dreadful, but for its producer. Dick landed on the front page of the papers when he disappeared after the opening night. With few tickets being sold and the theater owner about to evict them, the *Widow* company grew frantic when Dick couldn't be found to pay the bills. A nationwide dragnet went out, and one of Dick's associates at his airline company even made inquiries abroad. When Dick's yellow Rolls-Royce was found overturned in Long Island Sound, at the end of an abandoned pier, the worst was feared. But a few days later, the excitement subsided. Dick was discovered, not in Dakar or Timbuktu, but in a chop suey parlor in St. Louis, accompanied by a beautiful blonde. Surprised at all the concern, Dick said that he had simply gotten fed up with the Broadway scene, and was taking a brief vacation, going to the Dempsey-Tunney fight in Chicago and the races in St. Louis. He surmised that his sunken Rolls had been stolen, and was not at all distressed.

Two years later, in 1929, Dick was in the papers again. This time there was a real slaying, not a false alarm. But now Dick was the assailant instead of the victim. On holiday in England, Dick and a friend spent a rainy afternoon in a pub near Windsor Castle, in the course of which Dick downed five Pimm's No. 1 Cups, a gin and lemon concoction that was a favorite of old India hands during the British raj. Imperially inspired, Dick roared away from the pub in his Buick. A short distance down the road, he collided with a young motorcyclist, who died from injuries in the crash.

Dick did not stop after the collision, but was quickly apprehended and charged with drunken driving and manslaughter. He claimed that he had been blinded by oncoming headlights, denied he was drunk, and pleaded not guilty. For his trial Reynolds assembled a battery of Britain's greatest barristers, who brought some of the most eminent British physicians to the stand to argue the technicalities of the threshold of drunkenness. Despite his distinguished witnesses and counsel, Dick was convicted of the charges. The court, making a show of the equality of British justice, sentenced him to five months in Brixton Prison, in South London and a long way from Claridge's.

Dick served his term at "soft" labor, which included such tasks as cleaning cells and making beds, and was considered a model prisoner. Yet he was able to make the transition from prison stripes to pinstripe suits as if nothing had happened. The wild times began anew, though he did drive more carefully. When Smith was shot in July 1932, Dick was cruising off South Africa in his freighter-yacht. Instead of flying home, he sailed leisurely to Rio de Janeiro and arrived in Winston-Salem more than a month after the funeral. Given his own adverse press, Dick was instrumental in convincing his family to have the case dropped against Libby and Ab.

More trouble awaited Dick, now twenty-six, back in the States. A Viennese dancer named Johanna Rischke was suing him for $140,000 on the grounds that he fraudulently induced her to abandon her career in Europe for one on Broadway. The case was settled out of court but Dick's aunts and uncles were by now deeply disturbed by the beating the Reynoldses' reputation was taking, and began putting pressure upon the compulsive playboy to settle down.

A contrite Dick went all out to please his family. On Christmas

Day 1932, he announced his engagement to his childhood playmate from Winston-Salem, Elizabeth Dillard, twenty-four. The daughter of a local construction magnate, the sweet and petite Elizabeth rode horses, was a debutante, went to Sweetbrier, and was the guiding light of Winston-Salem's Junior League. In short, she was the perfect hometown belle. To the beaming Reynoldses, the match did much to compensate for the embarrassment and heartache of the past few years.

The union also contained an element of delayed gratification for the Reynoldses. When R.J., Sr., was building his tobacco empire, he did so in part by buying out his local competitors. One of his rivals was the now-defunct Taylor Brothers Tobacco Company, owned by Elizabeth Dillard's maternal grandfather, Will Taylor, an independent Scotch-Irishman who refused to be bought out, at any price, much to R.J.'s annoyance. Now love, not money, was bringing the two prominent families together.

For the next thirteen years, Dick continued to be a source of great pride to the Reynoldses. Marrying early in 1933, the new couple moved into Reynolda, where Dick sired four sons. He bowed out of the theater, sold his Reynolds Airways, and concentrated on solid North Carolina ventures, specifically furniture and, of course, tobacco. Because he had inherited his father's touch and, more important, his capital, Dick was a big success in increasing the family fortune. He also carried on the philanthropic heritage, directing the benefactions of the Z. Smith Reynolds Foundation to a diversity of areas, ranging from syphilis to symphonies and including the establishment in Winston-Salem of a major educational institution, Wake Forest College. As a token of its gratitude and esteem, Winston-Salem elected the reformed bon vivant as the city's mayor in 1941. (Dick was also active in politics as the treasurer of the Democratic National Committee.)

Dick's tenure was interrupted by World War II. He renewed his love affair with the sea as a Navy lieutenant-commander aboard an aircraft carrier in the Pacific. The return to the waves struck a lost chord; after the war Dick reverted to the decadent self-indulgence of times past. In 1946, he divorced Elizabeth Dillard, paying her an enormous settlement estimated at $11 million, a high price for his freedom.

Placing his many business ventures in the hands of his lieutenants, and with Reynolda in the hands of his ex-wife and family, Dick left staid Winston-Salem for the glitter of Manhattan. Several weeks later he was back in show business, and not long thereafter he remarried. The new bride was Marianne O'Brien, a twenty-three-year-old ravishing redhead and a Warner Brothers starlet.

After six years and two children, Reynolds returned to the divorce courts. He feared that Marianne was going to leave him for Porfirio Rubirosa. The marrying Rubirosa, that most financially successful of Latin lovers, had already enjoyed a fling in tobacco, as husband to Buck Duke's Doris. For Dick Reynolds, the merest possibility of being cuckolded by *any* Duke relation was ignominy of the worst sort. Marianne, like Porfirio, received a major fiscal souvenir of her tobacco alliance, a $2-million settlement that included an East Side Manhattan duplex and a Miami Beach palazzo.

Dick was not price sensitive where romance was concerned. The day after the divorce from Marianne was granted in 1952, the forty-six-year-old Reynolds returned to the altar with Mrs. Muriel Marston Greenough, thirty-six, an international socialite who lived in Oyster Bay, Long Island. Things began idyllically for the couple. Their nuptials were conducted at Sapelo, a 44,000-acre Georgia sea island entirely owned by Dick. This subtropical private paradise was crowned by a villa dwarfing most of those in Palm Beach and featuring a gold-plated indoor swimming pool. After Sapelo, Dick and Muriel continued on to England, to pick up Dick's new yacht, the *Aries,* for a round-the-world cruise.

But soon the effects of alimony battles, high living, and constant smoking began to catch up with the tobacco heir. He developed chronic emphysema and a host of other disorders. Muriel, in his mind, was less than sympathetic. After a few turbulent years, Dick had had enough of the childless and joyless combination. Well aware of his desperation, Muriel, through her Atlanta lawyers, set a monumental severance fee: $6 million. This was over and above the $1 million in jewelry and bonds Dick alleged that Muriel had already received as an incentive to leave gracefully. Even Dick, who had paid and paid, felt Muriel's de-

mands were excessive. He dug in for a legal battle of the same epic
proportions as the Cannon-Reynolds war. In 1962, the Georgia Supreme Court sided with Dick and awarded Muriel a paltry $5,000 a
month alimony. Having demanded and expected Sapelo Island and
more, a disappointed Muriel contested the ruling. Years later, the matter was still in the courts.

After Muriel had overturned a divorce Dick had obtained in 1959, a
second one was granted in 1961. Oblivious to Muriel's renewed opposition to the second decree and obviously intrepid where conjugality was
concerned, Dick married again. He was now fifty-five, a drawn and
haggard shell of his former rotund, robust self. Having gone through a
Southern belle, a Hollywood starlet, and an international jet-setter,
Dick completed his marital portfolio with a German scholar, Dr.
Annemarie Schmitt, thirty-one. The blond, brainy Annemarie had recently received her doctorate in philosophy from the University of
Freiburg. She met Dick when he was in Germany taking a much-
needed cure at a Bad Harzburg sanitarium. A brief courtship preceded
the 1961 wedding, which took place on a cruise ship in the South China
Sea.

At last Dick seemed content. But the cigarettes that had given him
his glamorous life ultimately killed him. He died in December 1964 of
chronic emphysema, in Lucerne, Switzerland, where he and Annemarie
then lived and where his body was cremated. The fifty-eight-year-old
Tar Heel had expressed no wish to return home, dead or alive. The day
he passed away, Annemarie gave birth to his first and only daughter. He
was potent to the end.

A final note. When the great grudge match between the Cannons
and the Reynoldses was declared a draw, there actually were some
winners, and some very big winners at that—the lawyers. Before this
case, the largest legal fees ever awarded in a North Carolina action
totaled a mere $10,000. The fees in the Cannon-Reynolds donnybrook
were over $3 million. Similarly, in Dick Reynolds's streak of divorces,
the lawyers again reaped a fabulous fiscal harvest, all from the discord of
the rich. In this way the rulers of the New South were sharing the

wealth and thereby bringing new members into their plutocratic fold. The first generation of Southern dynasties was founded on land; the second, on tobacco and textile manufacturing. The third may spring from legal fees.

Epilogue

Old families never die. They just fade away. The application of Douglas MacArthur's old soldier adage to the Southern aristocracy is sad but true. With only a few exceptions, the great dynasties that gave the South its special character now seem to exist in name only. The power is gone. The fading began with the Civil War, and has continued to the present day. After the Depression, most survivors of the old order could not even afford to live in regal decay. For the most part, they simply became poor people, with rich tales to tell. True enough, later generations produced accomplished doctors, lawyers, and businessmen. But such successes have been founded on the most conventional terms— white collars, not white knights. The great clans still have their hallowed names, but the mythic figures these families once produced are no more.

If one perseveres, however, these families can still be found. Take Natchez, for example. Elms Court, the plantation that had been taken away from Jane Surget Merrill because of her romance with Duncan Minor, now belongs to Mrs. Grace MacNeil, the descendant of the line of Surgets that dispossessed Miss Jennie. Mrs. MacNeil, a grande dame who has served as chairwoman of the American Girl Scouts, divides her time between Natchez and Princeton, New Jersey. Mrs. MacNeil's daughter, Beth, is a Radcliffe alumna and archeologist, one of the world's leading authorities on Greek pithos pots. When Beth and her classicist husband-to-be, Frank Boggess, first met in Athens, they were much too involved with Grecian urns to worry about genealogy. However, once Beth and Frank were married and moved to Mississippi, the Natchez family bug began to incubate.

To everyone's amazement, Frank was discovered to be a direct descendant of Don Estevan Minor, the Pennsylvanian Spanish royal governor and best friend of Beth's greatest great-grandfather, Pierre Surget. Frank was a member of the branch of the Minor family that had remained in the North. The Boggess-MacNeil wedding thus was a match between Natchez's first two families, even if the celebrants weren't aware at the time of how historic their nuptials really were. In the eyes of Natchezians, it is the most perfect of unions.

Of all the old Southern families, none has achieved a greater comeback than the Byrds of Virginia. The family had lived in unaccustomed obscurity since the American Revolution, when William Byrd III committed suicide. His Anglophilia proved fatally excessive. Byrd's applegrowing descendants in the Shenandoah Valley emerged from the shadows with Admiral Byrd of the Antarctic and his brother, Senator Harry Flood Byrd of the "Byrd machine." The political machine apparently keeps on rolling; Harry Flood Byrd, Jr., now sits, as his father did, in the U.S. Senate.

No member of that greatest of Virginia dynasties, the Randolphs, keeps as high a profile as the Byrds. There are Randolphs all over the country, every one intensely proud of his roots. Take Olivia Taylor, a regal octogenarian who lives in a Victorian mansion in Charlottesville, with a sweeping view across the Blue Ridge Mountains to her great-great-great-grandfather's Monticello. Surrounded by Randolph antiques, Randolph portraits, and Randolph genealogies, Miss Taylor knows more about Virginia history than almost anyone. That's because the Randolphs *are* Virginia history. Yet, although she is an insider, Miss Taylor is amused, rather than awed, by it all. To her, Mr. Jefferson is simply "Tommy Jeff."

Across the country in Los Angeles, there is a black descendant of the Randolph line. Elmer Roberts, an L.A. probation officer, can trace his ancestry to Sally Hemings, Jefferson's mistress. And back in Charlottesville, another Randolph scion, Rob Coles, is turning his ancestry into a form of show business. His fiery red hair and aquiline features make him a dead ringer for young Mr. Jefferson. Ever since the Bicentennial, Coles has been the star of a play called *Meet Thomas Jefferson,* which has been seen all over America. Actually preferring history to histrionics, Coles, an alumnus of the Jefferson-founded University of Virginia, is studying to become a historian. His field? Jeffersoniana, of course.

Tidewater Virginia, where the Byrds and Randolphs first rose to power, was one of the cradles of Southern civilization. The other was the Charleston low-country. That area is even less changed than the Tidewater. Charleston is a living museum. The gargantuan porticoed pastel houses seem immutable, as do the rolls of the St. Cecilia Society. The names remain the same. Elise Pinckney is a bulwark of the South Carolina Historical Society. Anna Rutledge has one of the grandest houses on the Battery, though she herself resides in the small kitchen building in the backyard. Peter Manigault is the president of the two Charleston newspapers. Alfred Huger practices law on Broad Street. The city is remarkably chauvinistic, so much so that when Charles Ravenel, whose Huguenot name is one of the oldest in Charleston, decided to run for Governor of South Carolina, he was decried as a carpetbagger, and disqualified by a five-year residency requirement, his family's ten generations notwithstanding. Ravenel had gone to Exeter on a scholarship as Charleston's best paper boy, and Harvard, and had worked as an investment banker on Wall Street before returning to his roots. In the eyes of locals, he should never have left at all.

One fine name conspicuous in its near-absence is Grimké. Most of the other elite families have Grimké blood, though no one ever seems to mention Sarah and Angelina in lists of venerated forebears. Iconoclasm is definitely not a virtue in this most traditional of cities. The only Grimké around is Frederick Grimké, who spent most of his life in New York as an engineer at Consolidated Edison and came home to Charleston for a gracious retirement. As for the black Grimkés, there are none left. Archie had no children. Frank had one daughter, who died a spinster.

In Columbia, South Carolina, the Hamptons have enjoyed a renaissance. Following the tradition of their crusading kinsman, Narciso Gonzales, who was killed by James Tillman for his redneck-baiting, the current-day Hamptons have become press lords. Ambrose Gonzales Hampton and Harry Elliott Rutledge Hampton coedit the *State,* founded by their Uncle Narciso. Their brother, Frank, raises prize dairy cattle and racehorses at Millwood, the original, restored plantation of Wade Hampton II.

While the Hamptons have recaptured much of the genteel tradition of the Old South, the Pitchfork Tillmans have retreated from the sound and fury that heralded the New South. Ben, Jr., the principal in the famous child custody case, settled into a quiet career as a civil servant. He died in 1950. The pitchfork apparently has not been handed down through the generations, but its rattle has inspired many a Southern politician, from Huey Long to George Wallace.

Down in Savannah, with its lush moss and luxurious townhouses, things still look as they did 150 years ago. Nonetheless, there is change. The houses are being increasingly occupied by disenchanted expatriate Yankees, in search of old-fashioned charm and elegance. Nearby Charleston seems too forbidding, but Savannah has the air of an open city. Although there are no more McAllisters, and one of the founding Sephardic clans, the Sheftalls, has been "born again" as Baptists and moved to Macon, the other Jewish founding family, the Minises, are still going strong. They easily made the transition from cotton brokerage to stock brokerage and continue to prosper. The current patriarch, Abraham Minis, a closet septuagenarian, spends much of his time big-game fishing off Tahiti. Mr. Minis is in the forefront of the Jewish elite on both his paternal and maternal lines. His mother was a member of the family of Sir Moses Montefiore, mightiest of British philanthropists. Everyone in Savannah addresses the city's most elegant patrician as A. Minis. His son is known as "B plus." No adverse reflection on the son is intended; Father is just a tough act to follow.

Other prominent Southern Jews have not fared as well. There are still Moseses in Spartanburg, but some of them have changed their name. Franklin J.'s scalawag shenanigans have never been forgotten in South Carolina. In New Orleans, there is no trace of the Judah P. Benjamins, other than a Bourbon Street bar named Judah P's in the French Quarter house where the Confederate statesman once lived. Judah's only daughter died in France without issue. There are some Beauregards and some Slidells in the New Orleans phone directory, but they are black. The Slidell tradition does live on overseas in the d'Erlangers, who left France for a castle in Tunisia. Rudolphe d'Erlanger, a recent graduate of Harvard and a member of its Porcellian Club, runs the small family office in London, where Slidell memorabilia are carefully preserved.

Even abroad, the Southern aristocracy sticks together. Rudolphe's godmother is none other than Nancy Lancaster, the niece of Lady Nancy Langhorne Astor. Mrs. Lancaster is the proprietress of Colefax and Fowler, one of the most fashionable of London decorating firms. More Langhorne descendants seem to live in England than in Charlottesville, though Langhorne Gibson, son of Dana and Irene, owns a farm in the shadow of Mirador, the Langhorne estate, and his daughter, Parthy, lives in an adjoining cottage where Irene came to die in 1954. Across the Atlantic, however, it's even more Virginian than Virginia. A visit to the Lancaster "cottage" (a former abbey) outside Oxford, or to the Chelsea flat of Mrs. Lancaster's sister, Alice Winn, is akin to a trip back to the Old Dominion. The Virginia accents are there, as are countless books about the South, cotillion photos, and troves of Mirador memories. Only the mint juleps are missing.

Just as William Byrd II shuttled back and forth between Virginia and England over two centuries ago, the Langhorne family has created its own Charlottesville-London axis. Other English Langhornes include Nancy Astor's sons, Michael and John Jacob, who have served in Parliament, and another son, David, the editor of the *London Observer,* as well as her niece, comedienne Joyce Grenfell, best remembered as the headmistress of an unruly girls' boarding school in *The Belles of St. Trinian's.* And Nancy's great-grandniece is Lady Charles Spencer-Churchill. Time and love seem to heal all rifts, even the chasm between Lady Nancy and Sir Winston.

Epilogue

In America, the Southern Astors are also alive and well, if not basking in the fin de siècle splendor of their forebears. Typical is William Astor Chanler III, twenty-nine, who works in the real estate department of New York's Manufacturers Hanover Trust Company. After work, which itself is a contemporary concession for the playboy Astor-Chanlers, he relaxes at the Racquet Club, or at his small studio apartment filled with priceless antiques and dominated by a giant portrait of his gorgeous Charlottesville grandmother, Beatrice Ashley.

The "marrying Wilsons" are in New York, too, though today they are, and have long been, the game rather than the hunter, where conjugality is concerned. Orme Wilson, Jr., is a diplomat at the United States Mission to the United Nations, and his Astor, Vanderbilt, and Goelet cousins are still the bedrock of New York society. Only the heirs of Ward McAllister are missing. Alas, no more *fêtes champêtres.* There is the California branch of the family, however, led by Decker McAllister, the retired board chairman of a scientific equipment manufacturing corporation. Such industrial lucre might have dismayed Uncle Ward, who didn't believe gentlemen should soil their hands, but today such big business keeps the McAllisters in the vanguard of San Francisco's forty-niner elite.

Of the founding families of the New South, most descendants seem to have remained below the Mason-Dixon line. The Dixie diaspora that occurred in the last half of the nineteenth century was largely a phenomenon of the antebellum aristocrats. The de Bardelebens, for instance, despite a new tradition of Princeton education, continue to reign as Birmingham's iron kings. The Candlers, even though they no longer dominate Coca-Cola, are nonetheless dominant figures in the Atlanta community. Asa Warren Candler and John Slaughter Candler II are two of the city's most powerful attorneys. The Reynoldses, who have quieted down in the most recent generation, occupy a similarly influential position in Winston-Salem. With the exception of Smith Bagley, an influential Washington host, the Reynoldses are rarely seen or heard. They devote their time to horses, trout fishing, and philanthropy, though not necessarily in that order. Only Zack Reynolds, who died in 1979 in a plane crash at age forty-one, seems to have inherited his father, R.J., Jr.'s, flamboyance. The owner of one of the world's largest collections of motorcycles, a skeet shooting champion, and an acrobatic stunt pilot, he perhaps signified the end of an era.

The Dukes are absentee dynasts. Buck's only child, Doris, followed the gossip-headlining tradition of her father and her Uncle Brodie with her amours, most notably with her marriage to Latin playboy Porfirio Rubirosa. The jet-set life kept Doris out of North Carolina. The Duke Biddles have become more Biddle than Duke, eschewing their Southern background for Main Line assimilation. Angier Biddle Duke, New York City's majordomo of civic affairs, began his diplomatic career as one of America's youngest ambassadors. He had no trouble making the transition from El Morocco to El Salvador, and later to Spain and Denmark. Duke served as the State Department's chief of protocol during the Kennedy years.

Josephine Drexel Biddle Duke breached all protocol, and occupied buildings as well as headlines when, as a senior at Barnard College, she joined Mark Rudd at the barricades in the 1968 Columbia riots. Josie Duke ultimately proved less true to her school than to her class by settling into a distinctly unrevolutionary blue-chip Philadelphia marriage. Compensating for the Duke disappearance from the South has been Doris's cousin, Mary Duke Biddle. After completing Miss Hewitt's classes in Manhattan, this Duke actually went to Duke. And she stayed in Durham, marrying in succession two prominent physicians from Duke Hospital and making her family's presence strongly felt in the state. Her current husband, James Semans, is widely known for his "Semans Technique" for dealing with impotence and frigidity.

Today, socially and economically, the South is wide open. Money, all by itself, provides entree as well as cachet. People who matter in the South are people whom no one ever heard about a generation before. People like the Memphis Wilsons of Holiday Inn fame. People like the Jarmans of Nashville who founded the giant Genesco conglomerate on shoe factories. The once lethargic charm of the South's cities is being obliterated by alien forces just as inexorable as Sherman in his march to the sea. Perhaps in exchange for Coca Cola, the South is receiving the skyscrapers of Park Avenue and the shopping centers of El Camino Real.

Nonetheless, despite such replicative progress, Southerners keep looking back. No sooner has the son of a tenant farmer made his fortune in real estate and bought his mock-antebellum mansion on Peachtree Street than the search for his roots begins. He hopes he will find a Civil War soldier, or better yet, a Revolutionary War combatant in his family's past. And should the armchair genealogist discover a Byrd or a Randolph, a Hampton or a Beauregard, he has found the Holy Grail, a link to the Southern aristocracy. Because of this legitimating factor, the cult of ancestry is Dixie's favorite obsession. No active accomplishment, no amount of wealth, can altogether overshadow mere descent, however tenuous, from one of the great Southern families.

These families created the South. They molded its character and captured its imagination. Southerners are a close-knit lot. *The* family is the South's most important institution, and the *great* families are its most cherished icons. Despite the beckoning future, Southerners enjoy living in the past. Despite every concept of democracy, Southerners enjoy doting on their aristocracy. Old times, it seems, are simply not forgotten.

Selected Bibliography

Amory, Cleveland. *Who Killed Society?* New York: Harper & Bros., 1960.

Asbury, Herbert. *The French Quarter.* New York: Alfred A. Knopf, 1936.

Astor, Michael. *Tribal Feeling.* London: John Murray, 1963.

Balsan, Consuelo Vanderbilt. *The Glitter and the Gold.* New York: Harper & Bros., 1952.

Birney, Catherine. *The Grimké Sisters.* New York: C. T. Dillingham, 1885.

Boyd, Julian. "The Murder of George Wythe." *William and Mary Quarterly,* 3rd series, vol. XII, October 1955.

Bridenbaugh, Carl. *Myths and Realities.* Baton Rouge: L.S.U. Press, 1952.

Bruce, William Cabell. *John Randolph of Roanoke.* New York: G. P. Putnam's Sons, 1922.

Candler, Charles H. *Asa Griggs Candler.* Atlanta: Emory University Press, 1950.

Cash, Wilbur J. *The Mind of the South.* New York: Alfred A. Knopf, 1941.

Cate, Wirt. *Lucius Lamar.* Chapel Hill: University of North Carolina Press, 1931.

Coulter, E. Merton. *The South During Reconstruction, 1865–1877.* Baton Rouge: L.S.U. Press, 1947.

Craven, Wesley. *The Southern Colonies in the Seventeenth Century, 1607–1689.* Baton Rouge: L.S.U. Press, 1949.

Daniels, Jonathan. *The Randolphs of Virginia.* New York: Doubleday Co., 1972.

de Leon, Thomas E. *Belles, Beaux and Brains of the 60s.* New York: G. W. Dillingham, 1907.

Dodd, William E. *The Cotton Kingdom.* New Haven: Yale University Press, 1921.

Downey, Fairfax. *Portrait of an Era.* New York: Chas. Scribner's Sons, 1936.

Durden, Robert. *The Dukes of Durham.* Durham: Duke University Press, 1975.

Eaton, Clement. *The Growth of Southern Civilization, 1790–1860.* New York: Harper & Row, 1961.

———. *A History of the Old South.* New York: Macmillan Co., 1949.

Eckenrode, H. J. *The Randolphs.* Indianapolis: Bobbs-Merrill, 1946.

Eliot, Elizabeth. *Heiresses and Coronets.* New York: McDowell, Obolensky, 1959.

Evans, Gladys, and Marshall, Theodora. *They Found It in Natchez.* New Orleans: Pelican Publishing Company, 1940.

Ferry, Henry J. "Francis James Grimké: Portrait of a Black Puritan." Ph.D. dissertation, Yale University, 1970.

Gamble, Thomas. "The McAllisters." *Savannah Morning News.* October 5, 1930.

Gregorie, Anne King. *History of Sumter County, South Carolina.* Sumter, S.C.: Library Board of Sumter County, 1954.

Grimké, Angelina Emily. *Appeal to the Christian Women of the South.* New York, 1836.

Hamer, Philip M., ed. *Tennessee: A History.* New York: American Historical Society, 1933.

Hatch Alden. *The Byrds of Virginia.* New York: Holt, Rinehart & Winston, 1969.

Hendrick, Burton J. *Statesmen of the Lost Cause.* New York: Literary Guild of America, 1939.

Henry, Robert S. *First with the Most.* Indianapolis: Bobbs-Merrill, 1944.

Herald, George, and Radin, Edward. *The Big Wheel: Monte Carlo's Opulent Century.* New York: Morrow, 1963.

Hoyt, Edwin P. *The Vanderbilts and Their Fortunes.* New York: Doubleday Co., 1962.

Israel, Lee. *Miss Tallulah Bankhead.* New York: G. P. Putnam's Sons, 1972.

Johnson, Allen, ed. *Dictionary of American Biography.* New York: Chas. Scribner's Sons, 1929.

Kane, Harnett. *Natchez on the Mississippi.* New York: William Morrow, 1949.

———. *Plantation Parade.* New York: William Morrow, 1949.

Kavaler, Lucy. *The Astors.* New York: Dodd, Mead, 1966.

Lerner, Gerda. *The Grimké Sisters from South Carolina.* Boston: Houghton Mifflin, 1967.

Lowe, David. *Ku Klux Klan: The Invisible Empire.* New York: W. W. Norton, 1967.

McAllister, Ward. *Society as I Have Found It.* New York: Cassell Publishing Co., 1890.

Meade, Robert Douthat. *Judah P. Benjamin.* New York: Oxford University Press, 1943.

Morris, Lloyd. *Incredible New York.* New York: Random House, 1951.

National Cyclopaedia of American Biography. New York: James T. White & Co., 1910.

O'Connor, Richard. *The Golden Summers: An Antic History of Newport*. New York: G. P. Putnam's Sons, 1974.

Owsley, Frank L. *King Cotton Diplomacy*. Chicago: University of Chicago Press, 1959.

Phillips, Ulrich B. *Life and Labor in the Old South*. Boston: Little, Brown, 1929.

Pickens, Monroe. *History of the Pickens Family*. Easly, South Carolina, privately printed, 1951.

Pollack, Barbara. *The Collectors: Dr. Claribel and Miss Etta Cone*. Indianapolis: Bobbs-Merrill, 1962.

Ravenel, Mrs. St. Julien. *Charleston: The Place and the People*. New York: Macmillan Co., 1925.

Rogers, George C. *Charleston in the Age of the Pinckneys*. Norman, Oklahoma: University of Oklahoma Press, 1969.

Ross, Ishbel. *First Lady of the South*. New York: Harper & Bros., 1958.

Rowland, Dunbar. *History of Mississippi*. Jackson: University of Mississippi Press, 1925.

Sears, Louis M. *John Slidell*. Durham: Duke University Press, 1925.

Simkins, Francis Butler. *A History of the South*. New York: Alfred A. Knopf, 1958.

——. *Pitchfork Ben Tillman*. Baton Rouge: L.S.U. Press, 1944.

Simkins, Francis Butler, and Woody, Robert Hilliard. *South Carolina During Reconstruction*. Chapel Hill: University of North Carolina Press, 1932.

Strode, Hudson. *Jefferson Davis*. New York: Harcourt, Brace and World, 1959.

Sydnor, Charles S. *The Development of Southern Sectionalism, 1819–1848*. Baton Rouge: L.S.U. Press, 1948.

Tallant, Robert. *The Romantic New Orleaneans*. New York: E. P. Dutton, 1950.

Tasistro, Louis F. *Random Shots and Southern Breezes*. New York: Harper & Bros., 1842.

Thomas, Lately. *A Pride of Lions*. New York: William Morrow, 1971.

——. *Sam Ward: King of the Lobby*. Boston: Houghton Mifflin, 1965.

Tilley, Nannie May. *Reynolds Homestead, 1814–1970*. Richmond: Robert Kline & Co., 1970.

Tinling, Marion, and Wright, Louis B., eds. *The Secret Diary of William Byrd of Westover, 1709–1712*. Richmond: The Dietz Press, 1941.

——. *William Byrd: The London Diary (1717–1721)*. New York: Oxford University Press, 1958.

Vanderbilt, Cornelius. *Queen of the Golden Age*. New York: McGraw-Hill, 1956.

Wallace, David D. *History of South Carolina*. New York: American Historical Society, 1934.

Wecter, Dixon. *The Saga of American Society*. New York: Chas. Scribner's Sons, 1937.

Wellman, Manley Wade. *Giant in Gray: Wade Hampton*. New York: Chas. Scribner's Sons, 1949.

Selected Bibliography

White, Laura A. *Robert Barnwell Rhett: Father of Secession.* New York, London: The Century Company, 1931.

Williams, J. Harry. *P.G.T. Beauregard.* Baton Rouge: L.S.U. Press, 1955.

Willson, Beckles. *John Slidell and the Confederates in Paris.* New York: AMS Press, 1970.

Winkler, John K. *Tobacco Tycoon.* New York: Random House, 1942.

Winn, Alice. *Always a Virginian.* Lynchburg, Va.,: J. P. Bell & Co., 1975.

Woodward, C. Vann. *Origins of the New South, 1877–1913.* Baton Rouge: L.S.U. Press, 1951.

Index

Index

Benjamin, Ninette, 104, 114–16
Benjamin, Philip, 100–102
Benjamin, Rebecca, 103
Benjamin family, 260
Benjamin on Sales (Benjamin), 115
Biddle, Anthony J. Drexel, 226
Biddle, Mary Duke, 226, 262
Bingaman, Adam, 16
Bird, John, 44, 45
Bizarre plantation, 55, 58, 59
Blacks
  disenfranchisement of, in South Carolina,
    208–9
  See also Abolitionism; Ku Klux Klan; Re-
    construction; Slavery
Bogges, Beth MacNeil, 257
Bogges, Frank, 257
Bonaparte, Prince Jerome, 139
Bonaparte, Napoleon, 97
Bonnet, Stede, 86
Bradford, Edward, 110
Brand, Robert, 202
Broadnax, Lydia, 65
Brooks, Phyllis Langhorne, 199, 202
Brooks, Preston "Bully," 124, 206
Brooks, Reggie, 199
Brown, Michael, 65
Bruce, William Cabel, 60
Buchanan, James, 110
Bull Durham, 220–21
Burns, Emily, 37–39
Byrd, Evelyn, 49, 51
Byrd, Harry Flood, Jr., 257
Byrd, Harry Flood, Sr., 257
Byrd, Lucy Parke, 47, 49
Byrd, Maria Taylor, 51
Byrd, Mary Horsmanden, 45
Byrd, Mary (Molly) Willing, 53
Byrd, Adm. Richard E., 257
Byrd, Thomas Taylor, 53
Byrd, Wilhelmina, 49, 51
Byrd, William, I, 44–45
Byrd, William, II, 42–52
  in England, 45–46, 48–51
Byrd, William, III, 51–53
Byrd, William, IV, 53
Byrd family, 44, 53, 257

Cabarrus Bank and Trust Company, 246
Calhoun, John C., 85–88

Candler, Allen, 215
Candler, Asa Griggs, 215–17
Candler, Asa Warren, 261
Candler, Daniel, 214
Candler, Elizabeth, 214
Candler, John Slaughter, I, 215
Candler, John Slaughter, II, 261
Candler, Lucy Howard, 215
Candler, Milton, 215
Candler, Samuel, 214, 215
Candler, Bishop Warren Akin, 215, 216
Candler, William, 214
Candler, Zachariah, 214
Candler family, 8, 214, 261
Cannon, Anne. *See* Reynolds, Anne Cannon
Cannon, Charles, 246
Cannon, James, 239
Cannon, Joseph F., 239, 240, 246, 247
Cannon family, 8
Cannon Mills, 239
Cardozo, Benjamin N., 154
Cardozo, Francis Louis, 154, 156
Carpenter, Mrs. J. Leslie, 34
Carter, Anne Byrd, 53
Carter, Col. Landon, 53
Carter, Maria Byrd, 53
Carter, Robert, 53
Carter family, 53–54
Catholicism, 3, 14, 19
Cecil, Lord Robert, 125, 131
Chamberlain, Daniel, 154, 156
Chanler, Beatrice Ashley, 195
Chanler, John Armstrong, 193–94
Chanler, John Winthrop, 193
Chanler, Maddie Ward, 193
Chanler, William Astor, 195
Chanler, William Astor, III, 261
Charleston, South Carolina, 4, 71–72, 82–86,
    101, 258
  closed-shop policy in, 3
  Denmark Vesey slave insurrection in
    (1822), 84
  economic decline of, 88–90, 92
  pirates and, 86–87
Charlottesville, Virginia, 192–95
Churchill, Winston, 200–201
Cigarettes, 221
Civil War, 2, 5, 90, 111–13, 117, 120–22, 234
  Natchez during, 17–19
  See also Confederate States of America

Index

Clay, Henry, 62, 63
Cleveland, Grover, 149, 157
Clift, Montgomery, 248
Cliveden Set, 201
Coca-Cola, 214-17
Coles, Rob, 258
Coltrane, Tom Gay, 241
Cone, Claribel, 218-19
Cone, Etta, 218-19
Cone, Helen Guggenheimer, 218
Cone, Herman, 218
Cone family, 8
Confederate States of America
  defeat of, 128-33
  European recognition of, 6, 112, 117,
    122-28
  Judah Benjamin and, 112-13
Coolidge, Ellen Randolph, 64
Cotton, 4, 15, 118, 125
Cox, Joshua, 234
Creoles, 3-4, 95, 98, 99
Custis, Frances Parke, 47-48

Dana, Charles A., 19-20, 22, 26
Dana, Rev. Charles Bacchus, 19-20, 26, 32-
  33
Dana, Richard H. (Dick), 11-12, 20-22, 25-
  34, 36-40
Dana, Richard Henry, 20
Davis, Jefferson, 89, 112, 113, 118-23, 127-
  29
  background and early life of, 118-19
  capture and incarceration of, 130-31
  death of, 132
  in Europe after Civil War, 131, 132
  marriages of, 119-20
  Mexican War and, 120
  secession favored by, 120, 121
Davis, Joseph, 118-20
Davis, Sarah, 119
Davis, Varina Anne (Winnie), 132
Davis, Varina Howell, 11, 32, 112, 119-21,
  130, 132-33
De Bardeleben, Ellen Pratt, 217
De Bardeleben, Henry Fairchild, 217-18
De Bardeleben family, 261
De Lara, Isidore, 192
De Marigny, Bernard, 98-99
Democratic Party, 153

Democratic Rifle Clubs, 155
Dockery, Alice, 25, 26
Dockery, Octavia, 11-12, 21, 25-34, 36, 38-
  40
Dockery, Brig. Gen. Thomas Paine, 21, 25,
  27, 32
Dorsey, Sarah, 132
Dugas, Douschka Pickens, 210-11
Dugas, George, 211
Duke, Alice Webb, 222-23
Duke, Angier, 226-27
Duke, Angier Biddle, 262
Duke, Benjamin Newton (Ben), 220, 221,
  224, 226-28
Duke, Brodie Leonidas, 220-24
Duke, James Buchanan (Buck), 220, 221,
  224-28, 237
Duke, Josephine Drexel Biddle, 262
Duke, Lillian McCredy, 224-26, 228
Duke, Mary, 226
Duke, Nanaline Inman, 226
Duke, Washington, 220, 221, 225
Duke, Wylanta Rochelle, 223-24
Duke family, 8, 219-28, 262
Duke University, 227-28
Duncan family, 15

Early, Gen. Jubal, 140
Elms Court, 17, 18, 22, 23, 256
Emory College, 216
England. See Great Britain
Episcopal Church, 19
Epistle to the Clergy of the Southern States
  (Sarah Grimké), 82
Erlanger, Emil, 126-27
Erlanger, Frederic, 126
Erlanger, Rudolphe d', 260

Family Circle Dancing Class, 176
Farmers' Association, 207
Fillmore, Millard, 110
Fish, Stuyvesant, 179
Fish, Mrs. Stuyvesant, 181
Flynn, Maurice "Lefty," 202
Forrest, Gen. Nathan Bedford, 143-45
Fort Pillow massacre, 144
400, the (society list), 179
Foxcroft School, 202

Index

Index